# CSET Mathematics Study Guide
## Subtests I, II, and III

Copyright 2012 by Christopher Goff

University of the Pacific

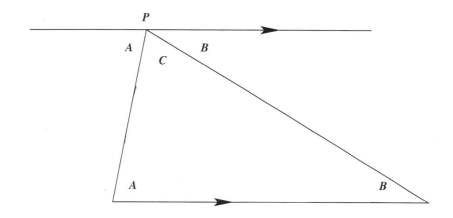

# Table Of Contents

# Subtest I:
# Algebra
# Number Theory

# 1.1 Algebraic Structures

## a. Know why the real and complex numbers are each a field, and that particular rings are not fields (e.g., integers, polynomial rings, matrix rings)

1. What is a field? What are some examples?

   A field is a set $F$ together with two operations (called $+$ and $\times$) satisfying the following properties. Suppose that $a$, $b$, and $c$ are elements of $F$.

   (a) $F$ is closed under $+$ and $\times$

   This means that $a + b$ and $a \times b$, also called $ab$, are elements of $F$. [The element $a \times b$ is often written $ab$. We will follow this conventional notation below.]

   (b) $+$ and $\times$ are associative

   This means that $(a + b) + c = a + (b + c)$ and $(ab)c = a(bc)$.

   (c) $+$ and $\times$ are commutative

   This means that $a + b = b + a$ and $ab = ba$.

   (d) $+$ and $\times$ have identity elements 0 and 1 in $F$, respectively

   This means that $a + 0 = a$ and $b \cdot 1 = b$.

   (e) every element has an additive inverse in $F$

   This means that for every $a$ in $F$, there is an element $-a$ **in** $F$ satisfying $a + (-a) = 0$.

   (f) every non-zero element has a multiplicative inverse in $F$

   If $b \neq 0$, then there is $\frac{1}{b}$ **in** $F$ satisfying $b(\frac{1}{b}) = 1$.

   (g) $\times$ distributes over $+$

   This means that $a(b + c) = ab + ac$.

   The most common fields we use are the rational numbers, the real numbers, and the complex numbers.

2. What is a ring? What are some examples?

   A ring is a set $R$ together with two operations (called $+$ and $\times$) satisfying the following properties.

   (a) $R$ is closed under $+$ and $\times$

   (b) $+$ and $\times$ are associative

   (c) $+$ is commutative

   (d) $+$ and $\times$ have identity elements 0 and 1 in $R$, respectively

   (e) every element has an additive inverse in $R$

   (f) $\times$ distributes over $+$

There are two key differences between the definition of a ring and the definition of a field: (1) rings do not necessarily have a commutative multiplication, and (2) rings do not necessarily contain multiplicative inverses. Notice that every field is a ring, but that there are rings which are not fields.

The most common rings we use (in addition to the fields listed above) are the integers, the set of square matrices of a given size (like all 2 by 2 matrices, for instance), and the set of polynomials with coefficients in another ring.

3.  What are some non-examples of fields and rings?

    The following common rings are not fields: integers, the set of square matrices of a given size (like all 2 by 2 matrices, for instance), and the set of polynomials with coefficients in another ring.

    The natural numbers are not a ring. The set of all quadratic polynomials is not a ring. See Sample Problems, below.

4.  Sample Problems

    (a)  Give an example of a ring that is not a field. integers, polynomials, set of square matrices *w/ coefficients*

    (b)  Why are the integers not a field?

    (c)  Why are the natural numbers not a ring?

    (d)  Why is the set of all quadratic polynomials not a ring?

    (e)  Write the multiplicative inverse of $3 - 2i$ in $a + bi$ form.

    (f)  Show that the set of 2 by 2 matrices with integer entries forms a non-commutative ring.

    (g)  Prove that the set of 2 by 2 invertible matrices with complex number entries is NOT a field.

    (h)  Write the multiplicative inverse of $x + yi$ in $a + bi$ form.

    (i)  What is the smallest field that contains 0 and 1?

    (j)  Using the field properties listed above, prove that $(a + b)c = ac + bc$.

    (k)  Let $F$ be the field of rational functions $\dfrac{p(x)}{q(x)}$, where $p(x)$ and $q(x)$ are any polynomials with real coefficients and $q(x) \neq 0$.

         i.   Show that $F$ contains a multiplicative identity element.

         ii.  Show that $F$ is closed under multiplication.

         iii. Show that $F$ is closed under addition.

         iv.  Show that every non-zero element of $F$ is invertible.

5.  Answers to Sample Problems

    (a)  Give an example of a ring that is not a field. Examples include: the integers, polynomials, and the set of all square matrices of a given size.

(b) Why are the integers not a field? Because not every integer has a multiplicative inverse *that is an integer*. For instance, the multiplicative inverse of 3 is $\frac{1}{3}$, which is not an integer.

(c) Why are the natural numbers not a ring? Because they do not contain an additive identity (although you might see a textbook which includes 0 in the natural numbers). Also, the additive inverses of natural numbers are not natural numbers. For instance, the additive inverse of 3 is $-3$, which is not a natural number.

(d) Why is the set of all quadratic polynomials not a ring? The set of quadratic polynomials is not closed under multiplication. For instance, if you multiply $x^2 + 1$ by $x^2 - 1$, you obtain $x^4 - 1$, which is not quadratic.

(e) Write the multiplicative inverse of $3 - 2i$ in $a + bi$ form.

$$\frac{1}{3 - 2i} \cdot \frac{3 + 2i}{3 + 2i} = \frac{3 + 2i}{9 - 4i^2} = \frac{3 + 2i}{9 + 4} = \frac{3}{13} + \frac{2}{13}i.$$

(f) Show that the set of 2 by 2 matrices with integer entries forms a non-commutative ring. We will show a few of the properties directly and leave the rest to the reader. To see the closure under addition, we technically should show that the sum

$$\begin{bmatrix} a & b \\ c & d \end{bmatrix} + \begin{bmatrix} a' & b' \\ c' & d' \end{bmatrix} = \begin{bmatrix} a + a' & b + b' \\ c + c' & d + d' \end{bmatrix}$$

is again a two by two matrix of integers. But since the integers are closed under addition, each entry of the new matrix is an integer. Hence the set of 2 by 2 matrices of integers is closed under addition. We will show multiplication as well (in part to remind the reader about how to multiply matrices).

$$\begin{bmatrix} a & b \\ c & d \end{bmatrix} \cdot \begin{bmatrix} a' & b' \\ c' & d' \end{bmatrix} = \begin{bmatrix} aa' + bc' & ab' + bd' \\ ca' + dc' & cb' + dd' \end{bmatrix}$$

Since the set of integers is closed under multiplication and addition, each entry in the product matrix is again an integer. Hence the set of 2 by 2 matrices with integer entries is closed under matrix multiplication.

We now check that matrix addition is commutative. Since

$$\begin{bmatrix} a & b \\ c & d \end{bmatrix} + \begin{bmatrix} a' & b' \\ c' & d' \end{bmatrix} = \begin{bmatrix} a + a' & b + b' \\ c + c' & d + d' \end{bmatrix} = \begin{bmatrix} a' & b' \\ c' & d' \end{bmatrix} + \begin{bmatrix} a & b \\ c & d \end{bmatrix},$$

it certainly follows that matrix addition is commutative.

Most of the other properties involve straightforward checks, under two conditions. First, the additive identity element of this ring is the *zero matrix*, $\begin{bmatrix} 0 & 0 \\ 0 & 0 \end{bmatrix}$, while the multiplicative identity element is the *identity matrix*, $\begin{bmatrix} 1 & 0 \\ 0 & 1 \end{bmatrix}$.

To show that this ring is not commutative, we need to give an example of two matrices that do not commute:

$$\begin{bmatrix} 0 & 1 \\ 0 & 0 \end{bmatrix} \cdot \begin{bmatrix} 0 & 0 \\ 1 & 0 \end{bmatrix} = \begin{bmatrix} 1 & 0 \\ 0 & 0 \end{bmatrix},$$

whereas

$$\begin{bmatrix} 0 & 0 \\ 1 & 0 \end{bmatrix} \cdot \begin{bmatrix} 0 & 1 \\ 0 & 0 \end{bmatrix} = \begin{bmatrix} 0 & 0 \\ 0 & 1 \end{bmatrix}$$

Since these answers are different, then certainly the two matrices $\begin{bmatrix} 0 & 1 \\ 0 & 0 \end{bmatrix}$ and $\begin{bmatrix} 0 & 0 \\ 1 & 0 \end{bmatrix}$ do not commute. Hence the ring of 2 by 2 matrices with integer entries is NOT commutative.

(g) Prove that the set of 2 by 2 invertible matrices with complex number entries is NOT a field. We will show that this set of matrices is not closed under addition. Recall that $1 = 1 + 0i$ is a complex number. We have

$$\begin{bmatrix} 1 & 0 \\ 0 & 1 \end{bmatrix} + \begin{bmatrix} -1 & 0 \\ 0 & -1 \end{bmatrix} = \begin{bmatrix} 0 & 0 \\ 0 & 0 \end{bmatrix},$$

which is clearly not an invertible matrix, even though each matrix summand is invertible. Another reason is that the additive identity, the zero matrix, is not invertible and is therefore not an element of the set of 2 by 2 invertible matrices with complex number entries. Hence the set of 2 by 2 invertible matrices with complex number entries is not a field.

(h) Write the multiplicative inverse of $x + yi$ in $a + bi$ form.

$$\frac{1}{x+yi} \cdot \frac{x-yi}{x-yi} = \frac{x-yi}{x^2 - i^2 y^2} = \frac{x-yi}{x^2 + y^2} = \frac{x}{x^2+y^2} - \frac{y}{x^2+y^2}i.$$

(i) What is the smallest field that contains 0 and 1? Since any field must be closed under addition and must contain additive inverses, we know that all positive and negative integers must lie in this field. Moreover, since fields must contain multiplicative inverses of all nonzero elements, we must have the numbers $\frac{1}{2}$, $\frac{1}{3}$, etc. in the field. Then, using closure under addition and multiplication, we can obtain any rational number. It turns out that the rational numbers form a field. Thus, the rational numbers are the smallest field containing zero and one (under usual operations). [If you want to use operations mod 2 ($1+1 = 0$), then you can make a field containing only 0 and 1!]

(j) Using the field properties listed above, prove that $(a+b)c = ac + bc$. We have $(a+b)c = c(a+b) = ca + cb = ac + bc$, where we have used the commutativity of multiplication and the distributive property in the way it was originally stated above.

(k) Let $F$ be the field of rational functions $\dfrac{p(x)}{q(x)}$, where $p(x)$ and $q(x)$ are any polynomials with real coefficients and $q(x) \neq 0$.

    i. Show that $F$ contains a multiplicative identity element. The element $1 = \frac{1}{1}$ is an element of $F$, because 1 is a (degree zero) polynomial.

    ii. Show that $F$ is closed under multiplication.

$$\frac{p(x)}{q(x)} \cdot \frac{a(x)}{b(x)} = \frac{p(x)a(x)}{q(x)b(x)}$$

Polynomials are closed under multiplication. Since $q(x)$ and $b(x)$ are not 0, then $q(x)b(x) \neq 0$. So the product of two elements of $F$ is another element of $F$.

iii. Show that $F$ is closed under addition.

$$\frac{p(x)}{q(x)} + \frac{a(x)}{b(x)} = \frac{p(x)b(x) + q(x)a(x)}{q(x)b(x)}$$

Again, since polynomials are closed under multiplication and addition, and since the denominator is not zero, the sum of two elements of $F$ is again an element of $F$.

iv. Show that every non-zero element of $F$ is invertible. If $\frac{p(x)}{q(x)} \neq 0$, then $p(x) \neq 0$. So that means that $\frac{q(x)}{p(x)}$ is an element of $F$. Multiplying, we get

$$\frac{p(x)}{q(x)} \cdot \frac{q(x)}{p(x)} = \frac{p(x)q(x)}{p(x)q(x)} = 1.$$

Hence, every non-zero element of $F$ is invertible.

## b. Apply basic properties of real and complex numbers in constructing mathematical arguments (e.g., if $a < b$ and $c < 0$, then $ac > bc$)

1. What are some basic properties of real and complex numbers?

The field properties are the most basic properties of real and complex numbers. In addition, for the real numbers there are properties of ordering, like the Trichotomy Axiom (mentioned below), and the following. Fill in the blanks.

(a) If $a < b$ and $c < d$, then $a + c \underline{<} b + d$.

(b) If $a < b$ and $c > 0$, then $ac \underline{<} bc$.

(c) If $a < b$ and $c < 0$, then $ac \underline{>} bc$.

(d) If $a \leq b$ and $b \leq a$, then $a \underline{=} b$.

(e) If $a < b$ and $b < c$, then $a \underline{<} c$.

(f) (Trichotomy) If $a$ and $b$ are real numbers, then exactly one of the following is true: $a < b$, $a > b$, or $a \underline{=} b$.

ANS: $<, <, >, =, <, =$.

There are also properties of equality. List as many as you can:

ANS: Reflexive, Symmetric, and Transitive Properties of Equality, Additive Property of Equality, Multiplicative Property of Equality

2. What is the definition of a rational number? ... of a complex number?

A rational number can be expressed as the ratio of two integers. So, any rational number can be written as $\frac{p}{q}$, where $p$ and $q$ are integers, and $q \neq 0$.

A complex number can be expressed as the sum of a real number and an imaginary number. So, any complex number can be written as $a+bi$, where $a$ and $b$ are real numbers and $i^2 = -1$. What is an imaginary number?

ANS: An imaginary number is one satisfying $x^2 \leq 0$. [There is sometimes a debate on whether $0$ is imaginary or not. I choose to think of $0$ as $0i$ in this case, making it imaginary. It's also real. No one said that numbers had to be either real or imaginary, but not both.]

3. Sample Problems

   (a) Explain why the solution to $3x - 5 = 4$ is $x = 3$ by showing each step. List all the properties you use.

   (b) Explain why the solution to $-3x - 5 < 4$ is $x > -3$ by showing each step. List all the properties you use.

   (c) What is proved by the following?

   Suppose that $\sqrt{2} = \frac{p}{q}$, where $\frac{p}{q}$ is written in lowest terms; i.e., $p$ and $q$ are integers that have no common factors other than 1. Then $2 = \frac{p^2}{q^2}$. Since $p$ and $q$ have no common factors, we must have $q = 1$ or else $\frac{p^2}{q^2}$ would not be an integer. So $q = 1$ and $p^2 = 2$. But this is impossible because there is no integer $p$ with $p^2 = 2$. $\square$

   (d) Show on a number line that if $a > b > 0$, then $-a < -b$.

   (e) Let $a$ and $b$ be integers with $b \neq 0$. Consider the following statement: If $\frac{a}{b} < 1$, then $a < b$.

      i. List some values for $a$ and $b$ that make the statement true.

      ii. List some values for $a$ and $b$ that make the statement false.

      iii. What is a condition on $a$ and/or $b$ that will make the statement necessarily true?

   (f) Using various ring properties and properties of equality, give reasons for the proof of the Multiplication Property of Zero: If $x$ is in a ring, then $0x = 0$.

      • $0 + 0 = 0$    additive identity
      • $(0 + 0)x = 0x$   multiplicative equality
      • $0x + 0x = 0x$   distributive
      • $0x + 0x = 0x + 0$   additive identity
      • $0x = 0$.   additive - equality

4. Answers to Sample Problems

   (a) Explain why the solution to $3x - 5 = 4$ is $x = 3$ by showing each step. List all the properties you use.

$$
\begin{aligned}
3x - 5 &= 4 && \text{Given}\\
(3x - 5) + 5 &= 4 + 5 && \text{Additive Property of Equality}\\
(3x - 5) + 5 &= 9 && \text{Arithmetic}\\
(3x + (-5)) + 5 &= 9 && \text{Definition of Subtraction}\\
3x + ((-5) + 5) &= 9 && \text{Associative Property of Addition}\\
3x + 0 &= 9 && \text{Additive Inverse}\\
3x &= 9 && \text{Additive Identity}\\
\tfrac{1}{3}(3x) &= \tfrac{1}{3}(9) && \text{Multiplicative Property of Equality}\\
\tfrac{1}{3}(3x) &= 3 && \text{Arithmetic}\\
\left(\tfrac{1}{3}\cdot 3\right) x &= 3 && \text{Associative Property of Multiplication}\\
1x &= 3 && \text{Multiplicative Inverse}\\
x &= 3 && \text{Multiplicative Identity}
\end{aligned}
$$

(b) Explain why the solution to $-3x - 5 < 4$ is $x > -3$ by showing each step. List all the properties you use.

$$
\begin{aligned}
-3x - 5 &< 4 && \text{Given}\\
(-3x - 5) + 5 &< 4 + 5 && \text{Additive Property of Inequality}\\
(-3x - 5) + 5 &< 9 && \text{Arithmetic}\\
(-3x + (-5)) + 5 &< 9 && \text{Definition of Subtraction}\\
-3x + ((-5) + 5) &< 9 && \text{Associative Property of Addition}\\
-3x + 0 &< 9 && \text{Additive Inverse}\\
-3x &< 9 && \text{Additive Identity}\\
-\tfrac{1}{3}(-3x) &> -\tfrac{1}{3}(9) && \text{Multiplicative Property of Inequality}\\
-\tfrac{1}{3}(-3x) &> -3 && \text{Arithmetic}\\
\left(-\tfrac{1}{3}\cdot -3\right) x &> -3 && \text{Associative Property of Multiplication}\\
1x &> -3 && \text{Multiplicative Inverse}\\
x &> -3 && \text{Multiplicative Identity}
\end{aligned}
$$

(c) What is proved by the following?

Suppose that $\sqrt{2} = \frac{p}{q}$, where $\frac{p}{q}$ is written in lowest terms; i.e., $p$ and $q$ are integers that have no common factors other than 1. Then $2 = \frac{p^2}{q^2}$. Since $p$ and $q$ have no common factors, we must have $q = 1$ or else $\frac{p^2}{q^2}$ would not be an integer. So $q = 1$ and $p^2 = 2$. But this is impossible because there is no integer $p$ with $p^2 = 2$. $\square$

This is a proof (by contradiction) that $\sqrt{2}$ is irrational. The proof started by assuming that $\sqrt{2}$ was rational and deduced a contradiction to that assumption. Hence $\sqrt{2}$ must be irrational.

(d) Show on a number line that if $a > b > 0$, then $-a < -b$. We are told that $a > b > 0$. On a number line, this looks like:

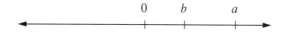

So, if we put in $-a$ and $-b$ as well, we get:

Clearly, $-a$ is to the left of $-b$, and thus $-a < -b$.

(e) Let $a$ and $b$ be integers with $b \neq 0$. Consider the following statement: If $\frac{a}{b} < 1$, then $a < b$.

   i. List some values for $a$ and $b$ that make the statement true. Answers may vary, although $b$ must be greater than zero.

   ii. List some values for $a$ and $b$ that make the statement false. Answers may vary, although $b$ must be less than zero.

   iii. What is a condition on $a$ and/or $b$ that will make the statement necessarily true? If $b$ is positive, then one can use the Multiplicative Property of Inequality to deduce that the statement must be true. Conversely, if $b < 0$, then the statement is false.

(f) Using various ring properties and properties of equality, give reasons for the proof of the Multiplication Property of Zero: If $x$ is in a ring, then $0x = 0$.

- $0 + 0 = 0$    Additive Identity (anything plus 0 equals itself)
- $(0 + 0)x = 0x$    Multiplicative Property of Equality
- $0x + 0x = 0x$    Distributive Property
- $0x + 0x = 0x + 0$    Additive Identity
- $0x = 0$.    Additive Property of Equality (in reverse)

## c. Know that the rational numbers and real numbers can be ordered and that the complex numbers cannot be ordered, but that any polynomial equation with real coefficients can be solved in the complex field

1. What does it mean to be "ordered?"

   A set is "totally ordered" (or just "ordered") if, given any two elements $a$ and $b$ in the set, either $a \leq b$ or $b \leq a$. Notice that because of the Trichotomy Axiom of real numbers, we know that if $x$ and $y$ are real numbers, either (i) $x < y$, (ii) $x > y$, or (iii) $x = y$. Thus, the real numbers, and any subset of the real numbers, is ordered.

2. Why can't the complex numbers be ordered?

   This question is misleading. The complex numbers can indeed be ordered, but not in a meaningful way. We will examine some of the consequences of trying to order the complex numbers in the sample problems.

3. Fundamental Theorem of Algebra

    We see in **1.2 Polynomial Equations and Inequalities** that the Fundamental Theorem of Algebra comes up. The Fundamental Theorem of Algebra says that if $f(x)$ is a polynomial with real coefficients, then $f(x)$ can be factored into linear and quadratic factors, each of which has real coefficients. Moreover, $f(x)$ can be factored entirely into linear factors if you allow your factors to have complex coefficients.

    [Mathematicians say: Every complex polynomial has a root in $\mathbb{C}$. A fancy way to say this is to say that $\mathbb{C}$ is an "algebraically closed" field.]

4. Sample Problems

    (a) Which of the following sets is an ordered field: complex numbers, rational numbers, integers, or natural numbers?

    (b) List three reasons why the set of 2 by 2 matrices with real number entries do not form an ordered field.

    (c) What is the maximum number of complex solutions to $x^{17} - 573x^9 + 54x^8 - 167x + 2 = 0$?

    (d) One way to order the complex numbers is as follows: $(a + bi) \lll (c + di)$ if (1) $a < c$ or (2) $a = c$ and $b < d$. In other words, compare the real parts to determine which is bigger. If they are the same, then move to the imaginary parts.

        i. Which is bigger, 2 or 20?
        ii. Which is bigger, $1 + 2i$ or $1 + 20i$?
        iii. Which is bigger, $2 + i$ or $-100 - 100i$?
        iv. Which is bigger, $100i$ or 1?
        v. What might be a disadvantage to this ordering?

    (e) Another way to order the complex numbers is by their magnitudes. The magnitude of $a + bi$ is $\sqrt{a^2 + b^2}$, which is a real number. So, $(a + bi) \lll (c + di)$ if $\sqrt{a^2 + b^2} < \sqrt{c^2 + d^2}$.

        i. Which is bigger, 2 or 20?
        ii. Which is bigger, $-2$ or $-20$?
        iii. Which is bigger, 5 or $3 + 4i$?
        iv. Which is bigger, $1 + i$ or $1 - i$?
        v. What might be a disadvantage to this ordering?

5. Answers to Sample Problems

    (a) Which of the following sets is an ordered field: complex numbers, rational numbers, integers, or natural numbers? The rational numbers, integers, and natural numbers are all ordered via $<$, because they are subsets of the (ordered) real numbers.

    (b) List three reasons why the set of 2 by 2 matrices with real number entries do not form an ordered field. It's certainly hard to order them (in a meaningful way), but the set of 2 by 2 real matrices do not even form a field. Indeed, matrices like $\begin{bmatrix} 1 & 0 \\ 0 & 0 \end{bmatrix}$ do not even have a multiplicative inverse.

(c) What is the maximum number of complex solutions to $x^{17} - 573x^9 + 54x^8 - 167x + 2 = 0$? Seventeen. The only time there may be fewer than 17 complex roots is if some of the roots have a multiplicity greater than one (like double roots, triple roots, etc.).

(d) One way to order the complex numbers is as follows: $(a + bi) \lll (c + di)$ if (1) $a < c$ or (2) $a = c$ and $b < d$. In other words, compare the real parts to determine which is bigger. If they are the same, then move to the imaginary parts.

    i. Which is bigger, 2 or 20? ANS: 20

    ii. Which is bigger, $1 + 2i$ or $1 + 20i$? ANS: $1 + 20i$

    iii. Which is bigger, $2 + i$ or $-100 - 100i$? ANS: $2 + i$

    iv. Which is bigger, $100i$ or 1? ANS: 1

    v. What might be a disadvantage to this ordering? One disadvantage is that complex numbers with large imaginary parts but small real parts might be considered smaller than numbers that have small imaginary parts and only slightly bigger real parts. This method seems to give undue importance to the real part of a complex number.

(e) Another way to order the complex numbers is by their magnitudes. The magnitude of $a + bi$ is $\sqrt{a^2 + b^2}$, which is a real number. So, $(a + bi) \lll (c + di)$ if $\sqrt{a^2 + b^2} < \sqrt{c^2 + d^2}$.

    i. Which is bigger, 2 or 20? ANS: 20

    ii. Which is bigger, $-2$ or $-20$? ANS: $-20$

    iii. Which is bigger, 5 or $3 + 4i$? ANS: same magnitude

    iv. Which is bigger, $1 + i$ or $1 - i$? ANS: same magnitude

    v. What might be a disadvantage to this ordering? One disadvantage is that it is not consistent with the ordering of real numbers. ($-20 > -2$, for instance.) Another disadvantage is that sometimes very different-looking complex numbers have the same magnitude.

# 1.2 Polynomial Equations and Inequalities

## a. Know why graphs of linear inequalities are half planes and be able to apply this fact (e.g., linear programming)

1. Why is the graph of a linear inequality a half plane?

   If you can solve the inequality for $y$, then it is clear that you are looking for values of $y$ either above $(y > f(x))$ or below $(y < f(x))$ the line. If $y$ doesn't appear in the equation, then the line must be vertical, and the inequality tells you if you are looking for points to the right $(x > a)$ or to the left $(x < a)$ of this line. In the following examples, the boundary lines have been labeled. Dotted boundary lines are not part of the solution set.

   **Examples:** $y \leq 5, \quad x > -2, \quad x + 2y \geq 3$

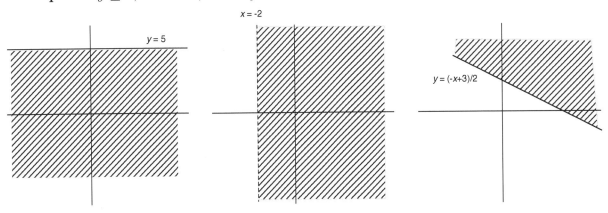

2. How do you apply linear inequalities?

   Linear programming can be used to solve optimization problems in many different fields. Usually, you are asked to maximize some quantity with respect to various linear constraints.

   **Simple(x) Example:** Say you have 20 days to knit hats and scarves for a friend's store. It takes you 1.5 days to knit a hat and only 1 day to knit a scarf. You plan to charge $20 per hat and $15 per scarf, but your friend says that she wants no more than 16 items from you. How many hats and how many scarves should you knit in order to maximize your revenue?

   ANS: Let $x$ be the number of hats knitted and $y$ the number of scarves knitted. So $x \geq 0$ and $y \geq 0$. Also, $x + y \leq 16$ because your friend only wants 16 items at most. The number of days it takes to knit hats is $1.5x$, while the number of days it takes to knit scarves is $y$. So $1.5x + y \leq 20$ since there are only 20 days to knit. If we graph all of these inequalities, we obtain a region of all the possible numbers of scarves and hats you could knit. The revenue function is $20x + 15y$, which we would like to maximize on the given region. According to the simplex method, since the revenue condition is linear, we need only check the corners of our region, which occur at any intersection point of two linear conditions.

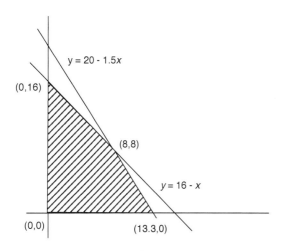

Checking, we get:

- no scarves and no hats yields 0 dollars of revenue
- 16 scarves and no hats yields $(16)(15) = 240$ dollars of revenue
- 8 scarves and 8 hats yields $8(15) + 8(20) = 280$ dollars of revenue
- 13 hats and no scarves yields $13(20) = 260$ dollars of revenue

So, to maximize revenue, you should knit eight scarves and eight hats.

3. Sample Problems

   (a) Sketch the solution to $y \leq 2x - 5$.
   (b) Sketch the solution to $2x + 3y > 6$.
   (c) Sketch all the complex numbers $a + bi$ with $a < 2b$.
   (d) Suppose that a company makes two kinds of puzzles: easy and hard. The company has 10 weeks to make puzzles before putting the products on the market. They can make 60 easy puzzles per week and 40 hard puzzles per week. They make \$12 profit on each easy puzzle and \$15 profit on each hard puzzle. Assuming that they can only put 500 puzzles on the market, how many of each should they make?

4. Answers to Sample Problems

   (a) Sketch the solution to $y \leq 2x - 5$.

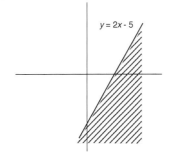

(b) Sketch the solution to $2x + 3y > 6$.

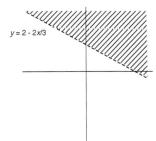

(c) Sketch all the complex numbers $a + bi$ with $a < 2b$.

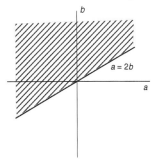

(d) Suppose that a company makes two kinds of puzzles: easy and hard. The company has 10 weeks to make puzzles before putting the products on the market. They can make 60 easy puzzles per week and 40 hard puzzles per week. They make \$12 profit on each easy puzzle and \$15 profit on each hard puzzle. Assuming that they can only put 500 puzzles on the market, how many of each should they make? 300 easy, 200 hard.

The corners of the region of interest are $(0, 0)$, $(0, 400)$, $(500, 0)$, and $(300, 200)$, where $x$ is the number of easy puzzles made and $y$ is the number of hard puzzles made. Checking each one, we obtain the maximum revenue at $(300, 200)$.

**b. Prove and use: the Rational Root Theorem for polynomials with integer coefficients; the Factor Theorem; the Conjugate Roots Theorem for polynomial equations with real coefficients; the Quadratic Formula for real and complex quadratic polynomials; the Binomial Theorem**

1. What is the Rational Root Theorem for polynomials with integer coefficients?

   If $f(x) = a_n x^n + a_{n-1} x^{n-1} + \ldots + a_1 x + a_0$, with each $a_i$ an integer, then the Rational Root Theorem says that the only possible rational roots are of the form $\pm \frac{p}{q}$, where $p$ is a divisor of $a_0$ and $q$ is a divisor of $a_n$.

   **Proof:** Suppose $\frac{p}{q}$ is a root of $f$. Then

   $$0 = f(p/q) = a_n(p/q)^n + a_{n-1}(p/q)^{n-1} + \ldots + a_1(p/q) + a_0.$$

   Multiply by $q^n$ to clear denominators. Then

   $$0 = a_n p^n + a_{n-1} p^{n-1} q + \ldots + a_1 p q^{n-1} + a_0 q^n.$$

   So $-a_0 q^n = a_n p^n + a_{n-1} p^{n-1} q + \ldots + a_1 p q^{n-1} = p(a_n p^{n-1} + a_{n-1} p^{n-2} q + \ldots + a_1 q^{n-1})$, which is clearly divisible by $p$. If we assume that $\frac{p}{q}$ is in lowest terms, then $p$ has no factors in common with $q^n$. So $p$ must be a divisor of $a_0$. Similarly, $-a_n p^n = q(a_{n-1}p^{n-1} + \ldots + a_1 pq^{n-2} + a_0 q^{n-1})$, which is divisible by $q$. Thus, $a_n$ must be divisible by $q$.    $\square$

**Alternate Explanation:** Factor $f(x)$ into factors with integer coefficients. If $\pm\frac{p}{q}$ is a root, then $(qx \mp p)$ is a factor. [See Factor Theorem, below.] So, when you multiply out all the factors, $q$ will be a factor of the leading coefficient, $a_n$, and $p$ will be a factor of the constant term, $a_0$. [To check this, try multiplying $(2x - 3)$ by any polynomial with integer coefficients. Then notice that the leading term is divisible by 2 and the constant term is divisible by 3.]

**Example:** List all possible rational roots of $g(x) = 2x^3 + 9x^2 + 7x - 6$.

ANS: Any rational root must be a factor of 6 divided by a factor of 2. The possibilities are: $\pm 1, \pm 2, \pm 3, \pm 6, \pm\frac{1}{2}, \pm\frac{3}{2}$.

2. What is the Factor Theorem?

The Factor Theorem says that $(x - b)$ is a factor of $f(x)$ if and only if $f(b) = 0$.

**Proof:** The Factor Theorem is just a special case of the Remainder Theorem, which says that if $f(x)$ is divided by $(x - b)$, then the remainder is $f(b)$. To see this, recall that if you divide $f(x)$ by $(x - b)$, you get a quotient polynomial $q(x)$ and a remainder polynomial $r(x)$ with the degree of $r(x)$ smaller than the degree of $(x - b)$. So $r(x)$ must be a constant, say $r$. Hence we have

$$f(x) = (x - b)q(x) + r.$$

Letting $x = b$ gives the Remainder Theorem: $f(b) = r$. Therefore, $f(b) = 0$ if and only if the remainder is zero, i.e., exactly when $(x - b)$ is a factor of $f(x)$.    $\square$

**Example:** Find the roots of $f(x) = x^5 + 8x^4 + 19x^3 + 8x^2 - 20x - 16$.

ANS: Using the Remainder Theorem (and synthetic substitution), we notice that both 1 and $-1$ are roots, which shortens the calculations:

| $x$ | 1 | 8 | 19 | 8 | $-20$ | $-16$ | |
|-----|---|---|----|----|-------|-------|-------------------|
| 1 | 1 | 9 | 28 | 36 | 16 | 0 | root |
| $-1$ | 1 | 8 | 20 | 16 | 0 | | root |
| $-1$ | 1 | 7 | 13 | 3 | | | (not a double root) |
| $-2$ | 1 | 6 | 8 | 0 | | | root |
| $-2$ | 1 | 4 | 0 | | | | double root |
| $-4$ | 1 | 0 | | | | | root |

(You can also try plugging in 1, $-1$, $-2$, and $-4$ into the polynomial to obtain zero. Review synthetic substitution if you wish to use it.) The roots are : 1, $-1$, $-2$, and $-4$, where $-2$ is a double root. This also means that

$$f(x) = x^5 + 8x^4 + 19x^3 + 8x^2 - 20x - 16 = (x - 1)(x + 1)(x + 2)^2(x + 4).$$

3. What is the Conjugate Roots Theorem for polynomial equations with real coefficients?

If $f(x)$ is a polynomial with *real* coefficients, and if $f(a + bi) = 0$, then the Conjugate Roots Theorem says that $f(a - bi) = 0$.

**Proof:** Since $f(x)$ has real coefficients, $f(x) = \overline{f}(x)$, where $\overline{f}(x)$ is the polynomial obtained by taking the complex conjugate of every coefficient of $f$. So

$$0 = f(a+bi) = \overline{f(a+bi)} = \overline{f}(\overline{a+bi}) = f(\overline{a+bi}) = f(a-bi). \quad \square$$

**Example:** Factor $g(x) = x^4 - 5x^3 + 9x^2 - 5x$ if you know that $g(2+i) = 0$.

ANS: Since $2+i$ is a root, the Conjugate Roots Theorem says that $2-i$ is also a root. This means that $(x - (2+i))$ and $(x - (2-i))$ are factors of $g(x)$. So

$$
\begin{aligned}
(x - (2+i))(x - (2-i)) &= x^2 - (2+i)x - (2-i)x + (2+i)(2-i) \\
&= x^2 - 4x + 5
\end{aligned}
$$

is also a factor of $g(x)$. Notice that $x$ is a factor as well. So, using long division, (or trial and error, or noticing that 1 is a root), we obtain

$$g(x) = x^4 - 5x^3 + 9x^2 - 5x = x(x-1)(x^2 - 4x + 5).$$

4. What is the Conjugate Roots Theorem for polynomial equations with rational coefficients? [**not specifically listed on CSET]

   If $f(x)$ is a polynomial with *rational* coefficients, and if $f(a + b\sqrt{n}) = 0$ (with $\sqrt{n}$ irrational), then the Conjugate Roots Theorem says that $f(a - b\sqrt{n}) = 0$.

   **Proof:** Abstract Algebra. Since $f$ has rational coefficients, $f$ doesn't change when you switch the irrational $\sqrt{n}$ with $-\sqrt{n}$. The proof then is similar to the one using complex conjugation, given above.

   **Example:** Suppose $f(x)$ is quadratic with $f(5 - \sqrt{5}) = 0$. Find a possible formula for $f(x)$.

   ANS: Let's find such an $f$ with rational coefficients, which means that we can require $f(5 + \sqrt{5}) = 0$ also. The simplest quadratic is thus

$$
\begin{aligned}
f(x) &= (x - (5 - \sqrt{5}))(x - (5 + \sqrt{5})) \\
&= x^2 - (5 - \sqrt{5})x - (5 + \sqrt{5})x + (5 - \sqrt{5})(5 + \sqrt{5}) \\
&= x^2 - 10x + 20.
\end{aligned}
$$

5. What is the Quadratic Formula for real and complex quadratic polynomials?

   If $ax^2 + bx + c = 0$ with $a \neq 0$, then $x = \dfrac{-b \pm \sqrt{b^2 - 4ac}}{2a}$.

   A Cubic Formula and a Quartic Formula also exist, but no Quintic Formula!

6. What is the Binomial Theorem?

$$(x+y)^n = \sum_{k=0}^{n} \binom{n}{k} x^{n-k} y^k,$$

where $\dbinom{n}{k} = \dfrac{n!}{k!(n-k)!}$ and is read "$n$ choose $k$." It is also the number of ways to choose $k$ objects from a set of $n$ objects.

The Binomial Theorem can be proved by mathematical induction.

**Proof:** We start by checking that the formula is true for $n = 1$.

$$\sum_{k=0}^{1} \binom{1}{k} x^{1-k} y^k = \binom{1}{0} x^1 y^0 + \binom{1}{1} x^0 y^1 = 1x + 1y = (x+y)^1.$$

Now we show that whenever the formula is true for some value of $n$ then it is also true for $n+1$. (Via induction, this will imply that the formula is true for any value of $n$.)

$$
\begin{aligned}
(x+y)^{n+1} &= (x+y)(x+y)^n \\
&= (x+y)\left( \sum_{k=0}^{n} \binom{n}{k} x^{n-k} y^k \right) \\
&= \sum_{k=0}^{n} \binom{n}{k} x^{n-k+1} y^k + \sum_{k=0}^{n} \binom{n}{k} x^{n-k} y^{k+1}
\end{aligned}
$$

We need to re-index the second summation in order to combine like terms correctly. Let $\ell = k+1$ so that the summation is from $\ell = 1$ to $\ell = n+1$. Then

$$
(x+y)^{n+1} = \sum_{k=0}^{n} \binom{n}{k} x^{n-k+1} y^k + \sum_{\ell=1}^{n+1} \binom{n}{\ell-1} x^{n-(\ell-1)} y^\ell
$$

Notice that we can combine the middle terms ($1 \leq k, \ell \leq n$) and notice that we have like terms now, if we match up $k$ in the first sum with $\ell$ in the second, but that the first and last terms need to be separated out.

$$
\begin{aligned}
(x+y)^{n+1} &= x^{n+1} + \left( \sum_{k=1}^{n} \left[ \binom{n}{k} + \binom{n}{k-1} \right] x^{n-k+1} y^k \right) + y^{n+1} \\
&= \sum_{k=0}^{n+1} \binom{n+1}{k} x^{n+1-k} y^k,
\end{aligned}
$$

which is exactly what we wanted to show. $\square$

**Example:** Expand $(x+2)^5$.

$$
\begin{aligned}
(x+2)^5 &= \sum_{k=0}^{5} \binom{5}{k} x^{5-k} 2^k \\
&= \binom{5}{0} x^5 2^0 + \binom{5}{1} x^4 2^1 + \ldots + \binom{5}{5} x^0 2^5 \\
&= x^5 + 5x^4(2) + 10x^3(4) + 10x^2(8) + 5x(16) + 1(32) \\
&= x^5 + 10x^4 + 40x^3 + 80x^2 + 80x + 32.
\end{aligned}
$$

7. Sample Problems

   (a) Show that in $x^2 + bx + c = 0$, the sum of the two roots is $-b$ and the product of the two roots is $c$.

   (b) Solve $z^2 - iz + 2 = 0$.

   (c) Let $2x^4 - x^3 - 20x^2 + 13x + 30 = 0$.

      i. List all possible rational roots.

      ii. Find all rational roots.

      iii. Find all roots.

   (d) Let $6x^4 + 7x^3 + 6x^2 - 1 = 0$.

      i. List all possible rational roots.

      ii. Find all rational roots.

      iii. Find all roots.

   (e) Factor $x^3 - x - 6$ if you know that one root is $-1 + i\sqrt{2}$.

   (f) Let $f(x) = x^2 - bx + (b-1)$. Find $f(1)$. Explain how the Factor Theorem allows you to factor $f(x)$. Then, factor $f(x)$.

   (g) Solve $x^2 + 3x = -5$.

   (h) Find the coefficient of $x^4$ in $(x-3)^6$.

   (i) Find the fifth term in the expansion of $(2x - y)^9$.

   (j) Derive the Quadratic Formula. [Hint: Complete the Square.]

   (k) Explain why the number of ways to choose $k$ objects from a group of $n$ is the same as the number of ways to choose $n - k$ objects from a group of $n$.

8. Answers to Sample Problems

   (a) Show that in $x^2 + bx + c = 0$, the sum of the two roots is $-b$ and the product of the two roots is $c$. The roots are $x = \frac{-b \pm \sqrt{b^2 - 4c}}{2}$. So,

$$\frac{-b + \sqrt{b^2 - 4c}}{2} + \frac{-b - \sqrt{b^2 - 4c}}{2} = \frac{-2b}{2} = -b,$$

and

$$\left(\frac{-b + \sqrt{b^2 - 4c}}{2}\right)\left(\frac{-b - \sqrt{b^2 - 4c}}{2}\right) = \frac{(-b + \sqrt{b^2 - 4c})(-b - \sqrt{b^2 - 4c})}{4}$$

$$= \frac{(-b)^2 - (b^2 - 4c)}{4} = \frac{4c}{4} = c.$$

   (b) Solve $z^2 - iz + 2 = 0$. Using the Quadratic Formula, we get

$$z = \frac{i \pm \sqrt{-1 - 4(2)}}{2} = \frac{i \pm \sqrt{-9}}{2} = \frac{i \pm 3i}{2} = 2i, -i.$$

(c) Let $2x^4 - x^3 - 20x^2 + 13x + 30 = 0$.

  i. List all possible rational roots. $\pm 1, \pm 2, \pm 3, \pm 5, \pm 6, \pm 10, \pm 15, \pm 30, \pm \frac{1}{2}, \pm \frac{3}{2}, \pm \frac{5}{2}, \pm \frac{15}{2}$.

  ii. Find all rational roots.

$$2x^4 - x^3 - 20x^2 + 13x + 30 = (x+1)(2x^3 - 3x^2 - 17x + 30) = (x+1)(x-2)(x+3)(2x-5)$$

  So, the rational roots are $-1, 2, -3, \frac{5}{2}$.

  iii. Find all roots. $-1, 2, -3, \frac{5}{2}$. We know the list is complete because the polynomial has degree 4.

(d) Let $6x^4 + 7x^3 + 6x^2 - 1 = 0$.

  i. List all possible rational roots. $\pm 1, \pm \frac{1}{2}, \pm \frac{1}{3}, \pm \frac{1}{6}$.

  ii. Find all rational roots.

$$6x^4 + 7x^3 + 6x^2 - 1 = (2x+1)(3x-1)(x^2 + x + 1)$$

  So, the rational roots are $-\frac{1}{2}$ and $\frac{1}{3}$.

  iii. Find all roots. $-\frac{1}{2}, \frac{1}{3}, \frac{-1 \pm i\sqrt{3}}{2}$.

(e) Factor $x^3 - x - 6$ if you know that one root is $-1 + i\sqrt{2}$. Since the coefficients are real, we know that another root is $-1 - i\sqrt{2}$. Hence

$$(x - (-1 + i\sqrt{2}))(x - (-1 - i\sqrt{2})) = (x + 1 - i\sqrt{2})(x + 1 + i\sqrt{2}) = (x+1)^2 + 2 = x^2 + 2x + 3$$

is a factor of $x^3 - x - 6$. So $x^3 - x - 6 = (x^2 + 2x + 3)(x - 2)$ by long division, or by guess and check, or by looking at the leading coefficient and constant term and deducing the linear factor.

(f) Let $f(x) = x^2 - bx + (b - 1)$. Find $f(1)$. Explain how the Factor Theorem allows you to factor $f(x)$. Then, factor $f(x)$.

$f(1) = 1 - b + (b - 1) = 0$. The Factor Theorem implies that $(x - 1)$ is thus a factor of $f(x)$. So

$$x^2 - bx + (b - 1) = (x - 1)(x - (b - 1)).$$

(g) Solve $x^2 + 3x = -5$. First, we set $x^2 + 3x + 5 = 0$ and use the Quadratic Formula.

$$x = \frac{-3 \pm \sqrt{9 - 4(5)}}{2} = \frac{-3 \pm \sqrt{-11}}{2} = \frac{-3 \pm i\sqrt{11}}{2}.$$

(h) Find the coefficient of $x^4$ in $(x - 3)^6$. 135. The $k = 2$ term is:

$$\binom{6}{2} x^{6-2}(-3)^2 = 15x^4(9) = 135x^4.$$

(i) Find the fifth term in the expansion of $(2x - y)^9$. The first term corresponds to $k = 0$ in the summation. So the fifth term corresponds to $k = 4$.

$$\binom{9}{4}(2x)^5(-y)^4 = \frac{(9)(8)(7)(6)(5!)}{(4)(3)(2)(1)(5!)}(32x^5)(y^4) = 4032x^5y^4.$$

(j) Derive the Quadratic Formula. [Hint: Complete the Square.]

$$ax^2 + bx + c = 0 \qquad \text{Given } (a \neq 0)$$

$$x^2 + \frac{b}{a}x = -\frac{c}{a} \qquad \text{Divide by } a \neq 0 \text{ and rearrange terms}$$

$$x^2 + \frac{b}{a}x + \frac{b^2}{4a^2} = -\frac{c}{a} + \frac{b^2}{4a^2} \qquad \text{Complete the square}$$

$$\left(x + \frac{b}{2a}\right)^2 = \frac{b^2 - 4ac}{4a^2} \qquad \text{Factor, obtain common denominator}$$

$$\left(x + \frac{b}{2a}\right) = \pm\frac{\sqrt{b^2 - 4ac}}{2a} \qquad \text{Take square root of each side}$$

$$x = -\frac{b}{2a} \pm \frac{\sqrt{b^2 - 4ac}}{2a} \qquad \text{Rearrange terms}$$

and thus $x = \dfrac{-b \pm \sqrt{b^2 - 4ac}}{2a}$.

(k) Explain why the number of ways to choose $k$ objects from a group of $n$ is the same as the number of ways to choose $n - k$ objects from a group of $n$. If you choose $k$ objects to include in your subgroup, then you could also think of that as simultaneously choosing $n - k$ objects to exclude from your subgroup. Each way to choose a few is also a way to exclude all the rest. Mathematically, this means $\dbinom{n}{k} = \dbinom{n}{n-k}$.

## c. Analyze and solve polynomial equations with real coefficients using the Fundamental Theorem of Algebra

1. What is the Fundamental Theorem of Algebra?

The Fundamental Theorem of Algebra says that if $f(x)$ is a polynomial with real coefficients, then $f(x)$ can be factored into linear and quadratic factors, each of which has real coefficients. Moreover, $f(x)$ can be factored entirely into linear factors if you allow your factors to have complex coefficients.

2. How do you use the Fundamental Theorem of Algebra to analyze polynomial equations?

The main way to use the Fundamental Theorem of Algebra is when determining the number of roots a polynomial has. For example, a polynomial of degree $n$ has at most $n$ roots. Combined with the previous theorems, we can often say more.

**Example:** Say $f$ has real coefficients and degree 5. If $2 - i$ is a root of $f$, then how many real roots can $f$ have? The answer is that $f$ has either one or three real roots. The reason for this is that because $f$ has real coefficients, the Conjugate Roots Theorem says that $2 + i$ is also a root. This accounts for 2 of the roots of $f$, leaving 3 more complex roots, some of which might (also) be real. Since the complex nonreal roots have to come in conjugate pairs, there are either zero or two more complex nonreal roots. Hence the number of real roots must be three or one. (This includes the multiplicity of a double or triple root, which would count as two or three roots, respectively.)

3. Sample Problems

    (a) Suppose $f(x)$ is a quartic polynomial with integer coefficients. If $f(1+i) = 0$ and $f(2 - \sqrt{3}) = 0$, then find a possible formula for $f(x)$.

    (b) How many real roots can $x^5 - 3x^2 + x + 1$ have? Be specific.

    (c) Find a possible formula for a polynomial $f(x)$ that satisfies: $f(-2) = f(3) = f(5) = 0$ and $f(0) = 15$.

    (d) If $x^2 - 5x + 6$ is a divisor of the polynomial $f(x)$, then what is the minimum degree of $f$? What is $f(2)$? What is $f(3)$? Suppose $f(4) = 0$. Find a formula for $f(x)$.

4. Answers to Sample Problems

    (a) Suppose $f(x)$ is a quartic polynomial with integer coefficients. If $f(1+i) = 0$ and $f(2 - \sqrt{3}) = 0$, then find a possible formula for $f(x)$. Since $f$ has rational coefficients, we can employ both forms of the Conjugate Roots Theorem, implying that $f$ has four roots. One possible formula for $f$ is thus:

$$f(x) = (x - (1+i))(x - (1-i))(x - (2 - \sqrt{3}))(x - (2 + \sqrt{3})),$$

    which equals $(x^2 - 2x + 2)(x^2 - 4x + 1) = x^4 - 6x^3 + 11x^2 - 10x + 2$.

    (b) How many real roots can $x^5 - 3x^2 + x + 1$ have? Be specific. This polynomial could have 1, 3, or 5 real roots. However, we can use synthetic substitution (or long division) to see that 1 is a double root. Thus the polynomial must have 3 or 5 real roots.

    (c) Find a possible formula for a polynomial $f(x)$ that satisfies: $f(-2) = f(3) = f(5) = 0$ and $f(0) = 15$. We know that $f$ must have factors $(x+2)$, $(x-3)$, and $(x-5)$. So we could guess $f(x) = (x+2)(x-3)(x-5)$, but this satisfies $f(0) = 30$, which is not what we want. So, we could multiply our guess by $\frac{1}{2}$, which doesn't change the roots. Thus a correct answer is

$$f(x) = \frac{1}{2}(x+2)(x-3)(x-5) = \frac{1}{2}(x^3 - 6x^2 - x + 30) = \frac{1}{2}x^3 - 3x^2 - \frac{1}{2}x + 15.$$

    (d) If $x^2 - 5x + 6$ is a divisor of the polynomial $f(x)$, then what is the minimum degree of $f$? What is $f(2)$? What is $f(3)$? Suppose $f(4) = 0$. Find a formula for $f(x)$. The minimum degree of $f$ would be 2. Since $2^2 - 5(2) + 6 = 0$, $f(2) = 0$. Similarly, $f(3) = 0$. If we also know that $f(4) = 0$, then $f$ must have a factor of $(x-4)$ as well, bringing its minimum degree up to 3. One possible formula for $f(x)$ is

$$(x^2 - 5x + 6)(x - 4) = x^3 - 9x^2 + 26x - 24.$$

## 1.3 Functions

**a. Analyze and prove general properties of functions (i.e., domain and range, one-to-one, onto, inverses, composition, and differences between relations and functions)**

1. What is a relation?

   A relation from a set $A$ to a set $B$ is a set of ordered pairs $(x, y)$, where $x \in A$ and $y \in B$.

   A relation on the real numbers is a subset of $\mathbb{R} \times \mathbb{R} = \mathbb{R}^2$.

2. What is a function? What are domain and range?

   A function $f$ from $A$ to $B$ is a relation from $A$ to $B$ that satisfies the following two properties:

   (a) for every element $x \in A$, there is an ordered pair $(x, y) \in f$. [We say that $y = f(x)$.]

   (b) if $(x, y) \in f$ and $(x, z) \in f$, then $y = z$.

   One of these properties talks about the *existence* of $f(x)$ and one talks about the *uniqueness* of $f(x)$, both of which are important in the definition of a function. Which is which?

   ANS: The first property establishes the existence of $f(x)$ and the second property establishes its uniqueness.

   The set $A$ is called the *domain* of $f$.

   The *range* of $f$ is NOT the set $B$, but rather $\{f(x) : x \in A\} \subseteq B$. The set $B$ is called a *codomain* of $f$.

   **Example:** $f : \mathbb{R} \to \mathbb{R}$ given by $f(x) = x^2$. The domain of $f$ is $\mathbb{R}$, but the range of $f$ is ....

   ANS: The range is $[0, \infty)$, the set of non-negative real numbers.

3. What is a one-to-one function?

   A function $f : A \to B$ is one-to-one if, for all $b \in B$, there is at most one $x \in A$ satisfying $f(x) = b$.

   (a) "Blob" Picture: If $f$ is one-to-one, then each element in the domain maps to a unique element in the range.

   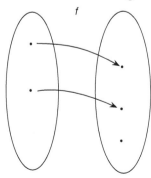

   one-to-one, but not onto

(b) Graphs and horizontal lines: If $f$ is one-to-one, then each horizontal line intersects the graph at most once. (Ex: $f(x) = \sqrt{x}$.)

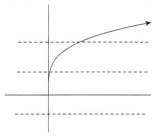

4. What is an onto function?

A function $f : A \to B$ is onto if, for all $b \in B$, there is at least one $x \in A$ satisfying $f(x) = b$.

(a) "Blob" Picture: If $f$ is onto, then each element in the codomain has at least one element mapping to it.

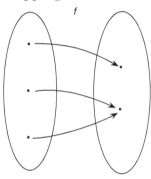

onto, but not one-to-one

(b) Graphs and horizontal lines: If $f$ is onto, then each horizontal line intersects the graph at least once. (Ex: $f(x) = x^3 - x$.)

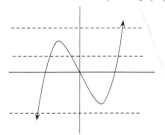

5. Making new functions from old functions

(a) shifts (translations)

To shift the graph of $y = f(x)$ up [resp. down] by $k$ units, you ___add___ [resp. _____] $k$ to the _____ of the function $f$. The new graph is $y = $ ___$f(x)+k$___ [resp. _____].

ANS: add, [subtract], output (or $y$-value), $f(x) + k$, [$f(x) - k$].

To shift the graph of $y = f(x)$ right [resp. left] by $k$ units, you _____*add*_____ [resp. _____] $k$ to the _____ of the function $f$. The new graph is $y = $ _$f(x+c)$_ [resp. _____].

ANS: subtract, [add], input (or $x$-value), $f(x - k)$, $[f(x + k)]$.

(b) stretches and smushes (dilations & compressions)

To stretch the graph of $y = f(x)$ vertically by a factor of $d$ units, you _$d($multip$)$_ the _____ of the function $f$ by $d$. The new graph is $y = $ _$d \cdot f(x)$_.

ANS: multiply, output, $df(x)$.

To stretch the graph of $y = f(x)$ horizontally by a factor of $d$ units, you _____ the _____ of the function $f$ by $d$. The new graph is $y = $ _____.

ANS: divide, input, $f(\frac{x}{d})$.

(c) reflections

To reflect the graph of $y = f(x)$ over the $x$-axis, you _*mult*_ the _*opp*_ of the function $f$ by $-1$. The new graph is $y = $ _$-f(x)$_.

ANS: multiply, output, $-f(x)$.

To reflect the graph of $y = f(x)$ over the $y$-axis, you _____ the _____ of the function $f$ by $-1$. The new graph is $y = $ _$f(-x)$_.

ANS: multiply (or divide!), input, $f(-x)$.

(d) sum, difference, product, quotient

You can add functions $f$ and $g$ to get a new function: $f + g$. The new function is defined by:

$$(f + g)(x) = f(x) + g(x).$$

The other operations are similar, except that there is one restriction when you divide two functions. What is it?

ANS: You are not allowed to divide by zero. If $g(a) = 0$, then $a$ cannot be in the domain of $(f/g)(x) = \frac{f(x)}{g(x)}$.

(e) composition

In addition to addition, subtraction, multiplication, and division, you can compose two functions to obtain a new one. That is, if $f : A \rightarrow B$ and $g : B \rightarrow C$, then you can compose them to get a new function $h : A \rightarrow C$ defined by $h(x) = g(f(x))$. We say $h = g \circ f$.

**Example:** $f(x) = x^2$ and $g(x) = x + 3$. Then $(g \circ f)(x) = x^2 + 3$ and $(f \circ g)(x) = (x + 3)^2 = x^2 + 6x + 9$. Notice that $f \circ g$ can be different from $g \circ f$.

(f) inverse functions

Also, if a function $f : A \rightarrow \text{range}(f)$ is one-to-one, then you can define a new function $f^{-1} : \text{range}(f) \rightarrow A$ according to:

$$f^{-1}(b) = x \quad \Longleftrightarrow \quad f(x) = b.$$

The roles of domain and range are swapped.

**Example:** $f(x) = \dfrac{3x-5}{7}$. Find $f^{-1}$.

ANS: The usual algorithm involves switching $x$ and $y$ and then solving for $y$. That is, instead of $y = \frac{3x-5}{7}$, we start with $x = \frac{3y-5}{7}$, which means $7x = 3y - 5$, or $y = \frac{7x+5}{3}$. So $f^{-1}(x) = \dfrac{7x+5}{3}$.

The graph of $f^{-1}$ can be obtained from the graph of $f$ by reflecting over the line $y = x$ (which essentially switches $y$ and $x$, thus swapping the domain and the range).

(g) identity function ($f(x) = x$)

The identity function is a boring function in one sense, but it plays a necessary role both in inverse functions and in function composition. How so?

ANS: The composition of a function and its inverse should be the identity function (because the inverse function "undoes" whatever the original function does). Also, the composition of any function $g$ with the identity function is equal to the function $g$. (The identity function is "inert" under composition.)

6. Sample Problems

(a) If $f(x) = 2x^2 - 8$ and if $g(x) = \sqrt{x}$, then what is the domain of $g(f(x))$?

(b) Let $f = \{(1,1),(2,3),(2,4),(3,1)\}$ and let $g = \{(4,3),(3,3),(2,1),(1,4)\}$

   i. Which set is a function?

   ii. What is the domain of that function? ... range ...?

   iii. Is that function one-to-one? Explain.

   iv. Is that function onto the set $\{1,3,4\}$? Explain.

(c) Fill in the table below. If there is not enough information, put a question mark.

| $x$ | 1 | 2 | 3 | 4 | 5 |
|---|---|---|---|---|---|
| $f(x)$ | 5 | 4 | 3 | 2 | 1 |
| $g(x)$ | 3 | 5 | 2 | 1 | 4 |
| $(f+g)(x)$ | | | | | |
| $(g/f)(x)$ | | | | | |
| $(g \circ f)(x)$ | | | | | |
| $(f \circ g)(x)$ | | | | | |
| $g^{-1}(x)$ | | | | | |

$3(3x-5)-5$

$9x - 9 - 5$

$3x-5 \quad\to$

$9x - 14$

$18 - 14 = 4$

(d) If $f(x) = 3x - 5$, then find $f(f(2))$ and $f^{-1}(2)$.

(e) Sketch the graph of $y = f(x) = |x|$ on the domain $[-2,2]$. Then sketch the following graphs, labeling the vertex and the endpoints.

   i. $y = f(x) - 3$

   ii. $y = f(x-3)$

   iii. $y = 3f(x)$

iv. $y = f(3x)$

v. $y = -f(x)$

vi. $y = f(-x)$

(f) Find formulas for the following (separate) transformations of $f(x) = x^3 - x$.

    i. Shift $f$ to the right 4 units and then up 2 units.

    ii. Stretch $f$ horizontally by a factor of 5 and then reflect in the $y$-axis.

    iii. Shift $f$ to the left 3 units, then reflect in the $x$-axis, and then compress vertically by a factor of 2.

(g) Give an example of functions $f$ and $g$ where $f \neq g$, neither function is the identity, but $f \circ g = g \circ f$.

(h) Find $f^{-1}(x)$ if $f(x) = \frac{5x-2}{3}$. Verify that $f(f^{-1}(x)) = x$ and that $f^{-1}(f(x)) = x$.

7. Answers to Sample Problems

(a) If $f(x) = 2x^2 - 8$ and if $g(x) = \sqrt{x}$, then what is the domain of $g(f(x))$? The set $(-\infty, -2] \cup [2, \infty)$.

(b) Let $f = \{(1,1), (2,3), (2,4), (3,1)\}$ and let $g = \{(4,3), (3,3), (2,1), (1,4)\}$

    i. Which set is a function? $g$. $f$ is not a function.

    ii. What is the domain of that function? $\{4, 3, 2, 1\}$ range? $\{1, 3, 4\}$.

    iii. Is that function one-to-one? Explain. NO. $g(4) = g(3) = 3$. Two elements of the domain map to the same element of the range, which means that $g$ is not one-to-one.

    iv. Is that function onto the set $\{1, 3, 4\}$? Explain. YES. Since $g$ maps to 1, 3, and 4, we say that $g$ is onto the set $\{1, 3, 4\}$.

(c) Fill in the table below. If there is not enough information, put a question mark.

| $x$ | 1 | 2 | 3 | 4 | 5 |
|---|---|---|---|---|---|
| $f(x)$ | 5 | 4 | 3 | 2 | 1 |
| $g(x)$ | 3 | 5 | 2 | 1 | 4 |
| $(f+g)(x)$ | 8 | 9 | 5 | 3 | 5 |
| $(g/f)(x)$ | 3/5 | 5/4 | 2/3 | 1/2 | 4 |
| $(g \circ f)(x)$ | 4 | 1 | 2 | 5 | 3 |
| $(f \circ g)(x)$ | 3 | 1 | 4 | 5 | 2 |
| $g^{-1}(x)$ | 4 | 3 | 1 | 5 | 2 |

(d) If $f(x) = 3x - 5$, then find $f(f(2))$ and $f^{-1}(2)$. Since $f(2) = 1$, $f(f(2)) = f(1) = -2$. We can find the inverse function directly or use the definition:

$$y = f^{-1}(2) \Leftrightarrow f(y) = 2.$$

So we need to solve $2 = f(y) = 3y - 5$, or $y = f^{-1}(2) = \frac{7}{3}$.

(e) Sketch the graph of $y = f(x) = |x|$ on the domain $[-2, 2]$. Then sketch the following graphs, labeling the vertex and the endpoints. Labels have been left off of the answers, but for the original graph, the vertex is at $(0, 0)$, and the endpoints are $(-2, 2)$ and $(2, 2)$.

   i. $y = f(x) - 3 = |x| - 3$, vertex: $(0, -3)$, endpts: $(-2, -1)$ and $(2, -1)$
   ii. $y = f(x - 3) = |x - 3|$, vertex: $(3, 0)$, endpts: $(1, 2)$ and $(5, 2)$
   iii. $y = 3f(x) = 3|x|$, vertex: $(0, 0)$, endpts: $(-2, 6)$ and $(2, 6)$
   iv. $y = f(3x) = |3x|$, vertex: $(0, 0)$, endpts: $(-\frac{2}{3}, 2)$ and $(\frac{2}{3}, 2)$
   v. $y = -f(x) = -|x|$, vertex: $(0, 0)$, endpts: $(-2, -2)$ and $(2, -2)$
   vi. $y = f(-x) = |-x| = |x|$ (same as original graph)

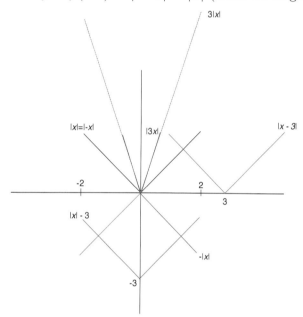

(f) Find formulas for the following (separate) transformations of $f(x) = x^3 - x$.

   i. Shift $f$ to the right 4 units and then up 2 units. $(x - 4)^3 - (x - 4) + 2$
   ii. Stretch $f$ horizontally by a factor of 5 and then reflect in the $y$-axis. $-(\frac{x}{5})^3 + \frac{x}{5}$
   iii. Shift $f$ to the left 3 units, then reflect in the $x$-axis, and then compress vertically by a factor of 2. $\frac{1}{2}[(-x + 3)^3 - (-x + 3)]$

(g) Give an example of functions $f$ and $g$ where $f \neq g$, neither function is the identity, but $f \circ g = g \circ f$. There are many answers. For example, $f(x) = x + 3$ and $g(x) = x - 5$. Also, $f(x) = px$ and $g(x) = qx$, where $p$ and $q$ are any real numbers with $p \neq q$.

(h) Find $f^{-1}(x)$ if $f(x) = \frac{5x-2}{3}$. Verify that $f(f^{-1}(x)) = x$ and that $f^{-1}(f(x)) = x$.

$$f^{-1}(x) = \frac{3x+2}{5}.$$

$$f(f^{-1}(x)) = f\left(\frac{3x+2}{5}\right)$$

$$= \frac{5\left(\frac{3x+2}{5}\right) - 2}{3} = \frac{3x+2-2}{3} = x.$$

$$f^{-1}(f(x)) = f^{-1}\left(\frac{5x-2}{3}\right)$$

$$= \frac{3\left(\frac{5x-2}{3}\right) + 2}{5} = \frac{5x-2+2}{5} = x.$$

## b. Analyze properties of polynomial, rational, radical, and absolute value functions in a variety of ways (e.g., graphing, solving problems)

1. Continuity and holes

   Polynomials and absolute value functions are continuous on the entire domain of real numbers. Rational functions are continuous everywhere except when the denominator is zero. Radical functions are continuous on their domains, but are not always defined for all reals.

   Examples include: $3x^3 - x$, $|x-4|$, $\dfrac{x+3}{x^2-4}$ (discontinuities at $x = \pm 2$), and $\sqrt{x-2}$ (not defined for $x < 2$).

2. Intercepts, horizontal and vertical

   Every function has exactly one vertical intercept, provided that $x = 0$ is in its domain. Functions can have several horizontal intercepts, which can be found by setting the value of the function to zero and solving for $x$. For example, $x^3 - 2x + 1$ has one vertical intercept at $y = 1$, and three horizontal intercepts: $\dfrac{-1 \pm \sqrt{5}}{2}$ and $1$.

3. Asymptotes, horizontal and vertical

   Polynomials, radicals, and absolute value functions have no asymptotes. Rational functions have horizontal asymptotes exactly when the degree of the numerator is less than or equal to the degree of the denominator. Rational functions can have vertical asymptotes or holes at the points where the denominator is zero. How can you tell which is which? (See example.)

   **Example:** $f(x) = \dfrac{x^2 + 4x + 4}{x^2 - 4}$ versus $g(x) = \dfrac{x^2 + 2x + 1}{x^2 - 4}$

   $f(x)$ can be factored and reduced to $\dfrac{x+2}{x-2}$, provided that $x \neq -2$. This means that there is a hole in the graph of $f$ at the point $\left(-2, \frac{-2+2}{-2-2}\right) = (-2, 0)$. The function $g(x)$ cannot be reduced, which means that the $(x+2)$ factor cannot be canceled. Thus $g(x)$ has a vertical asymptote at $x = -2$.

4. Sample Problems

(a) Solve for $x$: $\sqrt{x} + \sqrt{x+3} = 3$.

(b) Find the range of $f(x) = |2x - 5| + 3$ and sketch the graph of $y = f(x)$.

(c) Say that $y = f(x)$ is a cubic polynomial and that $f(3) = f(1) = f(-2) = 0$. Also, say that $f(0) = 12$. Find the formula for $f$.

(d) What is the [subtle] difference between $f(x) = x + 1$ and $g(x) = \dfrac{x^2 - 1}{x - 1}$? How does this show up on their graphs?

(e) Explain why the domain of $\sqrt{x}$ is $[0, \infty)$ but the domain of $\sqrt[3]{x}$ is all real numbers.

(f) Sketch a graph of $y = \dfrac{x^2 - 1}{x^2 - 4}$, labeling all intercepts and asymptotes.

(g) Sketch a graph of $y = \dfrac{1}{x^2 + 1}$, labeling all intercepts and asymptotes.

(h) Sketch $y = \sqrt{x}$. Then sketch its inverse graph and find the formula. What is the domain of $f^{-1}$ in this case?

(i) Explain why $f(x) = x^2$ is not invertible on its domain of all real numbers, but that it is invertible on the restricted domain $[0, \infty)$.

5. Answers to Sample Problems

(a) Solve for $x$: $\sqrt{x} + \sqrt{x+3} = 3$. $x = 1$

(b) Find the range of $f(x) = |2x - 5| + 3$ and sketch the graph of $y = f(x)$. The range is $[3, \infty)$.

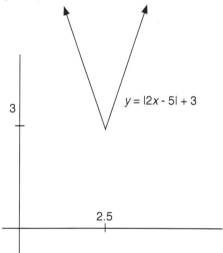

$y = |2x - 5| + 3$

3

2.5

(c) Say that $y = f(x)$ is a cubic polynomial and that $f(3) = f(1) = f(-2) = 0$. Also, say that $f(0) = 12$. Find the formula for $f$. $f(x) = 2(x-3)(x-1)(x+2) = 2x^3 - 4x^2 - 10x + 12$

(d) What is the [subtle] difference between $f(x) = x + 1$ and $g(x) = \dfrac{x^2 - 1}{x - 1}$? How does this show up on their graphs?

The only difference is that 1 is in the domain of $f$ but it is not in the domain of $g$. Other than that, the two functions are identical. This means that the graph of $y = g(x)$ is the line $x + 1$ except that it has a hole at the point $(1, 2)$.

(e) Explain why the domain of $\sqrt{x}$ is $[0, \infty)$ but the domain of $\sqrt[3]{x}$ is all real numbers. The square root of a negative number is not real, whereas the cube root of a negative number is negative. For example, since $(-2)^3 = -8$, $\sqrt[3]{-8} = -2$.

(f) Sketch a graph of $y = \dfrac{x^2 - 1}{x^2 - 4}$, labeling all intercepts and asymptotes.

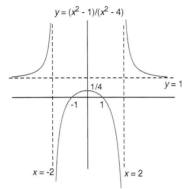

(g) Sketch a graph of $y = \dfrac{1}{x^2 + 1}$, labeling all intercepts and asymptotes.

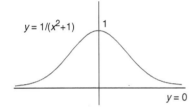

(h) Sketch $y = \sqrt{x}$. Then sketch its inverse graph and find the formula. What is the domain of $f^{-1}$ in this case? The domain of the inverse function is $[0, \infty)$.

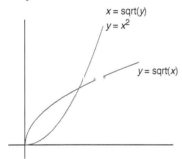

(i) Explain why $f(x) = x^2$ is not invertible on its domain of all real numbers, but that it is invertible on the restricted domain $[0, \infty)$. The function $f(x) = x^2$ is not one-to-one on its domain, $((-2)^2 = 2^2 = 4$, for instance), but it *is* one-to-one on its restricted domain. That means that $f$ is invertible if we only consider non-negative values of $x$.

## c. Analyze properties of exponential and logarithmic functions in a variety of ways (e.g., graphing, solving problems)

*** *For a quick review of logarithms, see the Miscellaneous Topics at the end of this book.*

1. How are exponential and logarithmic functions related?

The exponential and logarithmic functions are inverse functions of each other. So,

- $y = e^x \Leftrightarrow x = \ln y$,
- $y = 10^x \Leftrightarrow x = \log y$, and in general,
- $y = b^x \Leftrightarrow x = \log_b y$.

2. Continuity

   The basic exponential functions are continuous on the entire domain of real numbers.

   The basic logarithmic functions are continuous on their domains (positive real numbers).

3. Intercepts, horizontal and vertical

   The basic exponential functions have only one intercept, at $(0, 1)$.   opp

   The basic logarithmic functions have only one intercept, at $(1, 0)$.

4. Asymptotes, horizontal and vertical

   Exponential functions have one horizontal asymptote, at $y = 0$. As an example, $\lim\limits_{x \to -\infty} 2^x = 0$.

   Logarithmic functions have one vertical asymptote, at $x = 0$. For example, as $x \to 0^+$, $\ln x \to -\infty$.

5. Sample Problems

   (a) Explain the domains and ranges, intercepts, and asymptotes of basic exponential and logarithmic functions in terms of inverse functions.

   (b) Simplify, if possible:
   - i. $e^{\ln 4}$
   - ii. $\ln(e^{3x})$
   - iii. $\log 200 + \log 50$
   - iv. $\log_3(2) - \log_3(18)$
   - v. $\log_b 1$
   - vi. $\log_b 0$
   - vii. $10^{\log x + \log x^2}$

   (c) Solve for $x$: $3 - \log x = 10$.

   (d) Solve for $x$: $\ln 2^x = \ln 3$.

   (e) Suppose that the value of your \$20,000 car depreciates by 10% each year after you bought it. Find a formula for the value of your car $V$ as a function of $t$, the number of years since you bought it.

   (f) Suppose that you have money in a bank account earning 5% interest. Then the amount of money you have after $t$ years is given by $A(t) = P(1.05)^t$. where $P$ is the principal amount invested. Find the doubling time of this account. Leave logarithms in your answer.

   (g) Find a formula for an exponential function that passes through the point $(0, 4)$ and the point $(1, 8)$.

(h) Sketch a rough graph of $y = 5 - e^{-x}$. [Hint: Use transformations of a basic graph.] Name a real-world process you could model with a graph of this shape.

6. Answers to Sample Problems

(a) Explain the domains and ranges, intercepts, and asymptotes of basic exponential and logarithmic functions in terms of inverse functions.

| Feature | Exponential | Logarithmic |
|---|---|---|
| Domain | all reals | $x \geq 0$ |
| Range | $y \geq 0$ | all reals |
| Intercepts | $y = 1$ | $x = 1$ |
| Asymptotes | $y = 0$ | $x = 0$ |

Notice that switching $x$ and $y$ (reflecting over the line $y = x$) takes the domain of one function to the range of the other and vice versa. Also, the $y = 1$ intercept of a basic exponential function switches with the $x = 1$ intercept of a basic logarithmic function. Similarly, the horizontal asymptote of a basic exponential function switches with the vertical asymptote of a basic logarithmic function.

(b) Simplify, if possible:

    i. $e^{\ln 4} = 4$

    ii. $\ln(e^{3x}) = 3x$

    iii. $\log 200 + \log 50 = \log 10{,}000 = 4$

    iv. $\log_3(2) - \log_3(18) = \log_3 \frac{1}{9} = -2$

    v. $\log_b 1 = 0$

    vi. $\log_b 0$ is not defined.

    vii. $10^{\log x + \log x^2} = 10^{\log x^3} = x^3$

(c) Solve for $x$: $3 - \log x = 10$. $x = 10^{-7}$

(d) Solve for $x$: $\ln 2^x = \ln 3$. $2^x = 3$; $x = \log_2 3 = \frac{\ln 3}{\ln 2} = \frac{\log 3}{\log 2}$

(e) Suppose that the value of your \$20,000 car depreciates by 10% each year after you bought it. Find a formula for the value of your car $V$ as a function of $t$, the number of years since you bought it. $V(t) = 20{,}000(0.9)^t$

(f) Suppose that you have money in a bank account earning 5% interest. Then the amount of money you have after $t$ years is given by $A(t) = P(1.05)^t$. where $P$ is the principal amount invested. Find the doubling time of this account. Leave logarithms in your answer.

If $2P = P(1.05)^t$, then $2 = (1.05)^t$, or $t = \log_{1.05} 2 = \frac{\ln 2}{\ln 1.05} = \frac{\log 2}{\log 1.05}$.

(g) Find a formula for an exponential function that passes through the point $(0, 4)$ and the point $(1, 8)$. $y = 4 \cdot 2^x$

(h) Sketch a rough graph of $y = 5 - e^{-x}$. [Hint: Use transformations of a basic graph.] Name a real-world process you could model with a graph of this shape.

Using transformations: you can start with $y = e^x$, flip it over the $y$-axis to get $y = e^{-x}$, then flip it over the $x$-axis to get $y = -e^{-x}$. Finally, shift it up five units.

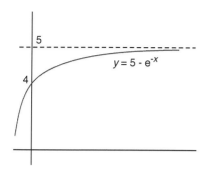

One possible process is heating an object. As the object sits in an oven (at a constant temperature), the object's temperature exponentially approaches the temperature of the oven. There are other valid answers.

## 1.4 Linear Algebra

**a. Understand and apply the geometric interpretation and basic operations of vectors in two and three dimensions, including their scalar multiples and scalar (dot) and cross products**

1. What is a vector?

   A vector is a mathematical object that has a magnitude and a direction. People often think of two-dimensional (2-D) vectors as arrows drawn on the plane, and three-dimensional (3-D) vectors as arrows in space. The starting point of a vector is not important to the definition. Consequently, vectors are often depicted in *standard position* (starting at the origin). The magnitude (or length) of $\vec{v}$ is often denoted $\|\vec{v}\|$.

2. What is a vector space?

   A vector space is a set (made up of elements called vectors) that is closed under an operation called vector addition (which is commutative and associative and has an identity and inverses) and under multiplication by a field of scalars (usually the real numbers) which has nice associative and distributive properties over vector addition. The main examples of vector spaces for us will be $\mathbb{R}^2$ (the Cartesian coordinate plane) and $\mathbb{R}^3$ (three-dimensional space).

3. How do you write vectors?

   There are three common main ways to write vectors:

   (a) as ordered $n$-tuples: $\langle 1, -2 \rangle$ or $\langle -3, 0, 4 \rangle$, [or sometimes as $(1, -2)$ or $(-3, 0, 4)$]
   
   (b) in terms of component vectors: $\vec{i} - 2\vec{j}$ or $-3\vec{i} + 4\vec{k}$, or

   (c) as columns: $\begin{bmatrix} 1 \\ -2 \end{bmatrix}$ or $\begin{bmatrix} -3 \\ 0 \\ 4 \end{bmatrix}$.

4. How do you add vectors? How do you multiply vectors by scalars?

   Algebraically, you can add vectors by adding their corresponding components. You can multiply a vector by a scalar by multiplying each of its components by that scalar. For example, if $\vec{v} = \langle 1, 4, -6 \rangle$ and $\vec{w} = \langle -3, 0, -2 \rangle$, then:

   $\vec{v} + \vec{w} = \langle 1 + (-3), 4 + 0, (-6) + (-2) \rangle = \langle -2, 4, -8 \rangle$,

   $2\vec{v} = \langle 2(1), 2(4), 2(-6) \rangle = \langle 2, 8, -12 \rangle$,

   and $\vec{v} - \vec{w} = \langle 1 - (-3), 4 - 0, (-6) - (-2) \rangle = \langle 4, 4, -4 \rangle$.

   Geometrically, you can add vectors by drawing one vector at the head of another. You can also multiply a vector by a scalar by scaling the vector by that amount. For example,

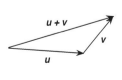
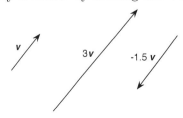

5. How do you "multiply" two vectors?

In general, you cannot multiply vectors, which is one of the ways that they are different from numbers. However, there are two specific products that are useful.

(a) Dot Product (scalar)

The dot product is defined for vectors in any dimension. The dot product of two vectors is always a scalar (and is never a vector). So it's also called the scalar product.

   i. Algebraic

   If $\vec{v} = \langle v_1, v_2, \ldots, v_n \rangle$ and $\vec{w} = \langle w_1, w_2, \ldots, w_n \rangle$, then

   $$\vec{v} \cdot \vec{w} = v_1 w_1 + v_2 w_2 + \ldots + v_n w_n.$$

   ii. Geometric

   The dot product of two vectors is the product of their lengths times the cosine of the angle between them. That is,

   $$\vec{v} \cdot \vec{w} = \|\vec{v}\| \|\vec{w}\| \cos \theta.$$

   iii. Why is the dot product important?

   The dot product is the easiest way to determine the angle between two vectors. So, it can be used to tell when two vectors are perpendicular. Also, the dot product of a vector with itself gives you the square of the length because $\theta = 0$ in this case. Physicists use the dot product to decompose a vector into its various components. For example, work is the dot product of the force vector with the displacement vector. Force that is perpendicular to the direction of motion ($\theta = 90°$) does not do any work.

(b) Cross Product (vector)

The cross product is only defined for three-dimensional vectors. The cross product of two vectors is always a vector (and is never a scalar). So it's also called the vector product.

   i. Algebraic

   If $\vec{v} = \langle v_1, v_2, v_3 \rangle$ and $\vec{w} = \langle w_1, w_2, w_3 \rangle$, then

   $$\vec{v} \times \vec{w} = \langle v_2 w_3 - v_3 w_2, v_3 w_1 - v_1 w_3, v_1 w_2 - v_2 w_1 \rangle.$$

   ii. Geometric

   The cross product of two vectors is a vector whose length is the product of the two vectors' lengths times the sine of the angle between them. That is,

   $$\|\vec{v} \times \vec{w}\| = \|\vec{v}\| \|\vec{w}\| \sin \theta.$$

   Also, the direction of the cross product is perpendicular to the two vectors and points in a direction determined by the Right Hand Rule. Using your right hand, point your fingers in the direction of $\vec{v}$. Keeping your fingers pointing that way, rotate your hand until curling your fingers would make them point in the direction of $\vec{w}$. Now your thumb points in the direction of $\vec{v} \times \vec{w}$.

iii. Why is the cross product important?

The cross product provides a vector that is perpendicular to the plane spanned by two given vectors. Physicists use the cross product with vector quantities and vector fields. For example, torque is the cross product of a force vector with a displacement vector on which the force acts. If a force pulls directly away from a point, $(\theta = 0°)$ then that point experiences zero torque from that force.

6. Sample Problems

(a) Draw a picture describing $\langle -3, 5 \rangle + \langle 3, -3 \rangle$.

(b) Draw a picture describing $3 \langle -1, 2 \rangle$.

(c) If $\vec{v}$ has magnitude 13 and points in a direction 135° counter-clockwise from the positive $x$-axis, then find the magnitude and direction of $2\vec{v}$ and $-3\vec{v}$.

(d) Find the magnitude and direction of $\vec{i} + \vec{j}$.

(e) Give an example showing that the two definitions of the dot product are the same.

(f) Give an example showing that the two definitions of the cross product are the same.

(g) (CSET Sample Test #11) Given any two unit vectors $\vec{a}$ and $\vec{b}$, explain why

$$-1 \le (\vec{a} \cdot \vec{b}) \le 1.$$

(h) Show on a graph that any vector $\vec{v} = v_1 \vec{i} + v_2 \vec{j}$ which is perpendicular to $2\vec{i} + \vec{j}$ has to satisfy $2v_1 + v_2 = 0$. [Hint: think of slopes.]

7. Answers to Sample Problems

(a) Draw a picture describing $\langle -3, 5 \rangle + \langle 3, -3 \rangle$.

(b) Draw a picture describing $3 \langle -1, 2 \rangle$.

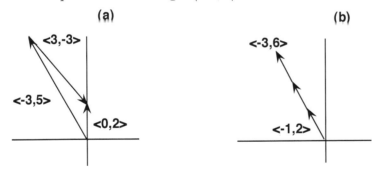

(c) If $\vec{v}$ has magnitude 13 and points in a direction 135° counter-clockwise from the positive $x$-axis, then find the magnitude and direction of $2\vec{v}$ and $-3\vec{v}$. $2\vec{v}$ has magnitude 26 and points 135° counter-clockwise from the positive $x$-axis, while $-3\vec{v}$ has magnitude 39, but points 315° counter-clockwise (or 45° clockwise) from the positive $x$-axis.

(d) Find the magnitude and direction of $\vec{i} + \vec{j}$. The magnitude is $\sqrt{2}$ and the direction is 45° counterclockwise from the positive $x$-axis.

(e) Give an example showing that the two definitions of the dot product are the same. There are many answers. Consider the example $\langle -1, 1 \rangle \cdot \langle 2, 0 \rangle$. Algebraically, the dot product is $(-1)(2) + (1)(0) = -2$. Geometrically, the magnitude of the first vector is $\sqrt{2}$ and the magnitude of the second vector is 2. The angle between them is $135°$. So the geometric version of the dot product is

$$(\sqrt{2})(2)(\cos 135°) = 2\sqrt{2}\left(-\frac{\sqrt{2}}{2}\right) = -2.$$

(f) Give an example showing that the two definitions of the cross product are the same. There are many answers. Consider the example $\langle 1, 1, 0 \rangle \times \langle 1, 0, 0 \rangle$. There is a $45°$ angle between these vectors. Algebraically, the cross product is $0\vec{i} + 0\vec{j} + (-1)\vec{k} = -\vec{k}$. Geometrically, the magnitude of the cross product is $(\sqrt{2})(1)(\sin 45°) = \sqrt{2}(\frac{\sqrt{2}}{2}) = 1$ and the direction is perpendicular to the $xy$-plane, in a direction given by the Right Hand Rule. Thus the geometric version of the cross product gives $-\vec{k}$ as well.

(g) (CSET Sample Test #11) Given any two unit vectors $\vec{a}$ and $\vec{b}$, explain why

$$-1 \le (\vec{a} \cdot \vec{b}) \le 1.$$

From the geometric version of the dot product, we know that

$$\vec{a} \cdot \vec{b} = \|\vec{a}\|\|\vec{b}\| \cos\theta,$$

where $\theta$ is the angle between $\vec{a}$ and $\vec{b}$. Since $\vec{a}$ and $\vec{b}$ are unit vectors, their magnitudes equal 1. So $\vec{a} \cdot \vec{b} = \cos\theta$, which is always between $-1$ and 1.

(h) Show on a graph that any vector $\vec{v} = v_1\vec{i} + v_2\vec{j}$ which is perpendicular to $2\vec{i} + \vec{j}$ has to satisfy $2v_1 + v_2 = 0$. [Hint: think of slopes.]

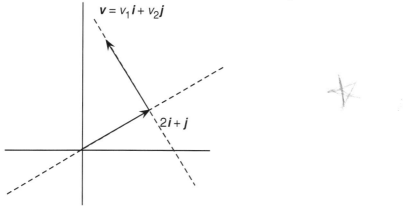

Notice that the slope of any vector $a\vec{i} + b\vec{j}$ is $\frac{\text{rise}}{\text{run}} = \frac{b}{a}$. So the slope of $2\vec{i} + \vec{j}$ is $\frac{1}{2}$. Since perpendicular lines have negative reciprocal slopes, the slope of $\vec{v}$ must be $-2$. So

$$-2 = \frac{v_2}{v_1} \Rightarrow -2v_1 = v_2 \Rightarrow 0 = 2v_1 + v_2.$$

**b. Prove the basic properties of vectors (e.g., perpendicular vectors have zero dot product)**

1. What are some basic properties of vectors?

   (a) Assume $\vec{v} \neq \vec{0} \neq \vec{w}$. Then $\vec{v} \cdot \vec{w} = 0$ if and only if $\vec{v} \perp \vec{w}$.

   **Proof:** From the geometric definition of the dot product (above),

   $$\vec{v} \cdot \vec{w} = \|\vec{v}\|\|\vec{w}\| \cos \theta,$$

   where $\theta$ is the angle between $\vec{v}$ and $\vec{w}$. Since the vectors have nonzero lengths, this dot product equals zero if and only if $\cos \theta = 0$. But this means $\theta = 90°$; that is, $\vec{v} \perp \vec{w}$.

   (b) Assume $\vec{v} \neq \vec{0} \neq \vec{w}$. Then $\vec{v} \times \vec{w} = \vec{0}$ if and only if $\vec{v}$ and $\vec{w}$ are parallel or anti-parallel.

   **Proof:** From the geometric definition of the cross product (above),

   $$\|\vec{v} \times \vec{w}\| = \|\vec{v}\|\|\vec{w}\| \sin \theta,$$

   where $\theta$ is the angle between $\vec{v}$ and $\vec{w}$. Since the vectors have nonzero lengths, this dot product equals zero if and only if $\sin \theta = 0$. But this means that either $\theta = 0°$, in which case $\vec{v}$ is parallel to $\vec{w}$, or that $\theta = 180°$, in which case $\vec{v}$ is anti-parallel to $\vec{w}$.

2. Sample Problems

   (a) Let $\vec{v} = 2\vec{i} - 3\vec{j}$ and let $\vec{w} = 7\vec{i} + \vec{j} - 3\vec{k}$. Find the following.

      i. $\vec{v} \cdot \vec{w}$

      ii. $\vec{v} \times \vec{w}$

      iii. $\|\vec{v}\|$ and $\|\vec{w}\|$

      iv. the angle between $\vec{v}$ and $\vec{w}$

   (b) Using the example above, show that $\vec{v} \times \vec{w}$ is perpendicular to $\vec{v}$ and to $\vec{w}$.

   (c) Show that $\vec{v} \times \vec{w}$ is always perpendicular to $\vec{v}$ and to $\vec{w}$.

   (d) Show that $(\vec{v} \times \vec{w}) = -(\vec{w} \times \vec{v})$.

   (e) Show that $\vec{u} \cdot (\vec{v} + \vec{w}) = \vec{u} \cdot \vec{v} + \vec{u} \cdot \vec{w}$. You can assume $\vec{u}$, $\vec{v}$, and $\vec{w}$ are two-dimensional. [The property is true in general.]

   (f) Show that $(\alpha\vec{v}) \cdot \vec{w} = \vec{v} \cdot (\alpha\vec{w}) = \alpha(\vec{v} \cdot \vec{w})$, where $\alpha$ is a scalar (real number). You can assume $\vec{v}$ and $\vec{w}$ are two-dimensional. [The property is true in general.]

   (g) Using the Law of Cosines [In $\triangle ABC$, $c^2 = a^2 + b^2 - 2ab \cos C$.], derive the geometric definition of the dot product. [Hint: draw a triangle of sides $\vec{v}$, $\vec{w}$, and $\vec{w} - \vec{v}$ and apply the formula for length: $\vec{v} \cdot \vec{v} = \|\vec{v}\|^2$.]

3. Answers to Sample Problems

   (a) Let $\vec{v} = 2\vec{i} - 3\vec{j}$ and let $\vec{w} = 7\vec{i} + \vec{j} - 3\vec{k}$. Find the following.

      i. $\vec{v} \cdot \vec{w} = 11$

      ii. $\vec{v} \times \vec{w} = 9\vec{i} + 6\vec{j} + 23\vec{k}$

iii. $\|\vec{v}\| = \sqrt{13}$ and $\|\vec{w}\| = \sqrt{59}$

iv. the angle between $\vec{v}$ and $\vec{w}$ is $\arccos\left(\dfrac{11}{\sqrt{767}}\right) \approx 1.16$ radians, or $66.6°$.

(b) Using the example above, show that $\vec{v} \times \vec{w}$ is perpendicular to $\vec{v}$ and to $\vec{w}$. Using the dot product, $\vec{v} \cdot (\vec{v} \times \vec{w}) = 2(9) + (-3)(6) = 18 - 18 = 0$. Similarly, $\vec{w} \cdot (\vec{v} \times \vec{w}) = 7(9) + 1(6) - 3(23) = 63 + 6 - 69 = 0$.

(c) Show that $\vec{v} \times \vec{w}$ is always perpendicular to $\vec{v}$ and to $\vec{w}$. We will show one directly and leave the other part to the reader.

$$
\begin{aligned}
\vec{v} \cdot (\vec{v} \times \vec{w}) &= \langle v_1, v_2, v_3 \rangle \cdot \langle v_2 w_3 - v_3 w_2, v_3 w_1 - v_1 w_3, v_1 w_2 - v_2 w_1 \rangle \\
&= v_1(v_2 w_3 - v_3 w_2) + v_2(v_3 w_1 - v_1 w_3) + v_3(v_1 w_2 - v_2 w_1) \\
&= v_1 v_2 w_3 - v_1 v_3 w_2 + v_2 v_3 w_1 - v_1 v_2 w_3 + v_1 v_3 w_2 - v_2 v_3 w_1 \\
&= 0 + 0 + 0 = 0.
\end{aligned}
$$

Hence, $\vec{v}$ is perpendicular to $\vec{v} \times \vec{w}$. The proof that $\vec{w}$ is perpendicular to $\vec{v} \times \vec{w}$ is similar.

(d) Show that $(\vec{v} \times \vec{w}) = -(\vec{w} \times \vec{v})$.

$$
\begin{aligned}
\vec{v} \times \vec{w} &= \langle v_2 w_3 - v_3 w_2, v_3 w_1 - v_1 w_3, v_1 w_2 - v_2 w_1 \rangle \\
&= \langle -(w_2 v_3 - w_3 v_2), -(w_3 v_1 - w_1 v_3), -(w_1 v_2 - w_2 v_1) \rangle \\
&= -\langle w_2 v_3 - w_3 v_2, w_3 v_1 - w_1 v_3, w_1 v_2 - w_2 v_1 \rangle = -(\vec{w} \times \vec{v}).
\end{aligned}
$$

(e) Show that $\vec{u} \cdot (\vec{v} + \vec{w}) = \vec{u} \cdot \vec{v} + \vec{u} \cdot \vec{w}$. You can assume $\vec{u}$, $\vec{v}$, and $\vec{w}$ are two-dimensional. [The property is true in general.]

Let $\vec{u} = \langle u_1, u_2 \rangle$, $\vec{v} = \langle v_1, v_2 \rangle$, and $\vec{w} = \langle w_1, w_2 \rangle$. Then $\vec{v} + \vec{w} = \langle v_1 + w_1, v_2 + w_2 \rangle$. So,

$$
\begin{aligned}
\vec{u} \cdot (\vec{v} + \vec{w}) &= u_1(v_1 + w_1) + u_2(v_2 + w_2) \\
&= u_1 v_1 + u_1 w_1 + u_2 v_2 + u_2 w_2 \\
&= (u_1 v_1 + u_2 v_2) + (u_1 w_1 + u_2 w_2) \\
&= \vec{u} \cdot \vec{v} + \vec{u} \cdot \vec{w}.
\end{aligned}
$$

(f) Show that $(\alpha \vec{v}) \cdot \vec{w} = \vec{v} \cdot (\alpha \vec{w}) = \alpha(\vec{v} \cdot \vec{w})$, where $\alpha$ is a scalar (real number). You can assume $\vec{v}$ and $\vec{w}$ are two-dimensional. [The property is true in general.]

Let $\vec{v} = \langle v_1, v_2 \rangle$ and $\vec{w} = \langle w_1, w_2 \rangle$. Then $\alpha \vec{v} = \langle \alpha v_1, \alpha v_2 \rangle$.

$$
\begin{aligned}
(\alpha \vec{v}) \cdot \vec{w} &= (\alpha v_1) w_1 + (\alpha v_2) w_2 \\
&= \alpha(v_1 w_1 + v_2 w_2) = \alpha(\vec{v} \cdot \vec{w}) \\
&= v_1(\alpha w_1) + v_2(\alpha w_2) = \vec{v} \cdot (\alpha \vec{w}).
\end{aligned}
$$

(g) Using the Law of Cosines [In $\triangle ABC$, $c^2 = a^2 + b^2 - 2ab \cos C$.], derive the geometric definition of the dot product. [Hint: draw a triangle of sides $\vec{v}$, $\vec{w}$, and $\vec{w} - \vec{v}$ and apply the formula for length: $\vec{v} \cdot \vec{v} = \|\vec{v}\|^2$.]

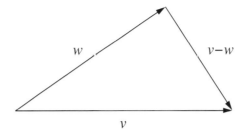

We'll begin with computing the length of the side $\vec{v} - \vec{w}$:

$$\begin{aligned} \|\vec{v} - \vec{w}\|^2 &= (\vec{v} - \vec{w}) \cdot (\vec{v} - \vec{w}) \\ &= \vec{v} \cdot \vec{v} - 2\vec{v} \cdot \vec{w} + \vec{w} \cdot \vec{w} \\ &= \|\vec{v}\|^2 + \|\vec{w}\|^2 - 2\vec{v} \cdot \vec{w}. \end{aligned}$$

Comparing this to the Law of Cosines, we see that the squares of the side lengths match up, giving $c^2 = a^2 + b^2 - 2\vec{v} \cdot \vec{w}$. Thus

$$-2ab\cos C = -2\vec{v} \cdot \vec{w},$$

which means $\vec{v} \cdot \vec{w} = ab\cos C = \|\vec{v}\|\|\vec{w}\|\cos C$, which is what we wanted.  □

## c. Understand and apply the basic properties and operations of matrices and determinants (e.g., to determine the solvability of linear systems of equations)

1. What is a matrix?

   A matrix is a rectangular array of numbers. Matrices can be very useful in solving systems of linear equations, among other applications.

2. How do you multiply matrices?

   You can multiply two matrices if the number of columns of the first matrix equals the number of rows of the second matrix. As an example,

   $$\begin{bmatrix} a & b \\ c & d \end{bmatrix} \begin{bmatrix} 1 & 2 & 3 \\ 4 & 5 & 6 \end{bmatrix} = \begin{bmatrix} a + 4b & 2a + 5b & 3a + 6b \\ c + 4d & 2c + 5d & 3c + 6d \end{bmatrix}.$$

   In general, if $A$ is an $m$ by $n$ matrix and $B$ is an $n$ by $p$ matrix, then $AB$ is an $m$ by $p$ matrix and the entry of $AB$ in row $i$ and column $j$ is given by:

   $$(AB)_{ij} = \sum_{k=1}^{n} A_{ik} B_{kj}.$$

3. What is the determinant of a matrix?

   The determinant of a square matrix is a specific number that encodes some of the properties of that matrix. For instance, if $\det M = 0$, then the matrix $M$ is not invertible. If $\det M \neq 0$, then there is a matrix $N$ satisfying $MN = NM = I$, where $I$ means the identity matrix (1s on the diagonal, 0s elsewhere). In this case, $N$ is also called $M^{-1}$, the inverse matrix of $M$.

For 2 by 2 matrices, the determinant is given by:

$$\det \begin{bmatrix} a & b \\ c & d \end{bmatrix} = \begin{vmatrix} a & b \\ c & d \end{vmatrix} = ad - bc.$$

Also, for 2 by 2 matrices, there is a relatively simple formula for finding the inverse matrix:

$$\begin{bmatrix} a & b \\ c & d \end{bmatrix}^{-1} = \left( \frac{1}{ad-bc} \right) \begin{bmatrix} d & -b \\ -c & a \end{bmatrix}, \text{ if } ad - bc \neq 0.$$

For 3 by 3 matrices, the determinant is given by:

$$\begin{vmatrix} a & b & c \\ d & e & f \\ g & h & i \end{vmatrix} = aei + bfg + cdh - bdi - afh - ceg.$$

One way to remember this formula involves recopying the first two columns and then looking along the diagonals of the resulting array.

$$\begin{array}{ccc|cc} a & b & c & a & b \\ d & e & f & d & e \\ g & h & i & g & h \end{array}$$

Multiplying along diagonals down and to the right, we get the terms $aei$, $bfg$, and $cdh$. These are the first three (positive) terms in the determinant formula. Multiplying down and to the left, we obtain the terms $bdi$, $afh$, and $ceg$, which are the next three (negative) terms in the determinant formula.

There is also a recursive way to find the determinant, called expansion by minors. This means that the determinant of a 3 by 3 matrix (for instance) can be written in terms of determinants of various 2 by 2 submatrices of the original matrix. The tricky part is that there is a factor of $(-1)^{r+c}$, where $r$ is the row number and $c$ the column number, counted from the upper left. We'll expand along the top row, although any row or column would work. Pick the first element, $a$, and then form a submatrix by deleting the row and column containing $a$. Continue throughout the row. See the example, below.

$$\begin{vmatrix} a & b & c \\ d & e & f \\ g & h & i \end{vmatrix} = (-1)^2 a \begin{vmatrix} e & f \\ h & i \end{vmatrix} + (-1)^3 b \begin{vmatrix} d & f \\ g & i \end{vmatrix} + (-1)^4 c \begin{vmatrix} d & e \\ g & h \end{vmatrix}$$

$$= a(ei - fh) - b(di - fg) + c(dh - eg)$$

$$= aei + bfg + cdh - afh - bdi - ceg.$$

Expansion by minors applies to larger matrices, whereas the trick of repeating the first two columns works only for 3 by 3 matrices.

4. How can you use a matrix to determine the solvability of a system of linear equations?

If you have a system of $n$ linear equations in $n$ variables, you can write it as $A\vec{x} = \vec{b}$, where $A$ is the square ($n$ by $n$) coefficient matrix, $\vec{x}$ is the vector of variables, and $\vec{b}$ is a column vector of right-hand sides to the equations. See Example, below. Method 1 uses row operations, which are really just manipulations of entire equations. For instance, you can multiply an equation by a constant. So, one valid row operation is to multiply the entire row by a constant.

If $A$ is invertible (that is, if $\det A \neq 0$), then there is exactly one solution to the system, namely $\vec{x} = A^{-1}\vec{b}$. Again, see Example, below, Method 2.

If $A$ is not invertible, then the situation is a little trickier. There might be no solutions (in which case the system of equations is *inconsistent*), or there might be an infinite number of solutions. An example of an inconsistent system is $x + y = 1; x + y = 2$. Clearly these two equations cannot simultaneously be true. An example of a system having an infinite number of solutions is $x + y = 1; 2x + 2y = 2$. This system has an entire line of solution points.

5. How can you use a matrix to solve a system of linear equations?

   **Example:** Solve the equations $2x + 3y = 5$ and $x - y = 5$ simultaneously.

   **Method 1 (row operations):**

   $$\begin{bmatrix} 2 & 3 & 5 \\ 1 & -1 & 5 \end{bmatrix} \sim \begin{bmatrix} 1 & -1 & 5 \\ 2 & 3 & 5 \end{bmatrix} \text{ (switch rows)}$$

   $$\sim \begin{bmatrix} 1 & -1 & 5 \\ 0 & 5 & -5 \end{bmatrix} \text{ (add } -2(\text{row 1}) \text{ to row 2)}$$

   $$\sim \begin{bmatrix} 1 & -1 & 5 \\ 0 & 1 & -1 \end{bmatrix} \text{ (divide row 2 by 5)}$$

   So the equations now read $x - y = 5$ and $y = -1$. We can substitute to find that $x = 4$.

   **Method 2 (inverse matrices):** First, rewrite the system of equations in matrix form:

   $$\begin{bmatrix} 2 & 3 \\ 1 & 1 \end{bmatrix} \begin{bmatrix} x \\ y \end{bmatrix} = \begin{bmatrix} 5 \\ 5 \end{bmatrix}.$$

   Using the formula for the inverse of a 2 by 2 matrix gives:

   $$\begin{bmatrix} 2 & 3 \\ 1 & -1 \end{bmatrix}^{-1} = \left( \frac{1}{(2)(-1) - (3)(1)} \right) \begin{bmatrix} -1 & -3 \\ -1 & 2 \end{bmatrix} = \begin{bmatrix} 1/5 & 3/5 \\ 1/5 & -2/5 \end{bmatrix}.$$

   So, we can multiply the original matrix equation on the left to obtain:

   $$\begin{bmatrix} 1/5 & 3/5 \\ 1/5 & -2/5 \end{bmatrix} \begin{bmatrix} 2 & 3 \\ 1 & -1 \end{bmatrix} \begin{bmatrix} x \\ y \end{bmatrix} = \begin{bmatrix} 1/5 & 3/5 \\ 1/5 & -2/5 \end{bmatrix} \begin{bmatrix} 5 \\ 5 \end{bmatrix},$$

   which simplifies to

   $$\begin{bmatrix} 1 & 0 \\ 0 & 1 \end{bmatrix} \begin{bmatrix} x \\ y \end{bmatrix} = \begin{bmatrix} x \\ y \end{bmatrix} = \begin{bmatrix} 4 \\ -1 \end{bmatrix}.$$

   Therefore, $(x, y) = (4, -1)$.

6. Sample Problems

   (a) Check the formula for the 2 by 2 inverse matrix by calculating $AA^{-1}$ and $A^{-1}A$.

   (b) Give an example of 2 by 2 matrices $A$ and $B$ satisfying $AB \neq BA$.

   (c) Solve the following system of equations: $4x - 3y = 15$ and $6x + y = 6$.

   (d) Solve the following system of equations: $x - y = 12$ and $-3x + 3y = 3$.

   (e) Describe how to solve the following system and set up the appropriate matrix equation, but do not actually solve the system.

$$\begin{aligned} 34x - 56y + 223z &= 217 \\ 24x + 25y - 100z &= 27 \\ -30x + 29y + 231z &= -429 \end{aligned}$$

   (f) Find the determinant of $\begin{bmatrix} 11 & 6 \\ 2 & -5 \end{bmatrix}$.

   (g) Find the determinant of $\begin{bmatrix} 4 & 3 & 7 \\ 5 & -5 & 4 \\ 0 & -9 & -8 \end{bmatrix}$.

   (h) Find $B$ so that $AB = C$, where $A = \begin{bmatrix} 3 & 5 \\ -3 & 4 \end{bmatrix}$ and $C = \begin{bmatrix} 9 \\ 9 \end{bmatrix}$.

   (i) Using $A$ and $C$ above, find $AC$, if possible. Then find $CA$, if possible.

7. Answers to Sample Problems

   (a) Check the formula for the 2 by 2 inverse matrix by calculating $AA^{-1}$ and $A^{-1}A$. We assume $ad - bc \neq 0$ so that the inverse of $A$ is defined.

$$\begin{bmatrix} a & b \\ c & d \end{bmatrix} \left( \frac{1}{ad - bc} \begin{bmatrix} d & -b \\ -c & a \end{bmatrix} \right) = \frac{1}{ad - bc} \begin{bmatrix} ad - bc & -ab + ba \\ cd - dc & -cb + da \end{bmatrix} = \begin{bmatrix} 1 & 0 \\ 0 & 1 \end{bmatrix},$$

$$\left( \frac{1}{ad - bc} \begin{bmatrix} d & -b \\ -c & a \end{bmatrix} \right) \begin{bmatrix} a & b \\ c & d \end{bmatrix} = \frac{1}{ad - bc} \begin{bmatrix} ad - bc & db - bd \\ -ca + ac & -bc + ad \end{bmatrix} = \begin{bmatrix} 1 & 0 \\ 0 & 1 \end{bmatrix}.$$

   (b) Give an example of 2 by 2 matrices $A$ and $B$ satisfying $AB \neq BA$. There are many answers.

$$\begin{bmatrix} 0 & 1 \\ 0 & 0 \end{bmatrix} \begin{bmatrix} 0 & 0 \\ 1 & 0 \end{bmatrix} = \begin{bmatrix} 1 & 0 \\ 0 & 0 \end{bmatrix}, \text{ but } \begin{bmatrix} 0 & 0 \\ 1 & 0 \end{bmatrix} \begin{bmatrix} 0 & 1 \\ 0 & 0 \end{bmatrix} = \begin{bmatrix} 0 & 0 \\ 0 & 1 \end{bmatrix}.$$

   (c) Solve the following system of equations: $4x - 3y = 15$ and $6x + y = 6$.

      Using matrices, we get

$$\begin{bmatrix} 4 & -3 \\ 6 & 1 \end{bmatrix} \begin{bmatrix} x \\ y \end{bmatrix} = \begin{bmatrix} 15 \\ 6 \end{bmatrix}.$$

The inverse of the coefficient matrix is $\dfrac{1}{22}\begin{bmatrix} 1 & 3 \\ -6 & 4 \end{bmatrix}$. So, multiplying both sides (on the left) by this inverse matrix gives:

$$\frac{1}{22}\begin{bmatrix} 1 & 3 \\ -6 & 4 \end{bmatrix}\begin{bmatrix} 4 & -3 \\ 6 & 1 \end{bmatrix}\begin{bmatrix} x \\ y \end{bmatrix} = \frac{1}{22}\begin{bmatrix} 1 & 3 \\ -6 & 4 \end{bmatrix}\begin{bmatrix} 15 \\ 6 \end{bmatrix} = \frac{1}{22}\begin{bmatrix} 33 \\ -66 \end{bmatrix} = \begin{bmatrix} 1.5 \\ -3 \end{bmatrix}.$$

So $x = 1.5$ and $y = -3$.

(d) Solve the following system of equations: $x - y = 12$ and $-3x + 3y = 3$.

Dividing the second equation by $-3$ gives $x - y = -1$. Hence there are no solutions to this system of equations. The system is inconsistent.

(e) Describe how to solve the following system and set up the appropriate matrix equation, but do not actually solve the system.

$$\begin{aligned} 34x - 56y + 223z &= 217 \\ 24x + 25y - 100z &= 27 \\ -30x + 29y + 231z &= -429 \end{aligned}$$

We can set up a matrix equation and then use row operations or finding an inverse matrix to reduce and solve the system. The corresponding matrix equation is:

$$\begin{bmatrix} 34 & -56 & 223 \\ 24 & 25 & -100 \\ -30 & 29 & 231 \end{bmatrix}\begin{bmatrix} x \\ y \\ z \end{bmatrix} = \begin{bmatrix} 217 \\ 27 \\ -429 \end{bmatrix}.$$

(f) Find the determinant of $\begin{bmatrix} 11 & 6 \\ 2 & -5 \end{bmatrix}$. $-67$

(g) Find the determinant of $\begin{bmatrix} 4 & 3 & 7 \\ 5 & -5 & 4 \\ 0 & -9 & -8 \end{bmatrix}$. $109$

(h) Find $B$ so that $AB = C$, where $A = \begin{bmatrix} 3 & 5 \\ -3 & 4 \end{bmatrix}$ and $C = \begin{bmatrix} 9 \\ 9 \end{bmatrix}$. In order for $AB$ to be a 2 by 1 matrix, we need $B$ to be a 2 by 1 matrix. Let $B = \begin{bmatrix} x \\ y \end{bmatrix}$ and solve. Or, find $A^{-1}$. Then $B = A^{-1}C$. In any case,

$$B = \begin{bmatrix} -\frac{1}{3} \\ 2 \end{bmatrix}.$$

(i) Using $A$ and $C$ above, find $AC$, if possible. Then find $CA$, if possible. $AC = \begin{bmatrix} 72 \\ 9 \end{bmatrix}$. The product $CA$ is not defined because $C$ has only one column, but $A$ has two rows.

# 3.1 Natural Numbers

## a. Prove and use basic properties of natural numbers (e.g., properties of divisibility)

1. What are the natural numbers?

$$\mathbb{N} = \{1, 2, 3, 4, 5, \ldots\}$$

   (Often, computer science books include zero in the natural numbers, but most mathematics books do not.) In higher mathematics, the natural numbers are built out of other objects, like sets. Then, the natural numbers are used to define the integers, which are then used to define the rational numbers, which are then used to define the real numbers, which are then used to define the complex numbers.

2. What are some axioms of the natural numbers?

   (Remember, axioms do not need to be proved.)

   The natural numbers are closed under addition and multiplication, which are commutative and associate operations in which multiplication distributes over addition. Also, the natural numbers are well ordered, which means that if $a$ and $b$ are natural numbers, then either $a \leq b$ or $b \leq a$. It also means that there is a smallest element.

3. What is division in the natural numbers (or integers)?

   There is a Division Algorithm in the integers that says the following. If $a$ and $b$ are natural numbers, then there exist *unique* integers $q$ and $r$ (called the *quotient* and *remainder*) satisfying

   (a) $a = qb + r$, and

   (b) $0 \leq r < b$.

   Usually, $a \geq b$, although that is not technically necessary. Also, $a$ could be any integer and division would still work.

4. What is divisibility in the natural numbers (or integers)?

   Let $a$ and $b$ be natural numbers [respectively, integers], with $b \neq 0$. We say $a$ is **divisible** by $b$, or $b$ **divides** $a$, or $b|a$, if there exists a natural number [resp., integer] $k$ satisfying $a = bk$. In other words, the remainder is zero when $a$ is divided by $b$.

5. What are some properties of divisibility?

   Let $a, b, c \in \mathbb{N}$.

   (a) $a|a$.

   (b) If $a|b$ and $b|c$, then $a|c$.

   (c) If $a|b$, then $a|bc$.

   (d) If $c|a$ and $c|b$, then $c|a + b$.

6. Sample Problems

   (a) Let $a, b \in \mathbb{N}$. Prove that the geometric mean of $a$ and $b$ is less than or equal to the arithmetic mean of $a$ and $b$; that is, $\sqrt{ab} \leq \frac{a+b}{2}$.

   (b) Let $a, b \in \mathbb{N}$. Prove that $\sqrt{ab} = \frac{a+b}{2}$ if and only if $a = b$.

   (c) Prove that a number is divisible by 4 if the number formed by its last two digits is divisible by 4.

   (d) Prove that a number is divisible by 3 if the sum of its digits is divisible by 3. (You may assume the number has three digits, although the property is true in general.)

   (e) Prove that there are an infinite number of Pythagorean triples.

7. Answers to Sample Problems

   (a) Let $a, b \in \mathbb{N}$. Prove that the geometric mean of $a$ and $b$ is less than or equal to the arithmetic mean of $a$ and $b$; that is, $\sqrt{ab} \leq \frac{a+b}{2}$.

   Since $a - b$ is a real number, $(a - b)^2 \geq 0$. So,

   $$\begin{aligned} a^2 - 2ab + b^2 &\geq 0 \\ a^2 + 2ab + b^2 &\geq 4ab \\ (a + b)^2 &\geq 4ab \\ a + b &\geq 2\sqrt{ab}, \end{aligned}$$

   where the last step follows because $ab > 0$. Dividing both sides by 2 gives the final result.

   (b) Let $a, b \in \mathbb{N}$. Prove that $\sqrt{ab} = \frac{a+b}{2}$ if and only if $a = b$.

   Multiplying both sides by 2 and then squaring both sides, we get $4ab = a^2 + 2ab + b^2$, or $0 = a^2 - 2ab + b^2 = (a - b)^2$. Thus $a - b$ must equal zero, that is, $a = b$.

   (c) Prove that a number is divisible by 4 if the number formed by its last two digits is divisible by 4.

   Since 100 is divisible by 4, we know that any number times 100 is also divisible by 4. (See properties of divisibility, above.) So we can disregard the digits in the hundreds place and higher, since they will not affect whether the overall number is divisible by 4. Only the tens and ones digits matter. As an example, consider $3424 = 34(100) + 24$. We know that 4 divides 100, and thus $34(100)$ as well. So, 3424 is divisible by 4 if and only if 24 is divisible by 4, which it is. So 3424 is divisible by 4.

   (d) Prove that a number is divisible by 3 if the sum of its digits is divisible by 3. (You may assume the number has three digits, although the property is true in general.)

   Let $h$, $t$, and $u$ be the hundreds, tens, and ones digits of the number $n$. Then

   $$n = 100h + 10t + u = (h + t + u) + 99h + 9t.$$

   Suppose that the digit sum of $n$ is divisible by 3. Then $h + t + u = 3k$ for some integer $k$. Then $n = 3k + 99h + 9t = 3(k + 33h + 3t)$. Clearly, $n$ is divisible by 3. As an aside, notice that a similar argument shows that $n$ is divisible by 9 if its digit sum is divisible by 9.

(e) Prove that there are an infinite number of Pythagorean triples.

The easy way to prove this is to prove that $(3, 4, 5)$ is a Pythagorean triple first $[3^2 + 4^2 = 9 + 16 = 25 = 5^2]$. Then we can show that $(3k, 4k, 5k)$ is another Pythagorean triple for any value of $k$. Indeed,

$$(3k)^2 + (4k)^2 = 9k^2 + 16k^2 = 25k^2 = (5k)^2.$$

So, $(6, 8, 10)$, $(9, 12, 15)$, etc. belong to an infinite chain of Pythagorean triples.

The harder way is to show that there are an infinite number of Pythagorean triples *which are not all multiples of each other*. Let's look at the difference between consecutive squares.

$$(n + 1)^2 - n^2 = n^2 + 2n + 1 - n^2 = 2n + 1$$

This means that every positive odd number, because it can be written as $2n + 1$, is the difference between two consecutive squares. For example, $4^2 - 3^2 = 16 - 9 = 7$. So $7 = 2(3) + 1$ is a difference of two consecutive squares. But 7 is not itself a perfect square, which means we do not get a Pythagorean triple in this case. However, $9 = 2(4) + 1$ is an odd number and a perfect square. In fact, $5^2 - 4^2 = 25 - 16 = 9 = 3^2$, which gives us the Pythagorean triple $(3, 4, 5)$. The next odd square is $25 = 2(12) + 1$. So $13^2 - 12^2 = 169 - 144 = 25 = 5^2$, giving $(5, 12, 13)$ as a Pythagorean triple. The next one in this sequence is $(7, 24, 25)$. Since there are an infinite number of odd perfect squares, we will get an infinite number of Pythagorean triples, no two of which are multiples of each other.

## b. Use the Principle of Mathematical Induction to prove results in number theory

1. What is Mathematical Induction?

   If you have a sequence of statements $(S_1, S_2, S_3, \dots)$ that satisfy the following properties: (1) that $S_1$ is true, and (2) that if $S_k$ is true, then it follows that $S_{k+1}$ is also true for all $k \in \mathbb{N}$, then the Principle of Mathematical Induction says that every statement in the sequence is true.

2. What is Complete Induction?

   If you have a sequence of statements $(S_1, S_2, S_3, \dots)$ that satisfy the following properties: (1) that $S_1$ is true, and (2) that if $S_j$ is true for all $j \leq k$, then it follows that $S_{k+1}$ is also true for all $k \in \mathbb{N}$, then the Principle of Complete Induction says that every statement in the sequence is true.

   The difference here is that in Complete Induction, you are allowed to assume that all the previous statements are true, rather than just the immediate predecessor. This can be very useful if one statement depends on several preceding statements.

3. How does one prove a result by induction?

   To prove a result by induction, one must prove the two parts of the principle. First, one must prove that $S_1$ is true. Second, one must prove that *if* $S_k$ is true, for some value of $k$, then $S_{k+1}$ must also be true.

4. Sample Problems (Prove the following statements.)

(a) $\displaystyle\sum_{i=1}^{n} i = \frac{n(n+1)}{2}$ for all $n \in \mathbb{N}$.

(b) The number $n^3 - n$ is divisible by 6 for any natural number $n$.

(c) $13 | (14^n - 1)$ for all $n \in \mathbb{N}$.

(d) $\displaystyle\sum_{i=1}^{n} i^2 = \frac{n(n+1)(2n+1)}{6}$ for all $n \in \mathbb{N}$.

(e) The sum of the even integers from 2 to $2n$ is $n(n+1)$.

(f) $\displaystyle\sum_{i=0}^{n} 2^i = 2^{n+1} - 1$ for all $n \in \mathbb{N}$.

5. Answers to Sample Problems

(a) $\displaystyle\sum_{i=1}^{n} i = \frac{n(n+1)}{2}$ for all $n \in \mathbb{N}$.

**Proof:** First, we must show that $\displaystyle\sum_{i=1}^{1} i = \frac{1(1+1)}{2}$. But $\displaystyle\sum_{i=1}^{1} i = 1 = \frac{1(2)}{2}$. So the statement $S_1$ is true.

**Aside:** What is the general statement, $S_n$?

ANS: $S_n$ is the statement we are asked to prove at the beginning, namely

$$\sum_{i=1}^{n} i = \frac{n(n+1)}{2} \text{ for all } n \in \mathbb{N}.$$

Second, we need to show that if $S_k$ is true for some $k$, then $S_{k+1}$ is also true. So, we assume that $S_k$ is true for some $k$. That is, $\displaystyle\sum_{i=1}^{k} i = \frac{k(k+1)}{2}$. This will come in handy later. Now we must prove that $S_{k+1}$ is true under this assumption. We will start by looking at the sum of $i$ as $i$ ranges from 1 to $k+1$ and we will algebraically manipulate it to fit the desired formula.

$$\begin{aligned}
\sum_{i=1}^{k+1} i &= \left(\sum_{i=1}^{k} i\right) + (k+1) \\
&= \frac{k(k+1)}{2} + (k+1) \\
&= (k+1)\left(\frac{k}{2}+1\right) \\
&= \frac{(k+1)(k+2)}{2},
\end{aligned}$$

which exactly proves that $S_{k+1}$ is true. Therefore, the Principle of Mathematical Induction implies that $S_n$ is true for all $n$, namely, that $\sum_{i=1}^{n} i = \frac{n(n+1)}{2}$. $\square$

(b) The number $n^3 - n$ is divisible by 6 for any natural number $n$.

**Proof:** $S_1$ says that $1^3 - 1$ is divisible by 6. That is true, because $1^3 - 1 = 0 = 6(0)$. Now assume that $k^3 - k$ is divisible by 6, which means that $k^3 - k = 6m$ for some integer $m$. Consider

$$(k+1)^3 - (k+1) = k^3 + 3k^2 + 3k + 1 - k - 1 = (k^3 - k) + 3k(k+1) = 6m + 3k(k+1),$$

where we used the assumption that $k^3 - k$ is divisible by 6. Notice that for any $k$, either $k$ or $k+1$ must be even, which means that $3k(k+1)$ is also divisible by 6. Thus, $(k+1)^3 - (k+1)$ is divisible by 6. Therefore, by the Principle of Mathematical Induction, $n^3 - n$ is divisible by 6 for all $n$. $\square$

(c) $13 | (14^n - 1)$ for all $n \in \mathbb{N}$.

**Proof:** Clearly, $14^1 - 1 = 13$ is divisible by 13. Let's now assume that $14^k - 1$ is divisible by 13. So, $14^k - 1 = 13m$ for some integer $m$. Then

$$14^{k+1} - 1 = 14(14^k) - 1 = (13+1)(14^k) - 1 = 13(14^k) + (14^k - 1) = 13(14^k) + 13m.$$

Since each term is divisible by 13, then $14^{k+1} - 1$ is also divisible by 13. Therefore, the Principle of Mathematical Induction says that $13 | (14^n - 1)$ for all $n \in \mathbb{N}$. $\square$

(d) $\sum_{i=1}^{n} i^2 = \frac{n(n+1)(2n+1)}{6}$ for all $n \in \mathbb{N}$.

**Proof:** When $n=1$, both sides are equal to 1. So assume that $\sum_{i=1}^{k} i^2 = \frac{k(k+1)(2k+1)}{6}$ for some $k \in \mathbb{N}$. Then

$$\begin{aligned} \sum_{i=1}^{k+1} i^2 &= \left( \sum_{i=1}^{k} i^2 \right) + (k+1)^2 \\ &= \frac{k(k+1)(2k+1)}{6} + (k+1)^2 \\ &= \left( \frac{k+1}{6} \right) [k(2k+1) + 6(k+1)] \\ &= \left( \frac{k+1}{6} \right) (2k^2 + 7k + 6) \\ &= \frac{(k+1)(k+2)(2k+3)}{6} = \frac{(k+1)((k+1)+1)(2(k+1)+1)}{6}, \end{aligned}$$

which is exactly the formula we wanted. Therefore, the Principle of Mathematical Induction says that $\sum_{i=1}^{n} i^2 = \frac{n(n+1)(2n+1)}{6}$ for all $n \in \mathbb{N}$. $\square$

(e) The sum of the even integers from 2 to $2n$ is $n(n+1)$.

This is the same proof as problem (a), above, except with both sides multiplied by 2.

(f) $\sum_{i=0}^{n} 2^i = 2^{n+1} - 1$ for all $n \in \mathbb{N}$.

**Proof:** Let $n = 1$. Then $\sum_{i=0}^{1} 2^i = 2^0 + 2^1 = 3 = 2^2 - 1$. So the statement is true when $n = 1$. Assume the statement is true for some $k \in \mathbb{N}$. That means that $\sum_{i=0}^{k} 2^i = 2^{k+1} - 1$.

Then

$$\sum_{i=0}^{k+1} 2^i = \left(\sum_{i=0}^{k} 2^i\right) + 2^{k+1}$$
$$= (2^{k+1} - 1) + 2^{k+1}$$
$$= 2(2^{k+1}) - 1 = 2^{k+2} - 1,$$

which is exactly the formula we wanted. Therefore the Principle of Mathematical Induction says that $\sum_{i=0}^{n} 2^i = 2^{n+1} - 1$ for all $n \in \mathbb{N}$.

## c. Know and apply the Euclidean Algorithm

1. What is the Euclidean Algorithm?

The Euclidean Algorithm is a procedure that returns the greatest common factor (or greatest common divisor, $GCD$) of two given natural numbers. The input is two natural numbers $a$ and $b$, with $a \geq b$. The output is the largest natural number which is a factor of both numbers.

2. How does the Euclidean Algorithm work?

The Euclidean Algorithm ($GCD$) is a recursive algorithm that can be summarized as follows:

To find the greatest common factor of $a$ and $b$ (where $a \geq b$), first divide $a$ by $b$ to find $q$ and $r$ satisfying $a = qb + r$ and $0 \leq r < b$. If $r = 0$, then $GCD(a,b) = b$. If $r \neq 0$, then $GCD(a,b) = GCD(b,r)$.

**Example:** Find $GCD(15,6)$.

ANS: Since $15 = 2(6) + 3$, then $r \neq 0$. So $GCD(15,6) = GCD(6,3)$. We repeat the algorithm. Since $6 = 2(3) + 0$, $GCD(6,3) = 3$. Thus $GCD(15,6) = 3$.

3. Why does the Euclidean Algorithm work?

Since $b > r$ at each step, meaning the next remainder $r' < r$, and so on, we have a descending chain of natural numbers: $b, r, r', \ldots$. But in the natural numbers, such a chain has to be finite. There are only a finite number of natural number solutions to $x < b$ for any value of $b$. Therefore the algorithm will eventually stop.

The algorithm stops at the right answer because the common factors of $a$ and $b$ are exactly the same as the common factors of $b$ and $r$. This is because $a = qb + r$, and thus $r = a - qb$. If $d$ is a factor of $a$ and $b$, then $d$ is a factor of $a - qb = r$ as well. Conversely, if $d$ is a factor of $b$ and $r$, then $d$ is a factor of $qb + r = a$. Since no common factors are gained or lost, the greatest common factor of the original two numbers is preserved through every step of the algorithm.

4. What is an application of Euclidean Algorithm?

   USEFUL FACT: The greatest common factor of $a$ and $b$ is the smallest natural number that can be written as $as + bt$, where $s$ and $t$ are suitably chosen integers. (The integers $s$ and $t$ are not unique, but you can find suitable values via the Euclidean Algorithm.)

5. Sample Problems

   (a) Find the greatest common factor of 123 and 24.

   (b) Find the greatest common factor of 55 and 34.

   (c) Find the greatest common factor of 91 and 35.

   (d) Show that the greatest common factor of $7n + 4$ and $5n + 3$ is 1 for all $n \in \mathbb{N}$.

6. Answers to Sample Problems

   (a) Find the greatest common factor of 123 and 24. 3
       Since $123 = 5(24) + 3$, $GCD(123, 24) = GCD(24, 3)$. Since $24 = 8(3)$, $GCD(24, 3) = 3$.

   (b) Find the greatest common factor of 55 and 34. 1
       $55 = 1(34) + 21; 34 = 1(21) + 13; 21 = 1(13) + 8; 13 = 1(8) + 5; 8 = 1(5) + 3;$
       $5 = 1(3) + 2; 3 = 1(2) + 1; 2 = 2(1) + 0.$

   (c) Find the greatest common factor of 91 and 35. 7
       $91 = 2(35) + 21; 35 = 1(21) + 14; 21 = 1(14) + 7; 14 = 2(7) + 0.$

   (d) Show that the greatest common factor of $7n + 4$ and $5n + 3$ is 1 for all $n \in \mathbb{N}$.
       $7n + 4 = 1(5n + 3) + (2n + 1); 5n + 3 = 2(2n + 1) + n + 1;$
       $2n + 1 = 2(n + 1) - 1; n + 1 = -(n + 1)(-1) + 0.$
       Or, $-5(7n + 4) + 7(5n + 3) = 1$, which means 1 is the greatest common factor. (See USEFUL FACT, above.)

**d. Apply the Fundamental Theorem of Arithmetic (e.g., find the greatest common factor and the least common multiple, show that every fraction is equivalent to a unique fraction where the numerator and denominator are relatively prime, prove that the square root of any number, not a perfect square number, is irrational)**

1. What is the Fundamental Theorem of Arithmetic?

   The Fundamental Theorem of Arithmetic states that if $n$ is a natural number, then $n$ can be expressed as a product of prime numbers. Moreover, there is only one way to do so, up to a permutation of the prime factors of $n$. (Here, we allow a "product" to consist of only one prime, or of no primes so that we can say that EVERY natural number, including 1, is a "product" of primes.)

2. What is a prime number?

   The number $n \in \mathbb{N}$ is **prime** if $n > 1$ and the only positive divisors of $n$ are 1 and $n$. As examples, 7 is prime but 9 is not, because 9 has 3 as a divisor.

3. Why is the Fundamental Theorem of Arithmetic true?

   The first sentence can be proved using Complete Induction. The second sentence can be proved by using the following Helpful Fact.

   **Helpful Fact:** Let $p$ be a prime. If $p|ab$, then $p|a$ or $p|b$.

   **Proof:** (of Helpful Fact) Suppose $p|ab$ but $p$ does not divide $a$. Then the greatest common factor of $p$ and $a$ must be 1, because there are no other factors of $p$. By the USEFUL FACT, above, there must be integers $s$ and $t$ satisfying $1 = as + pt$. Multiplying both sides by $b$, we get $b = bas + bpt$. Notice that $p|bas$ (because $p|ab$) and clearly $p|bpt$. Therefore, $p|b$.  □

4. How does one find the greatest common factor and the least common multiple, using the Fundamental Theorem of Arithmetic?

   Here, one can find the unique prime factorization of two numbers and use that information to determine the greatest common factor and the least common multiple. As an example, consider 12 and 18. We know $12 = 2^2 \cdot 3$ and $18 = 2 \cdot 3^2$. Both share a single factor of 2 and a single factor of 3. So, $2 \cdot 3 = 6$ is the greatest common factor. For the least common multiple, notice that we need factors of at least $2^2$ and $3^2$ in order to have both 12 and 18 as a factor. So, the least common multiple is $2^2 3^2 = 36$.

5. How can fractions be uniquely represented as a ratio of relatively prime integers? (What does relatively prime mean?)

   The numbers $a$ and $b$ are *relatively prime* if they have no common factors. This happens when $GCD(a, b) = 1$. If you are given a fraction, you can use the Fundamental Theorem of Arithmetic to write the numerator and denominator uniquely as products of primes. Then you can cancel any common factors between them. The resulting numerator and denominator will have no common factors, which makes them relatively prime.

6. What are some proofs that $\sqrt{2}$ is irrational?

   *** For a quick review of Proof by Contradiction, see the Miscellaneous Topics at the end of this book.

   (a) Euclid's proof

       (by contradiction) Assume that $\sqrt{2} = \frac{a}{b}$ and that $a$ and $b$ are relatively prime integers. Then $2b^2 = a^2$. Thus $a^2$ is even, which means that $a$ has to be even. (The square of an odd number is odd.) So, $a = 2c$ for some integer $c$. Then $2b^2 = 4c^2$, which means $b^2 = 2c^2$. Thus $b^2$ is even, which means that $b$ has to be even. But this is impossible, because $a$ and $b$ were chosen to be relatively prime; they can't both be even. Therefore, it must be impossible to write $\sqrt{2}$ as $\frac{a}{b}$, which means $\sqrt{2}$ is irrational.

   (b) Another proof

(by contradiction) Assume that $\sqrt{2} = \frac{a}{b}$. Then $2b^2 = a^2$. By the Fundamental Theorem of Arithmetic, the number on the left hand side of this equation must have an odd number of prime factors, and the number on the right hand side must have an even number of prime factors. This is impossible, because there is only one way to write a number (like $2b^2$) as a product of primes. Therefore, it must be impossible to write $\sqrt{2}$ as $\frac{a}{b}$, which means $\sqrt{2}$ is irrational.

7. Sample Problems

   (a) Consider $y = mx + b$, where $m$ and $b$ are rational numbers. Must there be a point on this line that has integer coordinates?

   (b) Consider $y = ax^2 + bx + c$, where $a$, $b$, and $c$ are rational numbers. Must there be a point on this parabola that has integer coordinates?

   (c) Prove that $\sqrt{5}$ is irrational.

   (d) Prove or disprove: If $x^2$ is rational, then $x$ is rational.

   (e) Prove or disprove: If $x^2$ is irrational, then $x$ is irrational.

   (f) If $n = 2^2 3^3 x^5 y z^2$ and $m = 2^3 3^2 x^3 y^2$, then find the greatest common factor of $n$ and $m$, and the least common multiple of $n$ and $m$.

   (g) Show that if $(x, y, z)$ is a Pythagorean triple, and if $f$ is a common factor of $x$, $y$, and $z$, then $(\frac{x}{f}, \frac{y}{f}, \frac{z}{f})$ is also a Pythagorean triple.

   (h) How many natural number solutions are there to $x + y = 12$? ...to $x + y = n \in \mathbb{N}$?

   (i) How many natural number solutions are there to $xy = 12$? ...to $xy = n \in \mathbb{N}$?

8. Answers to Sample Problems

   (a) Consider $y = mx + b$, where $m$ and $b$ are rational numbers. Must there be a point on this line that has integer coordinates?

   Not necessarily. For example, if $y = \frac{1}{3}x + \frac{1}{2}$, no matter what integer you plug in for $x$, $y$ will not come out to an exact integer.

   (b) Consider $y = ax^2 + bx + c$, where $a$, $b$, and $c$ are rational numbers. Must there be a point on this parabola that has integer coordinates?

   Not necessarily. The example given in the previous problem (with $a = 0$) still works. Also, if $a = b = c = \frac{1}{2}$, then for any integer $x$, $y$ is equal to an integer plus $\frac{1}{2}$.

   (c) Prove that $\sqrt{5}$ is irrational. We can mimic the proof given above that $\sqrt{2}$ is irrational.
   **Proof:** Assume that $\sqrt{5} = \frac{a}{b}$. Then $5b^2 = a^2$. By the Fundamental Theorem of Arithmetic, the number on the left hand side of this equation must have an odd number of prime factors, and the number on the right hand side must have an even number of prime factors. This is impossible, because there is only one way to write a number (like $5b^2$) as a product of primes. Therefore, it must be impossible to write $\sqrt{5}$ as $\frac{a}{b}$, which means $\sqrt{5}$ is irrational.

(d) Prove or disprove: If $x^2$ is rational, then $x$ is rational.

FALSE. Suppose $x^2 = 2$, which is rational. Then $x = \pm\sqrt{2}$, which was proven to be irrational. Thus the statement is false.

(e) Prove or disprove: If $x^2$ is irrational, then $x$ is irrational.

**Proof:** Assume that $x$ is rational. Then $x = \frac{p}{q}$ for some integers $p$ and $q$, with $q \neq 0$. Then $x^2 = \frac{p^2}{q^2}$, which is clearly rational. Therefore, by indirect reasoning (contrapositive), we have shown that if $x^2$ is irrational, then $x$ must be irrational too.

(f) If $n = 2^2 3^3 x^5 y z^2$ and $m = 2^3 3^2 x^3 y^2$, then find the greatest common factor of $n$ and $m$, and the least common multiple of $n$ and $m$.

The greatest common factor of $n$ and $m$ is $2^2 3^2 x^3 y$ and their least common multiple is $2^3 3^3 x^5 y^2 z^2$.

(g) Show that if $(x, y, z)$ is a Pythagorean triple, and if $f$ is a common factor of $x$, $y$, and $z$, then $(\frac{x}{f}, \frac{y}{f}, \frac{z}{f})$ is also a Pythagorean triple.

$$\left(\frac{x}{f}\right)^2 + \left(\frac{y}{f}\right)^2 = \frac{x^2 + y^2}{f^2} = \frac{z^2}{f^2} = \left(\frac{z}{f}\right)^2$$

(h) How many natural number solutions are there to $x + y = 12$? ...to $x + y = n \in \mathbb{N}$? For the first equation, $x$ can be any number between 1 and 11. So there are 11 solutions. (Some of these are essentially the same, like $1 + 11$ and $11 + 1$, but we ignore that similarity here because the solutions have distinct $x$-values.) For the second equation, then, there are $n - 1$ solutions.

(i) How many natural number solutions are there to $xy = 12$? ...to $xy = n \in \mathbb{N}$? For the first equation, there are 6 solutions, one for each factor of 12: $1, 2, 3, 4, 6, 12$. (Again, solutions are different if they have distinct $x$-values.) For the second equation, the answer is the number of factors of $n$. If $n$ is prime, for example, then the answer is 2.

# Miscellaneous Extra Review Topics

### a. Logarithms

1. What is a logarithm?

   A logarithm is an exponent. The logarithm base $b$ of $n$ is the exponent needed on $b$ to obtain $n$. In symbols:

   $$x = \log_b n \iff b^x = n.$$

   Any simple logarithmic equation can be transformed into an exponential equation according to the formula above. One consequence of this definition is that you cannot take the logarithm of a number unless that number is positive. This is because basic exponential functions only take positive values.

   **Example:** Find $\log_3 \frac{1}{81}$.

   Let $x = \log_3 \frac{1}{81}$. Then $3^x = \frac{1}{81} = \frac{1}{3^4} = 3^{-4}$. So, $x = -4$. Therefore, $\log_3 \frac{1}{81} = -4$.

2. What are some bases for logarithms?

   The bases most often used are 10 and $e$. Logs base 10 are called "common" logs and are written "log" (with no subscript). Logs base $e$ are called "natural" logs and are written "ln."

   **Aside:** By the way, $e \approx 2.718281828459045\ldots$ One reason $e$ is so useful has to do with calculus. The slope of the graph of $y = e^x$ at any point is equal to the $y$-coordinate of that point. So, $e^x$ is its own derivative. (See Derivatives, Test 3 materials.)

3. What are some properties of logarithms?

   The following properties hold for any base, $b$.

   (a) $x = \log_b n \iff b^x = n$ (the definition)

   (b) $\log_b(x^m) = m \log_b x$

   (c) $\log_b(xy) = \log_b x + \log_b y$

   (d) $\log_b x = \dfrac{\log x}{\log b} = \dfrac{\ln x}{\ln b} = \dfrac{\log_a x}{\log_a b}$ (for any base $a$) [Change of Base Formula]

   The following facts may help you solve log problems.

   (a) $\log_b 1 = 0$. (In particular, $\log 1 = \ln 1 = 0$.)

   (b) $\log_b b = 1$. (In particular, $\log 10 = \ln e = 1$.)

   (c) $\log_b 0$ is not defined.

   (d) $b^{\log_b x} = x$. (In particular, $10^{\log x} = e^{\ln x} = x$.)

   More properties can be found in the Sample Problems.

   **Example:** Simplify $\log 16 + \log 125 - \log 2$.

Answer: Using the properties, we can deduce that $\log_b \frac{x}{y} = \log_b x - \log_b y$. (See Sample Problems, below.) So, working backwards, we get

$$
\begin{aligned}
\log 16 + \log 125 - \log 2 &= \log \frac{(16)(125)}{(2)} \\
&= \log 1000 \\
&= \log 10^3 \\
&= 3 \log 10 \\
&= 3.
\end{aligned}
$$

4. Sample Problems

   (a) Simplify, if possible:

        i. $\log_4 64$

        ii. $\log_2 128$

        iii. $\log 0.000001$

        iv. $\ln e^{-1}$

        v. $\ln(-e)$

        vi. $\log_7 7$

        vii. $e^{\ln 4}$

        viii. $\log_2 5 - \log_2 40$

        ix. $\log_2 4^t$

        x. $e^{2 \ln w}$

        xi. $\log 10^{4x}$

        xii. $(\log e)(\ln 10)$ [Hint: Use the Change of Base Formula.]

   (b) Write as a single logarithm: $2 \ln w + 5 \ln x - \frac{1}{2} \ln y$.

   (c) Expand as a sum of logarithms of single variables: $\log_5 \left( \frac{x^7}{y^2 \sqrt[3]{z}} \right)$.

   (d) Solve for $x$: $\log_6 x + \log_6 (x + 5) = 1$.

   (e) Why does $\log_6 x - \log_6 (x + 5) = 1$ not have a real solution?

   (f) Using the log properties, show that $\log_b b^m = m$.

   (g) Using the log properties, show that $\log_b \frac{x}{y} = \log_b x - \log_b y$.

5. Answers to Sample Problems

   (a) Simplify, if possible:

        i. $\log_4 64 = 3$

        ii. $\log_2 128 = 7$

        iii. $\log 0.000001 = -6$

        iv. $\ln e^{-1} = -1$

v. $\ln(-e)$ is not defined.

vi. $\log_7 7 = 1$

vii. $e^{\ln 4} = 4$

viii. $\log_2 5 - \log_2 40 = \log_2(\frac{1}{8}) = -3$

ix. $\log_2 4^t = \log_2(2^{2t}) = 2t$

x. $e^{2\ln w} = e^{\ln w^2} = w^2$

xi. $\log 10^{4x} = 4x$

xii. $(\log e)(\ln 10) = \left(\dfrac{\ln e}{\ln 10}\right)(\ln 10) = 1$

(b) Write as a single logarithm: $2\ln w + 5\ln x - \frac{1}{2}\ln y$. $\ln\left(\dfrac{w^2 x^5}{\sqrt{y}}\right)$

(c) Expand as a sum of logarithms of single variables: $\log_5\left(\dfrac{x^7}{y^2\sqrt[3]{z}}\right)$.

$$7\log_5 x - 2\log_5 y - \frac{1}{3}\log_5 z$$

(d) Solve for $x$: $\log_6 x + \log_6(x+5) = 1$. $x = 1$ ($x = -6$ is extraneous)

$$\log_6 x + \log_6(x+5) = 1 \Rightarrow \log_6(x(x+5)) = 1 \Rightarrow x(x+5) = 6 \Rightarrow$$

$$\Rightarrow x^2 + 5x - 6 = 0 \Rightarrow (x+6)(x-1) = 0 \Rightarrow x = 1 \text{ or } -6$$

Checking both of these shows that $-6$ is extraneous.

(e) Why does $\log_6 x - \log_6(x+5) = 1$ not have a real solution? If we proceed as in the previous problem, we get $\frac{x}{x+5} = 6$, which has $x = -6$ as a solution. But since $\log_6(-6)$ is not defined, there is no solution to the original equation.

(f) Using the log properties, show that $\log_b b^m = m$. Answers may vary.

$$\log_b b^m = m(\log_b b) = m(1) = m.$$

(g) Using the log properties, show that $\log_b \frac{x}{y} = \log_b x - \log_b y$. Answers may vary.

$$\log_b \frac{x}{y} = \log_b(xy^{-1}) = \log_b x + \log_b(y^{-1}) = \log_b x - \log_b y.$$

## b. Proof by Contradiction

1. What is a proof by contradiction?

A proof by contradiction is a way to show that a statement is true by showing that it cannot be false. You assume that it is false, and then show that your assumption leads to a contradiction of some other mathematical fact or hypothesis of the problem.

**Aside:** This proof technique relies HEAVILY on the "Law of the Excluded Middle," which says that either a mathematical statement is true or else it is false. There is no room for any other outcome.

2. Sample Problems

   (a) Let $m$ be an integer and let $m^2$ be odd. Then $m$ is odd.

   (b) Let $r, s \in \mathbb{R}$ and let $r + s$ be irrational. Then $r$ is irrational or $s$ is irrational.

   (c) Let $m$ and $n$ be integers and let $mn$ be odd. Then $m$ is odd and $n$ is odd.

   (d) Suppose that $n$ is an integer which is not divisible by 3. Then $n$ is not divisible by 6.

   (e) Prove that $\log_2 3$ is irrational.

3. Answers to Sample Problems

   (a) Let $m$ be an integer and let $m^2$ be odd. Then $m$ is odd.

   **Proof:** Suppose that $m^2$ is odd, but $m$ is even. Then $m = 2k$ for some integer $k$. So $m^2 = 4k^2 = 2(2k^2)$, which is also even. But this contradicts our hypothesis that $m^2$ is odd. Therefore $m$ must be odd. $\square$

   (b) Let $r, s \in \mathbb{R}$ and let $r + s$ be irrational. Then $r$ is irrational or $s$ is irrational.

   **Proof:** Suppose that $r + s$ is irrational, but both $r$ and $s$ are rational. Then there exist integers $a$, $b$, $c$, and $d$ with $b \neq 0 \neq d$ such that $r = \frac{a}{b}$ and $s = \frac{c}{d}$. Then $r + s = \frac{a}{b} + \frac{c}{d} = \frac{ad+bc}{bd}$, which is clearly rational. But this contradicts our hypothesis that $r + s$ is irrational. Therefore $r$ is irrational or $s$ is irrational. $\square$

   (c) Let $m$ and $n$ be integers and let $mn$ be odd. Then $m$ is odd and $n$ is odd.

   **Proof:** Suppose that $mn$ is odd, but either $m$ or $n$ is even. Without loss of generality, say $m = 2k$ for some integer $k$. Then $mn = 2kn$, which is clearly even. But this contradicts our hypothesis that $mn$ is odd. So therefore $m$ and $n$ must be odd. $\square$

   (d) Suppose that $n$ is an integer which is not divisible by 3. Then $n$ is not divisible by 6.

   **Proof:** Suppose that $n$ is not divisible by 3, but that $n$ is divisible by 6. Then there exists an integer $k$ satisfying $n = 6k = 3(2k)$. Thus $n$ is also divisible by 3. But this contradicts our hypothesis that $n$ is not divisible by 3. Therefore, $n$ must not be divisible by 6. $\square$

   (e) Prove that $\log_2 3$ is irrational.

   **Proof:** Suppose that $\log_2 3$ is rational. Then $\log_2 3 = \frac{p}{q}$ for some integers $p$ and $q$ with $q \neq 0$. Then $2^{p/q} = 3$, or, raising both sides to the $q$-th power, $2^p = 3^q$. According to the Fundamental Theorem of Arithmetic, the only power of 2 that is also a power of 3 is the number $1 = 2^0 = 3^0$. So $p = q = 0$. But this contradicts the fact that $q \neq 0$. Therefore, $\log_2 3$ must be irrational. $\square$

# Subtest II:
# Geometry
# Probability and Statistics

## 2.1 Parallelism

**a. Know the Parallel Postulate and its implications, and justify its equivalents (e.g., the Alternate Interior Angle Theorem, the angle sum of every triangle is 180 degrees)**

1. Geometry Notation

   Before we begin, let's agree to some notation. Most of it is straightforward, but there are some important technicalities. There is a difference between a line segment and the length of the line segment. As a geometric object, the line segment between point $A$ and point $B$ will be denoted $\overline{AB}$. The length of this segment, also known as the distance from $A$ to $B$, is a positive real number denoted $AB$. Similarly, the angle with vertex at $A$ will be denoted $\angle A$ as a geometric object, but the measure of that angle in degrees, denoted $m\angle A$, is a number between 0 and 180.

2. What does "parallel" mean?

   This may seem like a simple question, but in geometry, two lines are "parallel" if and only if they do not intersect. There is no mention of "slope" until coordinate geometry. "Having the same slope" is a numerical, algebraic property. "Not intersecting" is a geometric property.

3. What is the Parallel Postulate? (What is Euclidean geometry?)

   Euclid's *Elements* comprise 13 books in which Euclid presents geometry from an axiomatic point of view. In particular, he builds geometry on a foundation of five postulates, 23 definitions, and five common notions. Euclid's postulates are:

   i. To draw a straight line from any point to any point.

   ii. To produce a finite straight line continuously in a straight line.

   iii. To describe a circle with any center and radius.

   iv. That all right angles equal one another.

   v. That, if a straight line falling on two straight lines makes the interior angles on the same side less than two right angles, the two straight lines, if produced indefinitely, meet on that side on which are the angles less than the two right angles.

   (Visit http://aleph0.clarku.edu/~djoyce/java/elements/elements.html for an online version of Euclid's *Elements*.)

   The fifth postulate is called Euclid's Parallel Postulate (but still not OUR Parallel Postulate). Notice that it is rather bulky. In our language, we might state Euclid's Fifth Postulate as: "If two lines are cut by a transversal, and same side interior angles add up to less than 180, then the two lines will eventually intersect on the side of the transversal on which the angle sum is less than 180." This is still not the Parallel Postulate as it appears in most school texts. In terms of the picture below, if $m\angle 1 + m\angle 4 < 180$, then $k$ and $m$ intersect on the left side of $t$.

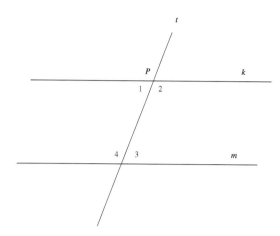

Euclidean geometry is the geometry described in Euclid's *Elements*. It is the geometry of flat planes on which the Fifth Postulate is assumed to be true.

4. What are some implications of the Parallel Postulate?

   One of the implications of Euclid's Parallel Postulate (and indeed equivalent to it) is Playfair's Postulate: "If $m$ is a line and $P$ is a point not on $m$, then there is exactly one line through $P$ that is parallel to $m$." In fact, THIS is the formulation which the CSET thinks of (and what the Geometry textbooks state) as the Parallel Postulate.

   > *The Parallel Postulate.* Through a given external point there is at most one line parallel to a given line.

   The following statements are equivalent to the Parallel Postulate. (This list is by no means complete.)

   (a) Euclid's Fifth Postulate

   (b) If two parallel lines are cut by a transversal, then alternate interior angles are congruent.

   (c) The angle sum of a triangle is 180.

   (d) If a line intersects one of two parallel lines, then it intersects the other.

   (e) If a line is perpendicular to one of two parallel lines, then it is perpendicular to the other.

   (f) Rectangles exist.

5. What is the Alternate Interior Angle Theorem? Why is it equivalent to the Parallel Postulate?

   The short answer is that the Alternate Interior Angle Theorem is the second of the equivalences listed above: "If two parallel lines are cut by a transversal, then alternate interior angles are congruent." The longer answer is that the "Alternate Interior Angle Theorem" is different in different textbooks. For instance, in *Roads to Geometry*, by Wallace and West (NJ: Pearson Education, 2004), their Alternate Interior Angle Theorem is the converse statement: "If two lines are cut by a transversal so that alternate interior angles are congruent, then the two lines are parallel." It is interesting to note that THIS statement can be proved *without* using Euclid's Parallel Postulate.

   Because our Alternate Interior Angle Theorem (AIAT) is equivalent to the Parallel Postulate, it is also equivalent to Euclid's Fifth Postulate (E5). This means two things:

- If E5 is true, then AIAT is true; AND

- If AIAT is true, then E5 is true.

**Sample Proof:** To prove the first item, we assume E5 is true. Then start with two parallel lines cut by a transversal. See figure below.

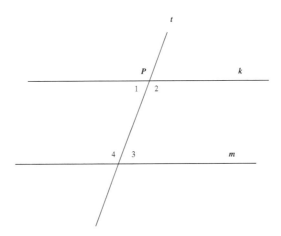

Suppose that angle 1 were less than angle 3. Then angle 2 would be greater than angle 4 (because of supplementary angle properties). So then angle 1 plus angle 4 would be less than angle 2 plus angle 3. In equations,

$$
\begin{aligned}
m\angle 1 + m\angle 4 &< m\angle 2 + m\angle 3 \\
m\angle 1 + m\angle 4 &< (180 - m\angle 1) + (180 - m\angle 4) \\
m\angle 1 + m\angle 4 &< 360 - (m\angle 1 + m\angle 4) \\
2(m\angle 1 + m\angle 4) &< 360,
\end{aligned}
$$

which means that the measure of angle 1 plus the measure of angle 4 is less than 180. Therefore, by E5, lines $k$ and $m$ would have to intersect on that side of $t$, contradicting the fact that they are parallel. So angle 1 cannot be less than angle 3. By a very similar argument, angle 1 cannot be greater than angle 3. So angle 1 must be congruent to angle 3. It then follows that angle 2 is congruent to angle 4.

To prove the other direction of this equivalence, see the exercises.

6. How does the fact that the angle sum of a triangle is 180 follow from the Parallel Postulate?

   In the picture below, we start with a triangle. Then we draw a line through $P$ that is parallel to the opposite side of the triangle. If we assume the Parallel Postulate, then there is only one such line, meaning that the two angles marked $A$ are congruent by the AIAT. Similarly, the two $B$ angles are congruent. So, the sum of $A$, $B$, and $C$ is clearly 180. Thus the Parallel Postulate implies that the sum of angles in a triangle is 180.

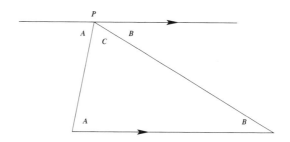

7. Sample Problems

   (a) State the converse of the Alternate Interior Angle Theorem.

   (b) Explain why Euclid's Fifth Postulate follows from the Alternate Interior Angle Theorem. (You may need the Exterior Angle Theorem, which says that an exterior angle of a triangle is always larger than either of the remote interior angles.)

   (c) Draw a picture of two parallel lines cut by a transversal. Label the eight angles formed.

      i. State the Alternate Interior Angle Theorem in terms of your diagram.
      ii. Create an Alternate Exterior Angle Theorem and its converse.
      iii. Create a Corresponding Angle Theorem and its converse.
      iv. Create a Same-side Interior Angle Theorem and its converse.
      v. List all equivalences among your theorems, the Alternate Interior Angle Theorem, and its converse.

   (d) If the Parallel Postulate were false, then what other statements would be false?

   (e) Explain why the Parallel Postulate implies that rectangles exist.

8. Answers to Sample Problems

   (a) State the converse of the Alternate Interior Angle Theorem.
      If two lines are cut by a transversal so that alternate interior angles are congruent, then the lines are parallel.

   (b) Explain why Euclid's Fifth Postulate follows from the Alternate Interior Angle Theorem. (You may need the Exterior Angle Theorem, which says that an exterior angle of a triangle is always larger than either of the remote interior angles.)

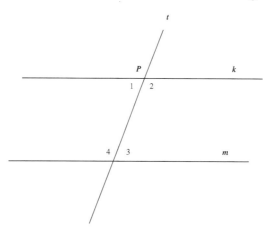

Suppose that two lines are cut by a transversal in such a way that same-side interior angles add up to less than 180. (In the diagram above, say $m\angle 1 + m\angle 4 < 180$.) We can also conclude that either $m\angle 1 < m\angle 3$ or $m\angle 4 < m\angle 2$. Without loss of generality, let's say that $m\angle 1 < m\angle 3$.

If alternate interior angles were congruent, then $m\angle 1 + m\angle 4$ would be 180. So, the alternate interior angles are not congruent. Thus, the lines $k$ and $m$ must intersect. Suppose they intersect on the *right* side of $t$.

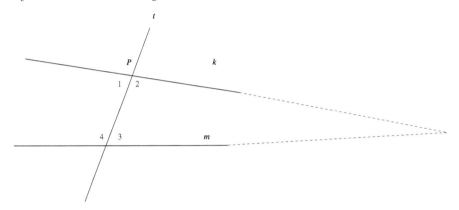

Then $\angle 1$ would be an exterior angle of the triangle formed by $k$, $m$, and $t$. Also, $\angle 3$ would be a remote interior angle in the same triangle, meaning that $m\angle 1 \geq m\angle 3$. This is a contradiction to the assumption that $m\angle 1 < m\angle 3$. So the intersection of $k$ and $m$ must happen on the *left* side of $t$, which is the side on which the same-side interior angles add up to less than 180.

(c) Draw a picture of two parallel lines cut by a transversal. Label the eight angles formed.

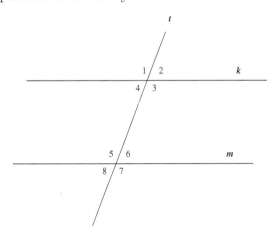

  i. State the Alternate Interior Angle Theorem in terms of your diagram.
    If $k \parallel m$, then $\angle 4 \cong \angle 6$ (or $\angle 3 \cong \angle 5$).

  ii. Create an Alternate Exterior Angle Theorem and its converse.
    Theorem: If $k \parallel m$, then $\angle 1 \cong \angle 7$ (or $\angle 2 \cong \angle 8$).
    Converse: If $\angle 1 \cong \angle 7$ (or if $\angle 2 \cong \angle 8$), then $k \parallel m$.

 iii. Create a Corresponding Angle Theorem and its converse.
    Theorem: If $k \parallel m$, then $\angle 1 \cong \angle 5$ (or $\angle 2 \cong \angle 6$, or $\angle 3 \cong \angle 7$, or $\angle 4 \cong \angle 8$).
    Converse: If $\angle 1 \cong \angle 5$ (or if $\angle 2 \cong \angle 6$, or if $\angle 3 \cong \angle 7$, or if $\angle 4 \cong \angle 8$), then $k \parallel m$.

    iv. Create a Same-side Interior Angle Theorem and its converse.

         Theorem: If $k \parallel m$, then $\angle 4$ and $\angle 5$ are supplementary, (or $\angle 3$ and $\angle 6$ are supplementary).

         Converse: If $\angle 4$ and $\angle 5$ are supplementary, (or if $\angle 3$ and $\angle 6$ are supplementary), then $k \parallel m$.

    v. List all equivalences among your theorems, the Alternate Interior Angle Theorem, and its converse.

         All the converse statements are equivalent to each other, but are not equivalent to any of the theorems. All the theorems above are equivalent to each other, and the theorems are also equivalent to Euclid's Fifth Postulate and the Parallel Postulate.

(d) If the Parallel Postulate were false, then what other statements would be false?

     If the Parallel Postulate were false, then every statement equivalent to it would also be false. So, triangle angle sums would not be 180, Euclid's Fifth Postulate would not be true, the Alternate Interior Angle Theorem would not be true, etc.

(e) Explain why the Parallel Postulate implies that rectangles exist.

     Let $k$ be a line and let $P$ be a point not on $k$. The Parallel Postulate says that there is only one line (call it $m$) through $P$ which is parallel to $k$. Draw line $m$. Let $Q$ be another point on $m$. Now draw the line $t$ through $P$ which is perpendicular to $k$. Call the point of intersection (of $t$ and $k$) $A$. By the Alternate Interior Angle Theorem (which is equivalent to the Parallel Postulate), $t \perp m$. The Parallel Postulate guarantees that there is only one line $s$ through $Q$ which is parallel to $t$. So $s \perp m$ and thus $s \perp k$ at some point $B$. By construction, then, $ABQP$ is a rectangle.

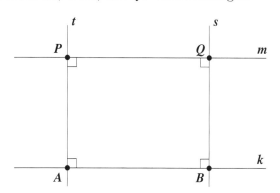

## b. Know that variants of the Parallel Postulate produce non-Euclidean geometries (e.g., spherical, hyperbolic)

1. What are some variations of the Parallel Postulate?

     There are two commonly-used variations:

     Variation #1: "Given a line $m$ and a point $P$ not on $m$, then there is no line through $P$ that is parallel to $m$."

     Variation #2: "Given a line $m$ and a point $P$ not on $m$, then there are at least two lines through $P$ that are parallel to $m$."

At this point, these axioms are just statements, mathematical statements which must be assumed to be true, just like the Parallel Postulate. Their "usefulness" is not part of their mathematical validity. Although, if they were not useful, we would probably not be studying them. [A technical note: some other axioms of Euclid contradict Variation #1, but we overlook that here.]

2. Why would you want to vary the Parallel Postulate?

As we stated earlier, Euclid's Fifth Postulate is rather bulky and difficult to follow, especially when compared to his other four postulates. Historically, many people tried to prove that Euclid's Parallel Postulate was unnecessary; that is, that it was a logical consequence of the other four. All such attempts were unsuccessful, although they did lead to a more thorough understanding of so-called *neutral* geometry (see below). It wasn't until the 1800s that some people began to ask the question, "What if the Parallel Postulate doesn't follow from the other four? Then could it be possible to build a geometric system in which the Parallel Postulate doesn't hold?" Thus began the investigation into "non-Euclidean" geometries, geometries which assumed a different version of the Parallel Postulate.

3. What are some non-Euclidean geometries?

The two main types of non-Euclidean geometry are called *elliptic* geometry, which assumes Variation #1, and *hyperbolic* geometry, which assumes Variation #2. In elliptic geometry, there are no parallel lines at all; any two lines intersect. In hyperbolic geometry, there are at least two lines through a given point which are parallel to a given line.

4. How can there be non-Euclidean geometries?

These non-Euclidean geometries exist because of undefined terms, such as *point*, *line*, *on*, and *through*, among others. So, one can create a model in which the axioms are consistent, but the notions of points and lines have changed. We'll discuss some geometries below – then we will draw pictures for each later. (See Sample Problems.)

In this vein, elliptic geometry is often called the geometry of the surface of a sphere, where a "point" is taken to mean a pair of antipodal points (opposite points, like the North and South poles) on the sphere and a "line" is taken to mean a great circle on the sphere (which means the center of the circle is the center of the sphere, like the Equator). So, two "points" determine a "line," and two "lines" intersect in a "point." Since any two great circles intersect, there are no parallel "lines." Moreover, studying elliptic geometry is like studying the geometry of the surface of the earth. [Technical notes: elliptic geometry is slightly different from spherical geometry in that elliptic geometry does not need spheres in order to exist. Also, elliptic geometry is not neutral in the sense that it violates some of the other theorems, definitions, or common notions of Euclid. But we'll ignore that here.]

In hyperbolic geometry, one can think of "points" as lying inside a given circle, and "lines" as being arcs inside the circle which intersect the circle at right angles. So, two points determine a line, and two intersecting lines determine a point. But, given a line $m$ and a point $P$ not on $m$, there are many lines through $P$ which do not intersect (and are therefore parallel to) $m$. It turns out that hyperbolic geometry shows up in Einstein's theory of relativity.

5. What is neutral geometry?

Neutral geometry is the study of geometry where one is not allowed to use the Parallel Postulate NOR any one of its variations. So, theorems proved in that geometry would apply to Euclidean as well as to non-Euclidean geometries. The following results are true in (or are axioms of) neutral geometry.

- Isosceles Triangle Theorem and its converse

- Triangle Inequality

- SSS, SAS, ASA, AAS, and HL triangle congruences

- If two lines are cut by a transversal so that alternate interior angles are congruent, then the lines are parallel.

6. Sample Problems

   (a) Draw a picture showing how Variation #1 works on the surface of a sphere.

   (b) Find a triangle in elliptic geometry and add up its angles. Do they add up to more than 180 or less than 180?

   (c) Draw a picture showing how Variation #2 works inside a given circle.

   (d) Find a triangle in hyperbolic geometry and add up its angles. Do they add up to more than 180 or less than 180?

   (e) Of the Corresponding Angle Theorem, the Same-side Interior Angle Theorem, etc., and their converses, which theorems on your list are neutral?

7. Answers to Sample Problems

   (a) Draw a picture showing how Variation #1 works on the surface of a sphere.

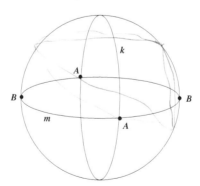

   Two "points" $A$ and $B$ determine a "line:" line $m$. Also, two "lines" $k$ and $m$ determine a "point:" point $A$. Notice that there are no parallel lines in this geometry.

   (b) Find a triangle in elliptic geometry and add up its angles. Do they add up to more than 180 or less than 180? more than 180. Consider a triangle with one vertex at the North Pole and one side on the Equator. Then the two base angles at the Equator must both be right angles, because longitude lines are perpendicular to the Equator. So the angles of this triangle add up to more than 180 degrees.

(c) Draw a picture showing how Variation #2 works inside a given circle.

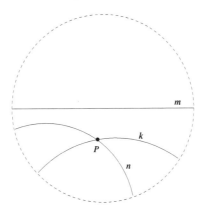

Notice that there are two lines ($k$ and $n$) through point $P$ which are "parallel to" (i.e. do not intersect) line $m$.

(d) Find a triangle in hyperbolic geometry and add up its angles. Do they add up to more than 180 or less than 180? less than 180. Triangles in hyperbolic geometry have concave sides, which means their angles at the vertices are smaller than in Euclidean triangles.

(e) Of the Corresponding Angle Theorem, the Same-side Interior Angle Theorem, etc., and their converses, which theorems on your list are neutral?

All of the converse statements are neutral. In other words, if you know that the alternate interior angles are congruent when two lines are cut by a transversal, then those two lines have to be parallel, even in neutral geometry. The other statements are similar.

# 2.2 Plane Euclidean Geometry

## a. Prove theorems and solve problems involving similarity and congruence

1. What does "congruent" mean? What does "similar" mean?

   Two line segments are congruent ($\cong$) if they have the same length. Two angles are congruent if they have the same measure. Two polygons are congruent if you can match up their vertices in sequence so that all corresponding sides and all corresponding angles are congruent.

   Two polygons are similar ($\sim$) if you can match up their vertices in sequence so that all corresponding angles are congruent, and so that all corresponding sides are in the same proportion.

2. What are the most common triangle congruence theorems?

   We say $\triangle ABC \cong \triangle DEF$ if and only if $\overline{AB} \cong \overline{DE}$; $\overline{AC} \cong \overline{DF}$; $\overline{BC} \cong \overline{EF}$; $\angle A \cong \angle D$; $\angle B \cong \angle E$; and $\angle C \cong \angle F$. This is a total of six conditions.

   However, in practice, you do not need to show all six. There are postulates or theorems that tell you when two triangles are congruent. They are: SAS (Side-Angle-Side), ASA, AAS, SSS, and for right triangles, HL (hypotenuse-leg).

3. What are the most common triangle similarity theorems?

   We say $\triangle ABC \sim \triangle DEF$ if and only if there is a value of $k > 0$ so that $AB = kDE$; $AC = kDF$; $BC = kEF$; $\angle A \cong \angle D$; $\angle B \cong \angle E$; and $\angle C \cong \angle F$. This is also a total of six conditions.

   However, in practice, you do not need to show all six. For triangles, any time their three angles are congruent, the triangles are similar. So, there is (in Euclidean geometry) an AA (Angle-Angle) Similarity Theorem. Other theorems include sss and sAs. (The lower-case "s" means that the corresponding sides are in the same proportion.) Also, there are lots of similarities available in right triangle $ABC$ (with right angle at $C$) if you draw altitude $\overline{CD}$. In particular, $\triangle ABC \sim \triangle CBD \sim \triangle ACD$.

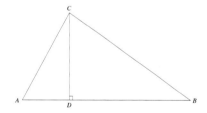

4. What does "CPCTC" mean?

   In my geometry class, this was our abbreviation for "corresponding parts of congruent triangles are congruent." It is most helpful in proofs.

5. Sample Problems

   (a) Complete the statement and then prove it: In parallelogram $ABCD$, $\triangle ABC \cong \triangle$_____.

   (b) Suppose that $X$ is the common midpoint of $\overline{AB}$ and $\overline{CD}$. Then $\triangle AXC \cong \triangle$_____. Prove it.

(c) The Isosceles Triangle Theorem says that if two sides of a triangle are congruent, then the angles opposite those sides are also congruent. Prove the Isosceles Triangle Theorem by drawing the angle bisector of the vertex angle.

(d) Prove that the diagonals of a rhombus bisect their vertex angles.

(e) True or false: Any two isosceles triangles must be similar. If true, prove it, and if false, give a counterexample.

(f) Draw $\triangle ABC$. On $\overline{AB}$, draw point $M$ so that $AM = 2MB$. On $\overline{AC}$, draw point $N$ so that $AN = 2NC$. Prove that $\overline{MN} \parallel \overline{BC}$.

(g) Draw an isosceles trapezoid and its two diagonals. The trapezoid is now divided into four triangular regions. Prove that two of these regions must be similar. Then prove that the other two regions must be congruent.

6. Answers to Sample Problems

(a) Complete the statement and then prove it: In parallelogram $ABCD$, $\triangle ABC \cong \triangle \underline{CDA}$.

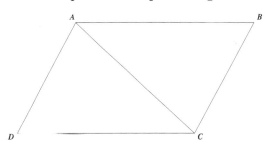

**Proof:** Draw diagonal $\overline{AC}$. Since $\overline{AB} \parallel \overline{CD}$, $\angle BAC \cong \angle DCA$. Also, since $\overline{AD} \parallel \overline{BC}$, $\angle BCA \cong \angle DAC$. And of course $\overline{AC} \cong \overline{AC}$. Therefore, by ASA, $\triangle ABC \cong \triangle CDA$. □

(b) Suppose that $X$ is the common midpoint of $\overline{AB}$ and $\overline{CD}$. Then $\triangle AXC \cong \triangle \underline{BXD}$. Prove it.

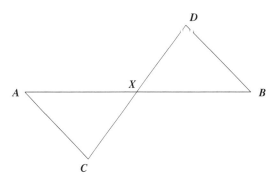

**Proof:** Draw $\overline{AC}$ and $\overline{BD}$. Since $X$ is the midpoint of $\overline{AB}$, $\overline{AX} \cong \overline{XB}$. Similarly, $\overline{CX} \cong \overline{XD}$. Also, $\angle AXC \cong \angle BXD$ because they are vertical. Therefore, by SAS, $\triangle AXC \cong \triangle BXD$. □

(c) The Isosceles Triangle Theorem says that if two sides of a triangle are congruent, then the angles opposite those sides are also congruent. Prove the Isosceles Triangle Theorem by drawing the angle bisector of the vertex angle.
Given: In $\triangle ABC$, $\overline{AB} \cong \overline{AC}$. Prove that $\angle B \cong \angle C$.

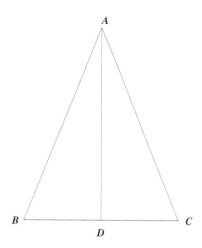

**Proof:** Draw $\overline{AD}$, the angle bisector of $\angle A$. This means that $\angle DAB \cong \angle DAC$. We are told that $\overline{AB} \cong \overline{AC}$, and clearly $\overline{AD} \cong \overline{AD}$. So, by *SAS*, $\triangle DAB \cong \triangle DAC$. Therefore, $\angle B \cong \angle C$ because CPCTC (corresponding parts of congruent triangles are congruent).

(d) Prove that the diagonals of a rhombus bisect their vertex angles.

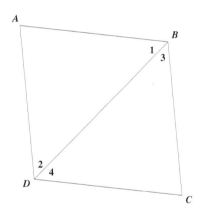

**Proof:** Since $ABCD$ is a rhombus, we know $\overline{AB} \cong \overline{BC} \cong \overline{CD} \cong \overline{DA}$ and clearly, $\overline{BD} \cong \overline{BD}$. Thus, by SSS, $\triangle ABD \cong \triangle CBD$. So, $\angle 1 \cong \angle 3$ and $\angle 2 \cong \angle 4$ by CPCTC. Therefore, $\overline{BD}$ bisects $\angle ABC$ and $\angle CDA$. A similar proof would show that the other diagonal bisects its vertex angles as well. $\square$

(e) True or false: Any two isosceles triangles must be similar. If true, prove it, and if false, give a counterexample. FALSE

Consider an isosceles triangle with a third side shorter than the other two. (See the picture used in the Isosceles Triangle proof, above.) This happens when the vertex angle is less than 60 degrees, because a vertex angle of 60 degrees would make our isosceles triangle into an equilateral triangle. Now consider the isosceles triangle with side lengths 1, 1, and $\sqrt{2}$. Then the third side is longer than the other two. (This happens to be a right triangle; its vertex angle is 90 degrees.) Since similar triangles must have congruent angles, there is no way that these two isosceles triangles can be similar.

(f) Draw $\triangle ABC$. On $\overline{AB}$, draw point $M$ so that $AM = 2MB$. On $\overline{AC}$, draw point $N$ so that $AN = 2NC$. Prove that $\overline{MN} \parallel \overline{BC}$.

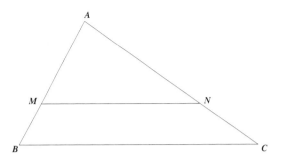

**Proof:** By the construction of $M$ and $N$, it follows that $AM = \frac{2}{3}AB$ and $AN = \frac{2}{3}AC$. Clearly $\angle A \cong \angle A$. Thus, by sAs, $\triangle AMN \sim \triangle ABC$. Hence, $\angle AMN \cong \angle ABC$, because corresponding angles of similar triangles are congruent. Therefore, $\overline{MN} \parallel \overline{BC}$, by the converse of the Corresponding Angle Theorem. (See previous section on Parallelism for the Corresponding Angle Theorem.)

(g) Draw an isosceles trapezoid and its two diagonals. The trapezoid is now divided into four triangular regions. Prove that two of these regions must be similar. Then prove that the other two regions must be congruent.

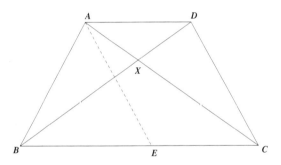

**Proof:** We are given isosceles trapezoid $ABCD$, in which $\overline{AD} \parallel \overline{BC}$ and $\overline{AB} \cong \overline{CD}$. By the Alternate Interior Angle Theorem, $\angle DAC \cong \angle BCA$. Also, $\angle AXD \cong \angle CXB$ because they are vertical. So, by AA, $\triangle AXD \sim \triangle CXB$. □

Now, draw $\overline{AE}$ parallel to $\overline{CD}$. Thus, $AECD$ is a parallelogram, and hence, $\overline{AE} \cong \overline{CD}$. By the transitive property of congruence, $\overline{AE} \cong \overline{AB}$. This makes $\triangle AEB$ isosceles, and so by the Isosceles Triangle Theorem, $\angle ABE \cong \angle AEB$. Because they are corresponding angles, $\angle AEB \cong \angle DCB$. By transitivity, then, $\angle ABC \cong \angle DCB$. Since $\overline{BC} \cong \overline{BC}$, SAS implies that $\triangle ABC \cong \triangle DCB$. Thus, $\angle BAC \cong \angle CDB$ by CPCTC. Moreover, $\angle AXB \cong \angle DXC$ because they are vertical. Therefore, by AAS, $\triangle AXB \cong \triangle DXC$. □

**b. Understand, apply, and justify properties of triangles (e.g., the Exterior Angle Theorem, concurrence theorems, trigonometric ratios, Triangle Inequality, Law of Sines, Law of Cosines, the Pythagorean Theorem and its converse)**

1. What does the Exterior Angle Theorem say?

   The Exterior Angle Theorem says (in Euclidean geometry) that the measure of an exterior angle of a triangle is equal to the sum of the measures of the other two remote interior angles.

In neutral geometry, you can say that the measure of an exterior angle is greater than the measure of either remote interior angle, but you cannot say that the sum of the two remote angles equals the exterior angle. That part is strictly Euclidean.

2. What do the concurrence theorems say?

There are several concurrence theorems for triangles. The medians of a triangle are concurrent at a point called the centroid, which also lies two-thirds of the distance along each median from its vertex end. The angle bisectors of a triangle are concurrent at the incenter. The perpendicular bisectors of the sides are concurrent at the circumcenter. The three altitudes of a triangle are concurrent at the orthocenter. There are more, but these are the most common.

3. What are the standard trigonometric ratios?

The six basic trigonometric ratios are sine, cosine, tangent, cotangent, secant, and cosecant (csc). Usually in Geometry, only sine, cosine, and tangent are used, while the others are written in terms of these three. [Incidentally, the word "cosine" is a contraction of "complement's sine." That is: $\cos(A) = \sin(90 - A)$. The other "co-" functions have a similar meaning.]

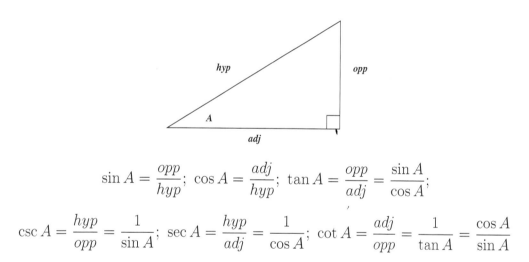

$$\sin A = \frac{opp}{hyp}; \quad \cos A = \frac{adj}{hyp}; \quad \tan A = \frac{opp}{adj} = \frac{\sin A}{\cos A};$$

$$\csc A = \frac{hyp}{opp} = \frac{1}{\sin A}; \quad \sec A = \frac{hyp}{adj} = \frac{1}{\cos A}; \quad \cot A = \frac{adj}{opp} = \frac{1}{\tan A} = \frac{\cos A}{\sin A}$$

4. What does the Triangle Inequality say?

The Triangle Inequality says that the sum of the lengths of ANY two sides of a triangle must be greater than the length of the third side.

5. What does the Law of Sines say? How do you justify it?

The Law of Sines says that in $\triangle ABC$, $\dfrac{\sin A}{a} = \dfrac{\sin B}{b} = \dfrac{\sin C}{c}$. To justify the Law of Sines, try calculating the area of the triangle three different ways (using its three different altitudes) and then set your areas equal to each other. (See area formulas, below.)

6. What does the Law of Cosines say? How do you justify it?

The Law of Cosines says that in $\triangle ABC$, $c^2 = a^2 + b^2 - 2ab(\cos C)$. To justify the Law of Cosines, we will use coordinate geometry, below.

7. What does the Pythagorean Theorem say?

   If $\wedge ABC$ has a right angle at $C$, then $a^2 + b^2 = c^2$.

8. What does the converse of the Pythagorean Theorem say?

   If $a^2 + b^2 = c^2$ in $\triangle ABC$, then $\triangle ABC$ has a right angle at $C$.

9. Sample Problems

   (a) Prove the Exterior Angle Theorem. Why is the Exterior Angle Theorem strictly a Euclidean theorem?

   (b) Show that a triangle's circumcenter is the center of its circumscribed circle.

   (c) Draw pictures showing that the circumcenter and orthocenter of a triangle could lie outside the triangle.

   (d) Write down all trigonometric ratios for a 30-60-90 triangle and a 45-45-90 triangle.

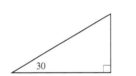 

   (e) Write down all the trigonometric ratios for a right triangle with legs 8 and 15.

   (f) Can you define all the trigonometric ratios for 0 and 90 degree angles? If so, do it, and if not, why not?

   (g) Explain how the Triangle Inequality follows from the saying "the shortest distance between two points is a straight line."

   (h) Explain why you cannot have a triangle of side lengths 3, 4, and 8.

   (i) What happens if you apply the Law of Cosines to a triangle that has a right angle at $C$?

   (j) Find the remaining sides of $\triangle DEF$ if $d = 4$, $m\angle E = 40$, and $m\angle F = 60$. (This is called *solving* the triangle.)

   (k) Prove the Pythagorean Theorem using similar triangles. [Hint: first, draw the altitude from the right angle. Then set up similarity ratios that lead to $a^2$ and $b^2$. Then add.]

10. Answers to Sample Problems

    (a) Prove the Exterior Angle Theorem. Why is the Exterior Angle Theorem strictly a Euclidean theorem?

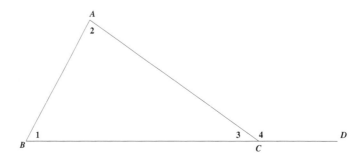

Given: $\triangle ABC$. Prove: $m\angle 4 = m\angle 1 + m\angle 2$.

**Proof:** Since $\angle 3$ and $\angle 4$ are supplementary, $m\angle 3 + m\angle 4 = 180$. So $m\angle 4 = 180 - m\angle 3$. In $\triangle ABC$, $m\angle 1 + m\angle 2 + m\angle 3 = 180$. Thus $m\angle 1 + m\angle 2 = 180 - m\angle 3$. By substitution, therefore, $m\angle 4 = m\angle 1 + m\angle 2$. $\square$

The Exterior Angle Theorem is strictly Euclidean because it relies on the Euclidean fact that the angles of a triangle add up to 180 degrees.

(b) Show that a triangle's circumcenter is the center of its circumscribed circle.

We will first prove a lemma: If $P$ is on the perpendicular bisector of $\overline{AB}$, then $\overline{PA} \cong \overline{PB}$.

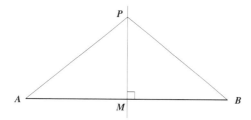

**Proof:** Draw the perpendicular bisector of $\overline{AB}$. By definition, it intersects $\overline{AB}$ at its midpoint, $M$, so that $\angle PMA$ and $\angle PMB$ are right angles. So $\angle PMA \cong \angle PMB$ and $\overline{AM} \cong \overline{BM}$. Clearly $\overline{PM} \cong \overline{PM}$. Thus, by SAS, $\triangle PMA \cong \triangle PMB$. Therefore $\overline{PA} \cong \overline{PB}$ by CPCTC. $\square$

The perpendicular bisectors of the sides of $\triangle ABC$ are concurrent at the circumcenter. Hence, if $P$ is the circumcenter, then $\overline{PA} \cong \overline{PB} \cong \overline{PC}$ by repeatedly invoking the lemma. Therefore, if we draw a circle with center $P$ and radius $PA$, the circle will pass through all three vertices of the triangle, circumscribing it.

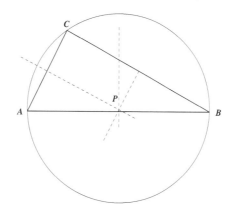

(c) Draw pictures showing that the circumcenter and orthocenter of a triangle could lie outside the triangle.

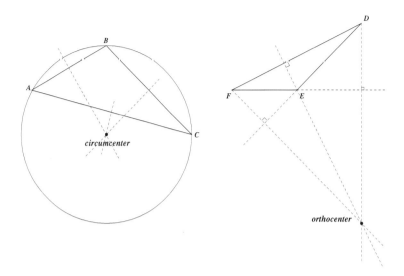

(d) Write down all trigonometric ratios for a 30-60-90 triangle and a 45-45-90 triangle.

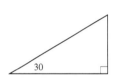 

| Angle $\theta$ | $\sin\theta$ | $\cos\theta$ | $\tan\theta$ | $\cot\theta$ | $\sec\theta$ | $\csc\theta$ |
|---|---|---|---|---|---|---|
| 30 | $\frac{1}{2}$ | $\frac{\sqrt{3}}{2}$ | $\frac{1}{\sqrt{3}}=\frac{\sqrt{3}}{3}$ | $\sqrt{3}$ | $\frac{2}{\sqrt{3}}=\frac{2\sqrt{3}}{3}$ | $2$ |
| 60 | $\frac{\sqrt{3}}{2}$ | $\frac{1}{2}$ | $\sqrt{3}$ | $\frac{1}{\sqrt{3}}=\frac{\sqrt{3}}{3}$ | $2$ | $\frac{2}{\sqrt{3}}=\frac{2\sqrt{3}}{3}$ |
| 45 | $\frac{\sqrt{2}}{2}$ | $\frac{\sqrt{2}}{2}$ | $1$ | $1$ | $\sqrt{2}$ | $\sqrt{2}$ |

(e) Write down all the trigonometric ratios for a right triangle with legs 8 and 15.

First, notice that the hypotenuse is $\sqrt{8^2+15^2}=\sqrt{289}=17$.

| Angle | $\sin\theta$ | $\cos\theta$ | $\tan\theta$ | $\cot\theta$ | $\sec\theta$ | $\csc\theta$ |
|---|---|---|---|---|---|---|
| opposite 8 | $\frac{8}{17}$ | $\frac{15}{17}$ | $\frac{8}{15}$ | $\frac{15}{8}$ | $\frac{17}{15}$ | $\frac{17}{8}$ |
| opposite 15 | $\frac{15}{17}$ | $\frac{8}{17}$ | $\frac{15}{8}$ | $\frac{8}{15}$ | $\frac{17}{8}$ | $\frac{17}{15}$ |

(f) Can you define all the trigonometric ratios for 0 and 90 degree angles? If so, do it, and if not, why not?

Think of what happens as the angle $A$ approaches 0 degrees. Then the opposite side shrinks to zero, and the adjacent side length approaches the length of the hypotenuse. So, $\sin(0)=0$ and $\cos(0)=1$. Thus, $\tan(0)=0$ and $\sec(0)=1$, but $\cot(0)$ and $\csc(0)$ are not defined because they have denominators equal to zero. Similarly, $\sin(90)=1$ and $\cos(90)=0$. So $\cot(90)=0$ and $\csc(90)=1$, while $\tan(90)$ and $\sec(90)$ are not defined.

(g) Explain how the Triangle Inequality follows from the saying "the shortest distance between two points is a straight line."

Consider two vertices of a triangle. There are two paths along the triangle leading from one vertex to the other. The first path is along the side joining the two vertices. The other path is along the other two sides, passing through the third vertex. According to the saying, the shortest path is the first one, the straight line joining the two vertices.

Therefore, the sum of the other two side lengths must be greater than the length of the third side. This is exactly what the Triangle Inequality says.

(h) Explain why you cannot have a triangle of side lengths 3, 4, and 8.

Think of attaching the sides of length 3 and 4 to the opposite ends of the side of length 8. Then it's clear that the sides of length 3 and 4 cannot reach each other. Even pointing directly toward each other, they have a total length of 7, which is less than 8, the distance between their fixed endpoints.

(i) What happens if you apply the Law of Cosines to a triangle that has a right angle at $C$?

The Law of Cosines says that in $\triangle ABC$, $c^2 = a^2 + b^2 - 2ab(\cos C)$. So, if $\angle C$ is a right angle, then $\cos C = 0$. Therefore, $c^2 = a^2 + b^2$, which is really the Pythagorean Theorem. Therefore, the Law of Cosines is a generalization of the Pythagorean Theorem to any triangle.

(j) Find the remaining sides of $\triangle DEF$ if $d = 4$, $m\angle E = 40$, and $m\angle F = 60$. (This is called *solving* the triangle.)

Since the angle sum of a triangle is 180, $m\angle D = 80$. Using the Law of Sines, we have

$$\frac{\sin 60}{f} = \frac{\sin 40}{e} = \frac{\sin 80}{4} \approx 0.2462.$$

Therefore, $e \approx 2.61$ and $f \approx 3.52$.

(k) Prove the Pythagorean Theorem using similar triangles. [Hint: first, draw the altitude from the right angle. Then set up similarity ratios that lead to $a^2$ and $b^2$. Then add.]

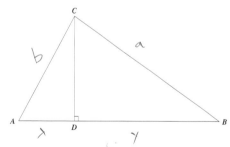

Let $a = BC$, $b = AC$, $c = AB$, $x = AD$, and $y = BD$. [Notice that $x + y = c$.] Recall that $\triangle ABC \sim \triangle CBD \sim \triangle ACD$. So, $\frac{c}{a} = \frac{a}{y}$ and $\frac{c}{b} = \frac{b}{x}$. After cross-multiplying, we get $a^2 = cy$ and $b^2 = cx$. Thus $a^2 + b^2 = cy + cx = c(y + x) = c^2$. □

## c. Understand, apply, and justify properties of polygons and circles from an advanced standpoint (e.g., derive the area formulas for regular polygons and circles from the area of a triangle)

1. What are some formulas for the area $A$ of a triangle?

There are many formulas, the most common of which is: $A = \frac{1}{2}bh$, where $b$ is the length of the base and $h$ the length of an altitude drawn to that base. There is a trigonometric formula for the area of $\triangle ABC$: $A = \frac{1}{2}ab\sin C$. There is also Heron's Formula, based only on the side lengths and the semiperimeter $s = \frac{1}{2}(a+b+c)$: $A = \sqrt{s(s-a)(s-b)(s-c)}$.

2. How do you use triangles to find the area of a regular polygon?

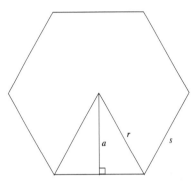

In the diagram, we are looking at a hexagon, but you can imagine the polygon to have any number of sides. Also, $r$ is called a *radius* and $a$ an *apothem*. The side length $s$ is just the perimeter of the polygon divided by $n$, the number of sides: $s = P/n$. Since the polygon is regular, drawing the radii will divide the polygon into $n$ congruent triangles, each with base $s$ and height $a$. So the total area of the polygon is: $A = n(\frac{1}{2}sa) = \frac{1}{2}aP$. Another way to see this formula is:

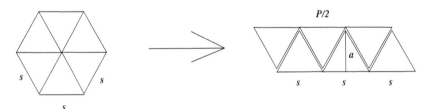

3. How do you use triangles to approximate the area of a circle?

Think of a regular polygon having more and more sides. As the number of sides increases, the polygon looks more and more like a circle. So, if you think about what happens, you can determine that the apothem approaches the radius ($a \to r$) and the perimeter approaches the circumference ($P \to 2\pi r$) as the number of sections increases (as $n \to \infty$). Therefore,

$$A = \frac{1}{2}aP \to \frac{1}{2}(r)(2\pi r) = \pi r^2.$$

4. Sample Problems

   (a) Find the area of a 3-4-5 triangle several different ways.

   (b) Find the area of an equilateral triangle of side length $s$. Compare it with the area of a square of side length $s$ and the area of a regular hexagon of side length $s$.

   (c) Find the area of a regular octagon of side length $s$.

   (d) In a regular $n$-gon, $a$, $r$, $P$, and $n$ are not independent quantities. Find the formula for the area in terms of $n$ and $a$. [Hint: You will need trigonometry.]

5. Answers to Sample Problems

(a) Find the area of a 3-4-5 triangle several different ways.

Notice that there is a right angle between the sides of length 3 and 4. Thus, if 4 is the base, then 3 is the height. So the area is $\frac{1}{2}(4)(3) = 6$.

Or, we can use the trigonometric formula, with any sides labeled $a$ and $b$. If we use the typical labeling for a right triangle, then $C$ is a right angle. So

$$\frac{1}{2}ab\sin C = \frac{1}{2}(3)(4)(\sin 90) = 6.$$

We could also use $a = 3$, $b = 5$, which means that $C$ is opposite the side of length 4. Thus $\sin C = \frac{4}{5}$. So

$$\frac{1}{2}ab\sin C = \frac{1}{2}(3)(5)\left(\frac{4}{5}\right) = 6.$$

We can also use Heron's formula, where $s = \frac{1}{2}(3 + 4 + 5) = 6$.

$$A = \sqrt{s(s-a)(s-b)(s-c)} = \sqrt{6(3)(2)(1)} = \sqrt{36} = 6.$$

(b) Find the area of an equilateral triangle of side length $s$. Compare it with the area of a square of side length $s$ and the area of a regular hexagon of side length $s$.

Using the trigonometric formula for area, we get $\frac{1}{2}(s)(s)(\sin 60) = \frac{\sqrt{3}}{4}s^2$. The area of a square of side length $s$ is $s^2$. A regular hexagon of side length $s$ is composed of six equilateral triangles of side length $s$. So, the area of a regular hexagon of side length $s$ is $6(\frac{\sqrt{3}}{4})s^2 = \frac{3\sqrt{3}}{2}s^2$.

(c) Find the area of a regular octagon of side length $s$.

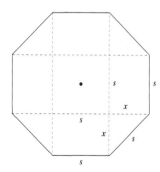

Notice that the regular octagon is made up of one square of side length $s$, four rectangles that are $s$ by $x$, and four half-squares of side length $x$. Also, the Pythagorean Theorem implies that $2x^2 = s^2$, which means $x = \frac{s}{\sqrt{2}}$. So the total area is

$$s^2 + 4sx + 2x^2 = s^2 + \frac{4s^2}{\sqrt{2}} + 2\left(\frac{s^2}{2}\right) = (2 + 2\sqrt{2})s^2.$$

(d) In a regular $n$-gon, $a$, $r$, $P$, and $n$ are not independent quantities. Find the formula for the area in terms of $n$ and $a$. [Hint: You will need trigonometry.]

We know that $A = \frac{1}{2}aP = \frac{1}{2}a(ns)$, where $s$ is the side length. Let $\theta$ be the angle formed at the center of the $n$-gon by a radius and an apothem. Then $\theta = \frac{360}{2n}$ and $\tan\theta = \frac{s}{2a}$. Hence, $s = 2a\tan\theta$. Therefore,

$$A = \frac{ans}{2} = \frac{an(2a\tan\theta)}{2} = a^2 n \tan\left(\frac{360}{2n}\right).$$

**d. Justify and perform the classical constructions (e.g., angle bisector, perpendicular bisector, replicating shapes, regular $n$-gons for $n$ equal to 3, 4, 5, 6, and 8)**

1. What makes a construction "classical?"

   The classical constructions are those that can be performed with a compass (for copying arcs of a given fixed length) and an unmarked straightedge (for drawing or extending lines if you are given two points). These were the geometry tools used by the ancient Greeks.

2. How do you copy an angle? Why does it work?

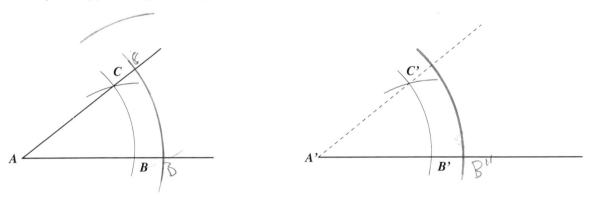

   To copy the given $\angle A$ onto the given line at $A'$, we first draw an arc through the sides of the angle. Label the points of intersection as $B$ and $C$. Using the same compass setting, swing an arc centered at $A'$. Label its point of intersection with the line as $B'$. Now set the compass to the distance $BC$. Keeping the same compass setting, swing an arc centered at $B'$ that intersects the first arc at a point $C'$. Then $\angle C'A'B' \cong \angle CAB$.

   The reason that $\angle C'A'B' \cong \angle CAB$ is because $AB = AC = A'B' = A'C'$ and $BC = B'C'$. So by SSS, $\triangle C'A'B' \cong \triangle CAB$. Therefore, $\angle A \cong \angle A'$ by CPCTC.

3. How do you bisect an angle? Why does it work?

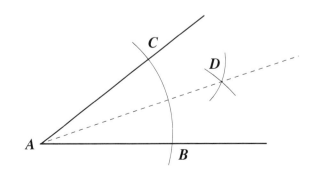

To bisect the given $\angle A$, we first draw an arc through the sides of the angle. Label the points of intersection as $B$ and $C$. Using a new compass setting that is at least half the distance $BC$, swing two arcs, one centered at $B$ and one centered at $C$, so that they intersect at a point $D$ in the interior of angle $A$. Then $\overrightarrow{AD}$ bisects angle $A$.

The reason that $\overrightarrow{AD}$ bisects angle $A$ is that $AB = AC$, $BD = CD$, and $AD = AD$. So, by SSS, $\triangle DAB \cong \triangle DAC$. Therefore, $\angle DAB \cong \angle DAC$ by CPCTC.

4. How do you perpendicularly bisect a line segment? Why does it work?

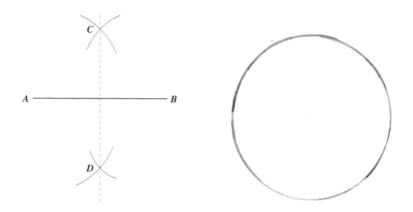

To perpendicularly bisect the given segment $\overline{AB}$, we first set the compass to a distance that is at least half of $AB$. Then swing arcs centered at $A$ on both sides of $\overline{AB}$. Using the same compass setting, swing arcs centered at $B$ on both sides of $\overline{AB}$ so that the new arcs intersect the old ones. Label the points of intersection $C$ and $D$. Then $\overline{CD}$ perpendicularly bisects $\overline{AB}$.

The reason that $\overline{CD}$ perpendicularly bisects $\overline{AB}$ is that $AC = AD = BC = BD$, which makes $ADBC$ a rhombus. The diagonals of a rhombus perpendicularly bisect each other.

5. How do you divide a segment into $n$ congruent pieces?

We will show how to trisect a line segment, but the process can be repeated for any positive integer $n$. We will also use the construction for copying an angle.

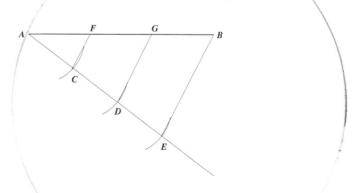

To trisect the given segment $\overline{AB}$, we first draw a line segment from $A$ in a different direction from $B$. Then we mark off three equal segments on this line: $AC = CD = DE$. Next, connect point $E$ to point $B$. Then, copy $\angle AEB$ so that it has a vertex at $D$ and then make another copy with its vertex at $C$. So $\angle ACF \cong \angle ADG \cong \angle AEB$. The points $F$ and $G$ trisect $\overline{AB}$.

The reason this construction works is that $\triangle ACF \sim \triangle ADG \sim \triangle AEB$ by AA. Moreover, the triangles' side lengths are in the proportion $1:2:3$. Therefore, $AF = FG = GB$.

6. How do you construct a regular hexagon?

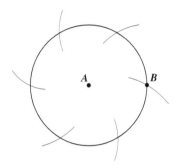

To construct a regular hexagon, draw a circle centered at some point $A$. Select a point $B$ on the circle. Using the same compass setting as you used to draw the circle, swing arcs around the circumference of circle $A$, starting at $B$. After six arcs, you should be back at $B$. The intersection points between the arcs and the circle are the vertices of a regular hexagon.

7. How do you double the number of sides in a given regular $n$-gon?

If you are given a regular $n$-gon, you could construct the circumscribing circle. Then, perpendicularly bisect any side (say $\overline{AB}$) of the $n$-gon. Now find the intersection point $C$ between the perpendicular bisector and the circumscribing circle. The length $AC$ (or $BC$) is the side length for the $2n$-gon. Use this as a new compass setting and proceed around the rest of the circle to construct all the vertices of the regular $2n$-gon.

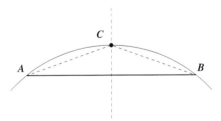

8. How do you construct a regular pentagon?

This is a surprisingly tricky construction. To present it here would go beyond the scope of this text. Suffice it to say that you must first construct a 72 degree angle in order to construct the regular pentagon. One hint is that $\cos 72 = \frac{\sqrt{5}-1}{4}$, which is a constructible length.

9. What constructions are not classical? Why not?

It is impossible to double the cube, square the circle, or trisect an arbitrary angle (though people tried for thousands of years). This means that a compass and straightedge cannot construct $\sqrt[3]{2}$ or $\sqrt{\pi}$, nor can they solve a general cubic equation. There is an algebraic proof of these facts that goes beyond many undergraduate mathematics curricula and certainly beyond this text, but suffice it to say that compasses and straightedges are good for finding distances, which means that rational numbers and square roots are OK, but it is not possible to construct irrational cube roots or $\sqrt{\pi}$.

Also, there are an infinite number of regular polygons which cannot be constructed, again, for algebraic reasons beyond the scope of this text. A regular 7-gon is not constructible; neither are a 9-gon, 11-gon, 13-gon, nor a 19-gon. Gauss constructed a regular 17-gon in his teens, but he was pretty smart!

10. Sample Problems

  (a) Practice your basic constructions. Look in a textbook for more fancy constructions. How do the compass and straightedge provide evidence for geometric proofs?

  (b) Inscribe an equilateral triangle in a circle.

  (c) Inscribe a square in a circle.

  (d) Suppose one of your students claims that they have constructed a regular polygon with 14 sides. Explain how you know that they must be wrong.

11. Answers to Sample Problems

  (a) Practice your basic constructions. Look in a textbook for more fancy constructions. How do the compass and straightedge provide evidence for geometric proofs?

  The compass copies distances. This means that it can be used to show that line segments are congruent. The straightedge can be used to draw the line between two points or to extend lines. Mathematicians have shown that every construction that can be done with a compass and straightedge can actually be done with a compass alone!

  (b) Inscribe an equilateral triangle in a circle.

  Use the construction given above for a regular hexagon inscribed in a circle. Then connect every other vertex to form an equilateral triangle.

  (c) Inscribe a square in a circle.

  There are a number of ways to do this. A direct way is to draw a diameter of the circle, then perpendicularly bisect the diameter to find the perpendicular diameter. The four endpoints of these diameters are the vertices of a square. See the picture below.

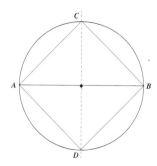

(d) Suppose one of your students claims that they have constructed a regular polygon with 14 sides. Explain how you know that they must be wrong.

If the student were correct, then by connecting every other vertex, the student would have constructed a regular 7-gon (heptagon), which is impossible to construct with a compass and straightedge. Therefore, the student must not be correct.

## e. Use techniques in coordinate geometry to prove geometric theorems

1. What is coordinate geometry? How does it work?

Coordinate geometry is the application of algebra to geometry. Often, we will place geometric objects on a Cartesian coordinate system and then use algebraic reasoning to discover, justify, show, or even prove a certain relationship.

Example: Show that the diagonals of a rectangle are congruent. To prove this, we first need to place an arbitrary rectangle on a coordinate system. Since rotating and translating the rectangle will not affect the length of its diagonals, we can place the rectangle so that its vertices are at $(0,0)$, $(a,0)$, $(a,b)$, and $(0,b)$.

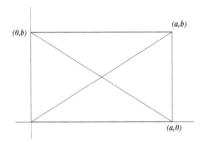

Using the distance formula, the length of the diagonal from $(0,0)$ to $(a,b)$ is found to equal $\sqrt{(a-0)^2 + (b-0)^2} = \sqrt{a^2 + b^2}$. The other diagonal has length $\sqrt{(a-0)^2 + (0-b)^2} = \sqrt{a^2 + b^2}$. Therefore, the diagonals of a rectangle are congruent.

Advice: if your proof requires midpoints, then start with points like $(2a, 2b)$ instead of $(a, b)$. You are still being completely arbitrary, but the math is easier.

2. Sample Problems

(a) Write down and memorize the Distance Formula, the Midpoint Formula, the Slope Formula, the Slope-Intercept equation of a line, and the Point-Slope equation of a line.

(b) Let $A = (2,3)$, $B = (-2,5)$, $C = (5,8)$, and $D = (1,10)$. Show that $ABDC$ is a parallelogram. Where is point $E$ if $ABCE$ is a parallelogram?

(c) Justify the Law of Cosines using the following picture.

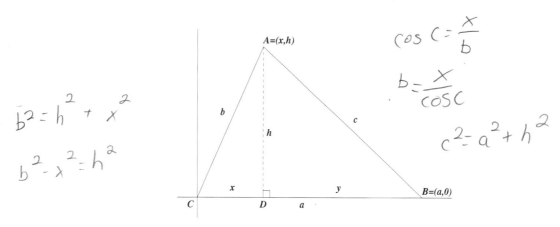

(d) Prove that the diagonals of a square are perpendicular to each other, bisect each other, and are the same length. How does the length of a diagonal compare with the length of a side of the square?

(e) Prove that the diagonals of a rectangle bisect each other. Is this true for any parallelogram? If so, prove it, and if not, give a counterexample.

(f) Show that if you join the four midpoints of the sides of a quadrilateral, then you form a parallelogram.

(g) Prove that the three medians of a triangle are concurrent.

3. Answers to Sample Problems

(a) Write down and memorize the Distance Formula, the Midpoint Formula, the Slope Formula, the Slope-Intercept equation of a line, and the Point-Slope equation of a line.

The distance between $(x_1, y_1)$ and $(x_2, y_2)$ is $\sqrt{(x_2 - x_1)^2 + (y_2 - y_1)^2}$.

The midpoint of the line segment between $(x_1, y_1)$ and $(x_2, y_2)$ is $\left(\dfrac{x_1 + x_2}{2}, \dfrac{y_1 + y_2}{2}\right)$.

The slope of the line passing through $(x_1, y_1)$ and $(x_2, y_2)$ is $\dfrac{y_2 - y_1}{x_2 - x_1}$.

If a line has slope $m$ and $y$-intercept $b$, then its equation is $y = mx + b$.

If a line has slope $m$ and passes through $(h, k)$, then its equation is $y - k = m(x - h)$.

(b) Let $A = (2, 3), B = (-2, 5), C = (5, 8)$, and $D = (1, 10)$. Show that $ABDC$ is a parallelogram. Where is point $E$ if $ABCE$ is a parallelogram?

(To see what's going on here, plot these points on a set of coordinate axes.) The slope of $\overline{AB}$ is $\frac{5-3}{-2-2} = -\frac{1}{2}$. The slope of $\overline{DC}$ is $\frac{10-8}{1-5} = -\frac{1}{2}$. So $\overline{AB} \parallel \overline{DC}$. The slope of $\overline{BD}$ is $\frac{10-5}{1-(-2)} = \frac{5}{3}$. The slope of $\overline{AC}$ is $\frac{8-3}{5-2} = \frac{5}{3}$. So $\overline{BD} \parallel \overline{AC}$. Therefore, $ABDC$ is a parallelogram.

Point $E$ must be located at $(9, 6)$ so that $ABCE$ is a parallelogram.

(c) Justify the Law of Cosines using the following picture.

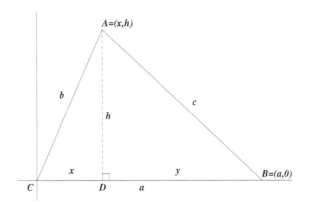

Notice that in right triangle $ADC$, $\cos C = \frac{x}{b}$. Thus $x = b \cos C$. Using the Distance Formula, we get $c = \sqrt{(x-a)^2 + (h-0)^2}$. So,

$$
\begin{aligned}
c^2 &= (x-a)^2 + (h-0)^2 = x^2 - 2ax + a^2 + h^2 \\
&= a^2 + (x^2 + h^2) - 2ax = a^2 + b^2 - 2ax,
\end{aligned}
$$

if we use the Pythagorean Theorem. Therefore, by substitution, $c^2 = a^2 + b^2 - 2ab \cos C$.
$\square$

(d) Prove that the diagonals of a square are perpendicular to each other, bisect each other, and are the same length. How does the length of a diagonal compare with the length of a side of the square?

On a coordinate grid, we can put the vertices of the square at $(0,0), (2s,0), (2s,2s)$, and $(0,2s)$, where $2s$ is the side length of the square. The diagonal through $(0,0)$ and $(2s,2s)$ has slope $\frac{2s-0}{2s-0} = 1$. The other diagonal has slope $\frac{0-2s}{2s-0} = -1$. Since the slopes are negative reciprocals of each other, the diagonals are perpendicular. Using the distance formula, the diagonals must be congruent. (This was already proven above for any rectangle.) To see that the diagonals bisect each other, we need to show that their midpoints are the same point. The midpoint of the diagonal through the origin is $(\frac{0+2s}{2}, \frac{0+2s}{2}) = (s,s)$, and the midpoint for the other diagonal is $(\frac{0+2s}{2}, \frac{2s+0}{2}) = (s,s)$ also. Therefore, the diagonals of a square bisect each other.

(e) Prove that the diagonals of a rectangle bisect each other. Is this true for any parallelogram? If so, prove it, and if not, give a counterexample.

We will show that it is true for any parallelogram, which means that it would certainly be true for any rectangle. Place the vertices of the parallelogram at $(0,0), (2a,0), (2b,2c)$, and $(2a+2b, 2c)$.

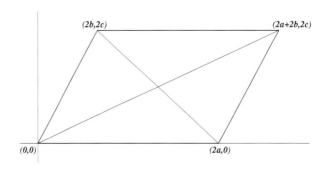

The midpoint of the diagonal that passes through the origin is $(\frac{0+2a+2b}{2}, \frac{0+2c}{2}) = (a+b, c)$. The midpoint of the other diagonal is $(\frac{2b+2a}{2}, \frac{2c+0}{2}) = (b+a, c)$. Since their midpoints coincide, the diagonals of a parallelogram bisect each other.

(f) Show that if you join the four midpoints of the sides of a quadrilateral, then you form a parallelogram.

In the following picture, we have drawn an arbitrary quadrilateral and labeled its vertices and the midpoints of its sides. We have also connected the midpoints.

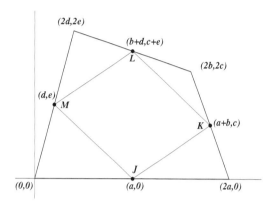

The slope of $\overline{JK}$ is $\dfrac{c-0}{a+b-a} = \dfrac{c}{b}$. The slope of $\overline{LM}$ is $\dfrac{c+e-e}{b+d-d} = \dfrac{c}{b}$.

The slope of $\overline{KL}$ is $\dfrac{c+e-c}{b+d-(a+b)} = \dfrac{e}{d-a}$. The slope of $\overline{MJ}$ is $\dfrac{e-0}{d-a} = \dfrac{e}{d-a}$.

Therefore $JKLM$ is a parallelogram.

(g) Prove that the three medians of a triangle are concurrent.

In the following picture, we have drawn an arbitrary triangle and labeled its vertices and the midpoints of its sides. We have also drawn in the medians. To prove that the medians are concurrent, we will find equations for all three lines, showing that they intersect. To make the calculations cleaner, we label the vertices with multiples of 6.

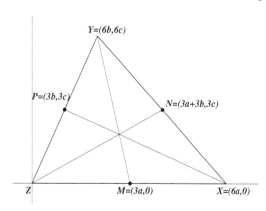

The slope of $\overline{ZN}$ is $\frac{3c}{3a+3b} = \frac{c}{a+b}$. So the equation of $\overline{ZN}$ is $y = (\frac{c}{a+b})x$.

The slope of $\overline{YM}$ is $\frac{6c}{6b-3a} = \frac{2c}{2b-a}$. So the equation of $\overline{YM}$ in Point-Slope form is $y = (\frac{2c}{2b-a})(x - 3a)$.

These two lines intersect at a point. To find it, substitute $y = (\frac{c}{a+b})x$ into the second equation, giving $(\frac{c}{a+b})x = (\frac{2c}{2b-a})(x - 3a)$. Cross-multiplying gives:

$$
\begin{aligned}
cx(2b - a) &= 2c(x - 3a)(a + b) = (2cx - 6ac)(a + b) \\
2bcx - acx &= 2acx - 6a^2c + 2bcx - 6abc \\
-3acx &= -6a^2c - 6abc \\
x &= 2a + 2b.
\end{aligned}
$$

Plugging this into the equation for $\overline{ZN}$ gives $y = 2c$. So the first two medians intersect at the point $(2a + 2b, 2c)$. If this point lies on the third median, then we will have proven that the medians are concurrent.

The slope of $\overline{XP}$ is $\frac{3c-0}{3b-6a} = \frac{c}{b-2a}$. So the Point-Slope form of $\overline{XP}$ is $y = (\frac{c}{b-2a})(x - 6a)$. If we plug in $x = 2a + 2b$, then we get

$$
y = \left(\frac{c}{b - 2a}\right)(2a + 2b - 6a) = \left(\frac{c}{b - 2a}\right)(2b - 4a) = 2c.
$$

So the point $(2a + 2b, 2c)$ is also on $\overline{XP}$. Therefore, the three medians of a triangle are concurrent. $\square$

# 2.3 Three-Dimensional Geometry

## a. Demonstrate an understanding of parallelism and perpendicularity of lines and planes in three dimensions

1. What does it mean for a line to lie in a plane? ...to be perpendicular to a plane? ...to be parallel to a plane?

   A line lies in a plane if every point on the line is also a point in the plane. A line $\ell$ is perpendicular to a plane $P$ if $\ell$ intersects $P$ at one point $A$ and if $\ell$ is perpendicular to any line through point $A$ that lies in plane $P$. [Aside: in advanced math, planes are described by their perpendicular lines, often called "normal vectors."] A line is parallel to a plane if the line and the plane do not intersect.

2. What does it mean for two planes to be parallel? ...perpendicular?

   Two planes are parallel if they do not intersect. Also, two planes are parallel if they are both perpendicular to the same line. Two planes are perpendicular if they intersect at a right angle.

   In other words, suppose plane $P$ is perpendicular to line $\ell$ and plane $Q$ is perpendicular to line $m$. Then plane $P$ is parallel to plane $Q$ if lines $\ell$ and $m$ are parallel, and $P$ is perpendicular to $Q$ if $\ell$ is perpendicular to $m$.

3. Are all non-intersecting pairs of lines "parallel?"

   No, just because two lines in space do not intersect does not mean they are "parallel." In space, we have the possibility of "skew" lines. The difference is this: if two lines are parallel, then there exists a plane containing both of them, whereas skew lines lie on parallel planes but never on the same plane.

4. Sample Problems

   (a) Explain why skew lines cannot intersect.

   (b) In what ways can two or three lines intersect on a plane?

   (c) In what ways can two or three lines intersect in space?

   (d) In what ways can two or three planes intersect in space?

   (e) In what ways can a line and a plane intersect in space?

   (f) How many points determine a line? ...a plane? ...space?

5. Answers to Sample Problems

   (a) Explain why skew lines cannot intersect.

   Skew lines cannot intersect because they lie on parallel planes, which by definition do not intersect.

   (b) In what ways can two or three lines intersect on a plane?

   On a plane, two lines could be parallel, or they could intersect in one point. Three lines could all be parallel, or two could be parallel and one a transversal, or any two of them could intersect in distinct points, or the three lines might be concurrent at a single point.

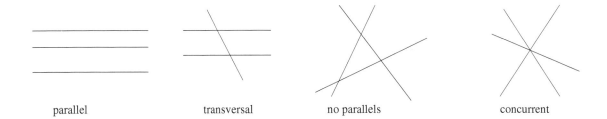

parallel      transversal      no parallels      concurrent

(c) In what ways can two or three lines intersect in space?

In space, two lines could be parallel or skew, in which case they do not intersect. If they are neither parallel nor skew, then the two lines intersect in one point. Three lines could exhibit the same behavior as in the previous problem, or if two of the lines are skew, then the third line could intersect one of them, both of them, or neither of them.

(d) In what ways can two or three planes intersect in space?

In space, two planes could be parallel, or else they could intersect in a line. Three planes could all be parallel, or two could be parallel and one could intersect each of the others in a line, or all three planes could intersect in a single point (like two walls and the floor intersect at the corner of a room), or the three planes could intersect in a line, or the three planes could intersect two at a time, with the three resulting lines of intersection being parallel.

(e) In what ways can a line and a plane intersect in space?

Either a line is parallel to a plane or else it intersects that plane in a single point.

(f) How many points determine a line? ...a plane? ...space?

Two points determine a line. Three non-collinear points determine a plane. Four non-coplanar points determine space.

## b. Understand, apply, and justify properties of three-dimensional objects from an advanced standpoint (e.g., derive the volume and surface area formulas for prisms, pyramids, cones, cylinders, and spheres)

1. What are the volume and surface area of a cube?

   If a cube has side length $s$, then its volume is $s^3$ and its surface area is $6s^2$ because it has six squares for its sides.

2. What are the other solids and what are their volume and surface area formulas?

   The other solids (roughly in order of increasing complexity) are:

   - rectangular prism - congruent rectangle bases lying in parallel planes (one directly aligned with the other) with corresponding vertices joined, making four rectangular lateral faces

   - prism - congruent polygon bases lying on parallel planes with corresponding vertices joined, making parallelogram lateral faces (PRISMS CAN BE SLANTED!)

   - pyramid - polygon base with each vertex joined to a point (called "the" vertex) on a different plane, making triangular lateral faces (PYRAMIDS CAN BE SLANTED!)

- cylinder - congruent circular bases lying on parallel planes, joined by one lateral face (CYLINDERS CAN BE SLANTED!)

- cone - a circular base joined to a vertex on a different plane, making one curved lateral face (CONES CAN BE SLANTED!)

- sphere - the set of all points in space which lie a certain distance (called the radius) from a given point (called the center)

| Solid | Volume | Surface Area, if not slanted |
|:---:|:---:|:---:|
| prism | $Bh$, where $B$ is area of base | $2B + Ph$, where $P$ is perimeter of base |
| pyramid | $\frac{1}{3}Bh$ | $B$ plus areas of triangle sides |
| cylinder | $\pi r^2 h$ | $2\pi r^2 + 2\pi rh$ |
| cone | $\frac{1}{3}\pi r^2 h$ | $\pi r^2 + \pi r\ell$, where $\ell$ is slant height |
| sphere | $\frac{4}{3}\pi r^3$ | $4\pi r^2$ |

3. How are these volume formulas obtained?

You can obtain all of the volume formulas using calculus. However, you can also find convincing geometric justifications as well. Euclid finds the volumes of the Platonic solids in Book XIII of the *Elements*.

The volumes of a prism and a cylinder are of the form $Bh$, where $B$ is the area of the base. This is plausible because each slice perpendicular to the height has exactly the same area.

To find the volume of a pyramid, you can subdivide a cube into 3 congruent pyramids of the same base area and height as the original cube, which explains why $\frac{1}{3}$ shows up in the volume of a pyramid.

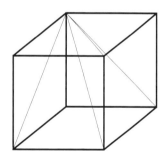

The relationship of a cone to a cylinder is analogous to the relationship of a pyramid to a prism of the same base and height. So, the volume of a cone is one-third that of the cylinder of the same base and height.

Archimedes found the volume of a sphere by showing that the ratio of the volume of a sphere to the volume of its circumscribing cylinder is 2:3. He was so proud of this result that he reportedly wanted it put on his tombstone.

Here's how it works. Archimedes noticed that if you take a double cone, a sphere, and a cylinder, all of the same radius $r$ and height $2r$, and if you take circular slices through all three of them at the same height, then the area of the cylinder slice is the sum of the areas of the double cone slice and the sphere slice.

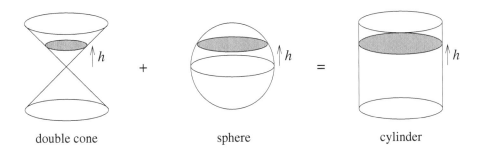

double cone          sphere          cylinder

To see this, assume that the double cone, sphere, and cylinder are centered at a height of zero. Hence for the cone, if the slice is at height $h$, then the radius of the slice is $h$. For the sphere, however, the radius of the slice is $\sqrt{r^2 - h^2}$, since the side view of the sphere is a circle. So the sum of the areas of these slices is

$$\pi h^2 + \pi(\sqrt{r^2 - h^2})^2 = \pi h^2 + \pi(r^2 - h^2) = \pi r^2,$$

which is precisely the area of the cylinder slice at height $h$.

So, by Cavalieri's Principle[1], the volume of the cylinder is the sum of the volumes of the sphere and the volume of the cone. In other words:

$$(\pi r^2)(2r) = V_{sph} + 2\left(\frac{1}{3}\pi r^2 r\right).$$

From this, one obtains $V_{sph} = 2\pi r^3 - \frac{2}{3}\pi r^3 = \frac{4}{3}\pi r^3$.

4. How are these surface area formulas obtained?

The surface areas of a prism or a pyramid are found by adding up the areas of their polygonal faces. If the pyramid is not slanted, then its slant height $\ell$ (the height of each triangular face) is constant. In this case, its surface area would be $B + \frac{1}{2}P\ell$, where $B$ is the area of the base and $P$ is the perimeter of the base.

For a cylinder, the surface has three faces, two circular bases plus one lateral side. If you think of a soup can label, this lateral side can be "unrolled" into a rectangle whose dimensions are the circumference of the base ($2\pi r$) and the height $h$. So the surface area of a cylinder is $2\pi r^2 + 2\pi rh$. For a cone, if we use an analogous argument as in the pyramid case, we find that its surface area is $\pi r^2 + \frac{1}{2}P\ell = \pi r^2 + \pi r\ell$, because the perimeter $P$ equals $2\pi r$, the circumference of the base.

For a sphere, calculus can be used to find its surface area somewhat directly, although Archimedes certainly knew the formula. One can project the sphere onto the lateral side of its circumscribing cylinder (like projecting the surface of Earth onto a rectangular map) in such a way that areas are preserved. The lateral side of the cylinder of radius $r$ and height $2r$ has area $(2\pi r)(2r) = 4\pi r^2$. Hence, $4\pi r^2$ is the surface area of a sphere of radius $r$.

5. Sample Problems

---

[1]Cavalieri's Principle says that if you take two solids and if parallel planes through those solids always intersect both solids so that the areas of intersection are equal, then the volumes of the solids must be equal.

(a) Find the volume of the Great Pyramid of Cheops, with square base of side length 754ft, and a height of 482ft.

(b) Find the surface area of the four sides of the Great Pyramid of Cheops (not the base).

(c) Find the volume of an equilateral triangular prism with base side length 4cm and height 5cm.

(d) Find the volume of a pyramid with an equilateral triangle base of side length 4cm and height 5cm.

(e) Find the volume of a cylindrical soda can of height 12cm and base diameter 6.5cm. Assuming 1 cubic cm holds 1mL of liquid, and 1mL equals 0.0338 fluid oz, how many ounces would this can hold?

(f) Find the volume and surface area of a cone of radius 5 and height 5.

(g) Several of the formulas involve the height. The volume formulas still work if the solid is slanted, provided the height is measured perpendicularly to the base. Justify this using Cavalieri's Principle.

(h) Which volume formulas take the form: volume equals area of base times height? ... volume equals one-third area of base times height?

(i) Suppose that a can of tennis balls is a cylinder that is just large enough to hold three spherical tennis balls. Find the ratio of the total volume of the tennis balls to the total volume of the can if a tennis ball has radius 3cm.

(j) In the previous problem, what is the surface area of the three tennis balls? What is the lateral surface area of the can (not including the bases)? What is the ratio of the two?

(k) Do your answers to the previous two questions really depend on the radius of the tennis balls? [What would Archimedes say?]

6. Answers to Sample Problems

(a) Find the volume of the Great Pyramid of Cheops, with square base of side length 754ft, and a height of 482ft.

The volume of a pyramid is $\frac{1}{3}Bh$, where $B$ is the area of the base. So,

$$V = \frac{1}{3}(754)^2(482) \approx 91{,}340{,}000 \text{ cubic feet.}$$

(b) Find the surface area of the four sides of the Great Pyramid of Cheops (not the base).

We know that the sides are triangles, but we don't know the height of each triangle. (The slant height of the pyramid is the height of each triangular side.) A cut-away side view shows how we can use the Pythagorean Theorem to determine the slant height.

So $\ell^2 = (482)^2 + (377)^2$, or $\ell \approx 612$ feet. Therefore, the total surface area of the sides of the Great Pyramid is

$$4 \left[ \frac{1}{2}(754)(612) \right] \approx 923{,}000 \text{ square feet.}$$

(c) Find the volume of an equilateral triangular prism with base side length 4cm and height 5cm.

The volume of a prism is $Bh$, where $B$ is the area of the base. Using trigonometry (or the 30-60-90 right triangle ratios), we find $B = \frac{\sqrt{3}}{4}s^2$, where $s$ is the side length of the triangle. So, the volume is

$$\frac{\sqrt{3}}{4}(4^2)(5) = 20\sqrt{3} \approx 34.6 \text{ cm}^3.$$

(d) Find the volume of a pyramid with an equilateral triangle base of side length 4cm and height 5cm.

The volume of a pyramid is one-third of its corresponding prism. So the answer to this problem is one-third of the answer to the previous problem: $V = \frac{20\sqrt{3}}{3} \approx 11.5 \text{ cm}^3$.

(e) Find the volume of a cylindrical soda can of height 12cm and base diameter 6.5cm. Assuming 1 cubic cm holds 1mL of liquid, and 1mL equals 0.0338 fluid oz, how many ounces would this can hold?

The radius of the can is 3.25 cm. So the volume is $\pi r^2 h = \pi(3.25)^2(12) \approx 398 \text{ cm}^3$. The can holds $398(0.0338) \approx 13.5$ fluid ounces.

(f) Find the volume and surface area of a cone of radius 5 and height 5.

The volume is $\frac{1}{3}\pi r^2 h = \frac{1}{3}\pi(25)(5) \approx 131$ cubic units. The surface area is $\pi r^2$ (for the base) plus $\pi r \ell$, where $\ell$ is the slant height. Since the radius is equal to the height, this cone has a 45 degree slant angle. So, $\ell = 5\sqrt{2}$. Therefore, the surface area is

$$\pi(25) + \pi(5)(5\sqrt{2}) = \pi(25 + 25\sqrt{2}) \approx 190 \text{ square units.}$$

(g) Several of the formulas involve the height. The volume formulas still work if the solid is slanted, provided the height is measured perpendicularly to the base. Justify this using Cavalieri's Principle.

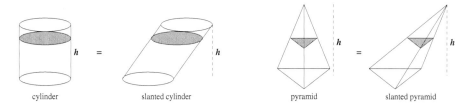

Since the area of each slice is the same in the solid as it is in the slanted version of the solid, Cavalieri's Principle says that the volumes of the two solids have to be equal to each other.

(h) Which volume formulas take the form: volume equals area of base times height? ...volume equals one-third area of base times height?

The volumes of prisms and cylinders are of the form $V = Bh$, where $B$ is the area of the base. The volumes of pyramids and cones are of the form $V = \frac{1}{3}Bh$.

(i) Suppose that a can of tennis balls is a cylinder that is just large enough to hold three spherical tennis balls. Find the ratio of the total volume of the tennis balls to the total volume of the can if a tennis ball has radius 3cm.

Notice that the height of the can is 18cm.

$$V_{sphs} = 3\left(\frac{4}{3}\pi \cdot 3^3\right) = 108\pi \text{ cm}^3$$
$$V_{cyl} = \pi(3^2)(18) = 162\pi \text{ cm}^3$$

The ratio is therefore $108\pi : 162\pi = 2 : 3$.

(j) In the previous problem, what is the surface area of the three tennis balls? What is the lateral surface area of the can (not including the bases)? What is the ratio of the two?

$$SA_{sphs} = 3(4\pi \cdot 3^2) = 108\pi \text{ cm}^2$$
$$SA_{cyl} = 2\pi(3)(18) = 108\pi \text{ cm}^2$$

The ratio is therefore $1 : 1$.

(k) Do your answers to the previous two questions really depend on the radius of the tennis balls? [What would Archimedes say?]

Archimedes knew that these ratios did not depend on the radius of the spheres. To be more general, let's assume a radius $r$.

$$V_{sphs} = 3\left(\frac{4}{3}\pi r^3\right) = 4\pi r^3$$
$$V_{cyl} = \pi r^2(6r) = 6\pi r^3$$
$$SA_{sphs} = 3(4\pi r^2) = 12\pi r^2$$
$$SA_{cyl} = 2\pi r(6r) = 12\pi r^2$$

Therefore, in general, the ratio $V_{sphs} : V_{cyl} = 2 : 3$ and the ratio $SA_{sphs} : SA_{cyl} = 1 : 1$.

## 2.4 Transformational Geometry

**a. Demonstrate an understanding of the basic properties of isometries in two- and three- dimensional space (e.g., rotation, translation, reflection)**

1. What is an isometry?

   An isometry is a function that maps points on the plane (or in space) to other points on the plane (or in space) in such a way that all distances are preserved. So, if we call our isometry $F$, then the distance between points $A$ and $B$ is equal to the distance between $F(A)$ and $F(B)$. A common notation is to use primes for the transformed points. So, under an isometry, $A'B' = AB$. The most common isometries are rotations, reflections in a line (or in a plane), and translations.

2. What are the basic properties of isometries?

   Because isometries preserve lengths, they also preserve any geometric property that follows from lengths, such as congruence of triangles, and thus of angles, polygons, and solids, too. Areas and volumes are also preserved by isometries.

3. Sample Problems

   (a) What information is necessary to describe a rotation? ... a translation? ... a reflection?

   (b) Prove that if $T$ is an isometry, then $\triangle ABC \cong \triangle T(A)T(B)T(C)$.

   (c) Draw and label an equilateral triangle. List all the different isometries that don't really change the equilateral triangle. (Such an isometry is called a *symmetry*.) Repeat for a square, a rectangle, and a parallelogram.

   (d) Justify the Isosceles Triangle Theorem using transformational geometry.

   (e) If you draw a diagonal of a parallelogram, you obtain two congruent triangles. What isometry maps one of these triangles to the other?

   (f) Is the composition of two isometries another isometry? Explain.

4. Answers to Sample Problems

   (a) What information is necessary to describe a rotation? ... a translation? ... a reflection?

   To describe a rotation, you need to state the center of rotation and the angle of rotation. (Or, in three dimensions, you need to state an axis of rotation and an angle of rotation.) To describe a translation, you need to give a vector of translation; that is, you need to state a direction in which to translate and how far to move in that direction. To describe a reflection, you need to state a line of reflection. (Or, in three dimensions, you need to state a plane of reflection.)

   (b) Prove that if $T$ is an isometry, then $\triangle ABC \cong \triangle T(A)T(B)T(C)$.
   **Proof:** Since $T$ is an isometry, $AB = T(A)T(B)$, $AC = T(A)T(C)$, and $BC = T(B)T(C)$. Therefore, by SSS, $\triangle ABC \cong \triangle T(A)T(B)T(C)$. $\square$

(c) Draw and label an equilateral triangle. List all the different isometries that don't really change the equilateral triangle. (Such an isometry is called a *symmetry*.) Repeat for a square, a rectangle, and a parallelogram.

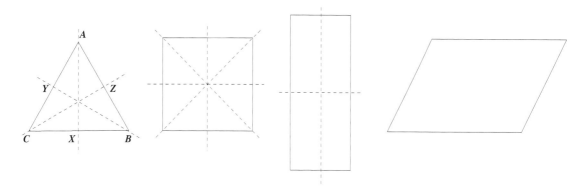

In the triangle above, there are six symmetries: three reflections in the dashed lines $\overline{AX}$, $\overline{BY}$, and $\overline{CZ}$; and rotations by 120 degrees, 240 degrees, and 0 degrees. Even though rotation by zero degrees doesn't really do anything, it is an important symmetry of the triangle, in roughly the same way that zero is an important concept in addition.

In the square, there are eight symmetries: four reflections in the dashed lines, and four rotations, by 90, 180, 270, and 0 degrees.

In the rectangle, there are four symmetries: two reflections in the dashed lines, and rotations by 180 and 0 degrees.

In the parallelogram, there are only two symmetries: rotations by 180 and 0 degrees.

(d) Justify the Isosceles Triangle Theorem using transformational geometry.

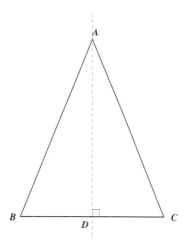

**Proof:** The hypothesis is that $\overline{AB} \cong \overline{AC}$. Let $\overline{AD}$ be the perpendicular bisector of $\overline{BC}$. Let $R$ represent reflection in $\overline{AD}$. Then it is clear that $R(B) = C$, $R(C) = B$, and $R(A) = A$. Since $R$ is an isometry, $\angle ABC \cong \angle R(A)R(B)R(C) = \angle ACB$.  □

(e) If you draw a diagonal of a parallelogram, you obtain two congruent triangles. What isometry maps one of these triangles to the other? a 180 degree rotation around the center of the parallelogram.

(f) Is the composition of two isometries another isometry? Explain.

Yes, the composition of two isometries is another isometry. If $F$ and $G$ both preserve distances, then doing $F$ followed by $G$ would still preserve distances. Consider $G(F(A))G(F(B))$. Since $G$ preserves distances, $G(F(A))G(F(B)) = F(A)F(B)$. Since $F$ preserves distances, $F(A)F(B) = AB$. So, $G(F(A))G(F(B)) = AB$. Therefore, $G$ composed with $F$ (denoted $G \circ F$) is an isometry.

## b. Understand and prove the basic properties of dilations (e.g., similarity transformations or change of scale)

1. What is a dilation?

   A dilation (or similarity transformation, or change of scale) is a function that maps the points of the plane (or space) to other points of the plane (or space) in such a way that the lengths between any two points are multiplied by a constant value. So, if $S$ is a similarity transformation with a scale factor $k$, then the distance between $S(A)$ and $S(B)$ is $k$ times the distance between $A$ and $B$. Or, $A'B' = kAB$. By the way, I'm used to "dilation" only referring to a specific type of similarity transformation with $k > 1$. If $k < 1$, I would call it a "contraction" because distances are getting smaller, but "dilation" seems rather common for both types.

2. What are some basic properties of similarity transformations?

   The main property is that a similarity transformation preserves angles. So, the image of a triangle under a similarity transformation is a similar triangle. This explains why we use the term "similarity transformation." Another important property is that if you dilate by a scale factor $k$, then areas are multiplied by the factor $k^2$ and volumes by $k^3$.

3. How do you prove properties of similarity transformations?

   Let's see if we can prove that angles are preserved by a similarity transformation. Consider $\triangle ABC$ and its image, $\triangle A'B'C'$. By the properties of a similarity transformation,

   $$A'B' = kAB; \ A'C' = kAC; \ B'C' = kBC.$$

   So, by the SSS Similarity Theorem, $\triangle ABC \cong \triangle A'B'C'$. Hence $\angle ABC \cong \angle A'B'C'$, because corresponding angles of similar triangles are congruent.

4. Sample Problems

   (a) Sketch square $ABCD$ and its image under a dilation of scale factor two ...
      i. centered at the center of the square.
      ii. centered at point $A$.
      iii. centered at the midpoint of $\overline{CD}$.

   (b) Consider $\triangle ABC$ with $a = 3$, $b = 4$, and $c = 5$. Draw altitude $\overline{CD}$. Find the scale factor of the contraction that maps ...
      i. $\triangle ABC$ to $\triangle CBD$.

    ii. $\triangle ABC$ to $\triangle ACD$.

(c) Is the composition of two similarity transformations another similarity transformation? Explain. If so, what is its scale factor?

(d) Is the composition of a similarity transformation and an isometry another similarity transformation? Explain. If so, what is its scale factor?

(e) Join the midpoints of the sides of a square to obtain a smaller square. What is the exact similarity transformation that maps the first square to the second square? Is there more than one right answer?

(f) What scale factor is needed for a similarity transformation to transform a square into a square with twice the area?

(g) What scale factor is needed for a similarity transformation to transform a cube into a cube with twice the volume?

5. Answer to Sample Problems

(a) Sketch square $ABCD$ and its image under a dilation of scale factor two ...

    i. centered at the center of the square.

    ii. centered at point $A$.

    iii. centered at the midpoint of $\overline{CD}$.

In each picture, $A'B'C'D'$ is the image of $ABCD$ after the transformation.

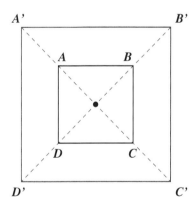 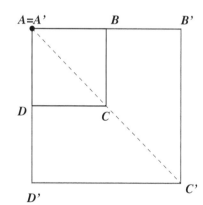 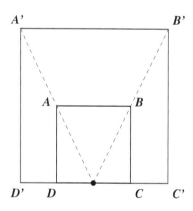

(b) Consider $\triangle ABC$ with $a = 3$, $b = 4$, and $c = 5$. Draw altitude $\overline{CD}$. Find the scale factor of the contraction that maps ...

    i. $\triangle ABC$ to $\triangle CBD$. $\frac{3}{5}$

    ii. $\triangle ABC$ to $\triangle ACD$. $\frac{4}{5}$

(c) Is the composition of two similarity transformations another similarity transformation? Explain. If so, what is its scale factor?

The composition of two similarity transformations is a similarity transformation and the scale factor of the composition is the product of the scale factors of the individual similarity transformations. If $S_1$ is a similarity transformation with scale factor $k_1$ and $S_2$ is a similarity transformation with scale factor $k_2$, then $S_1 \circ S_2$ is a similarity transformation with scale factor $k_1 k_2$.

(d) Is the composition of a similarity transformation and an isometry another similarity transformation? Explain. If so, what is its scale factor?

The composition of a similarity transformation and an isometry is another similarity transformation. Moreover, the composition has a scale factor equal to the scale factor of the first similarity transformation. If $S$ is a similarity transformation with scale factor $k$ and $T$ is an isometry, then $S \circ T$ is a similarity transformation with scale factor $k$.

(e) Join the midpoints of the sides of a square to obtain a smaller square. What is the exact similarity transformation that maps the first square to the second square? Is there more than one right answer?

There are several right answers. This transformation is composed of a dilation and a rotation. The dilation is centered at the center of the square and has a scale factor of $\frac{1}{\sqrt{2}} = \frac{\sqrt{2}}{2}$. This is followed by a rotation of 45 degrees around the center of the square.

(f) What scale factor is needed for a similarity transformation to transform a square into a square with twice the area? $\sqrt{2}$

(g) What scale factor is needed for a similarity transformation to transform a cube into a cube with twice the volume? $\sqrt[3]{2}$

# 4.1 Probability

## a. Prove and apply basic principles of permutations and combinations

1. What are permutations and combinations?

   A permutation is a partial sequence of elements from a set. The order of that sequence is important. For instance, a permutation problem might involve determining the number of ways that you can rank the students in your class. If you have ten students, then there would be 10! or 3,628,800 ways to rank your students. If you want to know how many ways you can choose the top three students, there are $10 \times 9 \times 8 = 720$ ways to do so. In general, the number of ways to rank $k$ objects from a set of $n$ objects is often denoted $_nP_k$ and is equal to $\dfrac{n!}{(n-k)!}$.

   A combination is a selection of a certain number of elements from a set. The order in which the selection is chosen is not important. The number of ways to choose $k$ objects from a set of $n$ objects is often denoted $_nC_k$ (read "$n$ choose $k$") or $\dbinom{n}{k}$ and is equal to $\dfrac{n!}{k!(n-k)!}$.

2. What are the basic rules of counting?

   There are a few "axioms" of counting:

   - If there are $n$ total outcomes, and if $k$ of those outcomes meet condition $A$, then the number of outcomes than do NOT meet condition $A$ is $n - k$.

   - If two choices are independent of each other, and there are $m$ ways to make the first choice and $n$ ways to make the second choice, then the total number of ways to make both choices is $mn$.

   - The total number of events that meet condition $A$ or condition $B$ is the total number that meet $A$ plus the total number that meet $B$ minus the number that meet both $A$ and $B$ (due to overcounting).

   As an example of this last rule, suppose you want to count the number of students in your class who are either 14 years old or female. Then you could add the total number of students who are 14 years old to the total number of female students, but then you would have to subtract the number of female students who are 14 years old because you would have counted them twice.

3. What are the basic principles of permutations and combinations?

   Permutations often use multiplication. To count the number of ways to pick first, second, and third place from 10 students, we start by seeing that there are 10 ways to choose the first place student. After that, there are 9 contestants from which to choose the second place student. Then, there are only 8 left from which to choose the third place student. So, there are $(10)(9)(8) = 720 = {_{10}P_3}$ ways to choose the top three places.

   Combinations are similar, except that order doesn't matter. So, if we were to count the number of ways to pick a committee of 3 students from a class of 10, we are not interested in ranking them. We could still count them using the rankings above, but then we are overcounting because sometimes different rankings will be made up of the same three people. In fact, there are $3! = 6$ ways to rank three people, and so we have overcounted the number of combinations by a factor of 6. Therefore, there are only $\frac{720}{6} = 120 = {}_{10}C_3$ possible committees of three students from a class of ten.

4. Sample Problems

   (a) How many ways are there to select a three-course meal from 6 appetizers, 3 entrées, and 5 desserts?

   (b) How many California license plates are there (assuming 4 numbers and 3 letters each)?

   (c) How many ways are there to pick a committee of 4 students from a class of 33?

   (d) How many ways are there to pick a committee of 4 students consisting of 2 girls and 2 boys from a class of 12 girls and 21 boys?

   (e) Explain why ${}_9C_5 = \dfrac{{}_9P_5}{5!}$

   (f) Suppose that you want a password that is 8 characters long, and that you are allowed to choose from a total of 100 characters.

       i. How many possible passwords are there?

       ii. Now suppose that a hacker can check 1 million passwords a second. How long would it take the hacker to go through all the passwords?

       iii. How often should you change your password, or should you not really worry?

5. Answers to Sample Problems

   (a) How many ways are there to select a three-course meal from 6 appetizers, 3 entrées, and 5 desserts? $(6)(3)(5) = 90$

   (b) How many California license plates are there (assuming 4 numbers and 3 letters each)? $(10^4)(26^3) = 175,760,000$

   (c) How many ways are there to pick a committee of 4 students from a class of 33? ${}_{33}C_4 = 40,920$

   (d) How many ways are there to pick a committee of 4 students consisting of 2 girls and 2 boys from a class of 12 girls and 21 boys? $({}_{12}C_2)({}_{21}C_2) = 13,860$

   (e) Explain why ${}_9C_5 = \dfrac{{}_9P_5}{5!}$

       The number ${}_9P_5$ counts how many ways there are to rank 5 people from a group of 9. However, if we are interested in combinations, then we do not care about the actual ranking. For example, the ranking $A, B, C, D, E$ is different from the ranking $A, B, C, E, D$, but as far as combinations are concerned, these two sets of five elements are the same. So to calculate ${}_9C_5$, we need to divide ${}_9P_5$ by the total number of ways in which 5 people can be ranked, which is $5!$.

   (f) Suppose that you want a password that is 8 characters long, and that you are allowed to choose from a total of 100 characters.

i. How many possible passwords are there? $100^8 = 10^{16}$

ii. Now suppose that a hacker can check 1 million passwords a second. How long would it take the hacker to go through all the passwords? $10^{10}$ seconds, which is over 317 years

iii. How often should you change your password, or should you not really worry? If you change your password each year, then the hacker has only a 0.3% chance of finding your password each year.

## b. Illustrate finite probability using a variety of examples and models (e.g., the fundamental counting principles)

1. What is finite probability?

   Finite probability measures the probability of certain outcomes when there are only a finite number of outcomes possible. In finite probability, if all possible outcomes are equally likely, then the probability of an outcome $A$ is the ratio of the number of outcomes in which $A$ occurs to the total number of outcomes. For example, if you roll a die, what is the likelihood of rolling a multiple of 3? Since there are two multiples of 3 out of six possible rolls, the probability of rolling a multiple of 3 is $\frac{2}{6} = \frac{1}{3}$.

2. What are the basic principles of probability?

   There are a few "axioms" of probability:

   - If the probability of event $A$ is $P(A)$, then the probability that $A$ does not happen $(\overline{A}$, called the *complement* of $A$) is: $P(\overline{A}) = 1 - P(A)$.

   - If two events ($A$ and $B$) are *independent* of each other, then the probability of both occurring ($A$ AND $B$) is: $P(A \cap B) = P(A)P(B)$. This is called the *Multiplication Rule*.

   - If $A$ and $B$ are two events, then the probability of either one of them happening ($A$ OR $B$) is: $P(A \cup B) = P(A) + P(B) - P(A \cap B)$, where, as in the counting case, we subtract the probability of both $A$ and $B$ happening due to having counted it twice.

   - In the special case when two events ($A$ and $B$) are *mutually exclusive*, then the probability that either one of them occurs ($A$ OR $B$) is: $P(A \cup B) = P(A) + P(B)$. This is called the *Addition Rule*.

3. What are some common examples and models for finite probability?

   The simplest example is flipping a coin, which is a good model for an event to occur with probability $p = \frac{1}{2}$. Another simple example involves rolling a die, in which the numbers 1 through 6 come up, each with probability $p = \frac{1}{6}$. Rolling two dice is slightly more complicated, because then different sums have different probabilities, based on the number of ways they can occur. (See the Sample Problems.) Finally, a standard deck of 52 playing cards is often used as a model for finite probability. In a standard deck, there are four suits, each with 13 cards. In fact, in poker, the ranking of poker hands is determined by their relative likelihoods.

4. Sample Problems

(a) Suppose you flip a penny, a quarter, and a nickel. What is the probability that all three come up heads? ...that two come up heads? Explain (in terms of the symmetry of heads and tails) why your two answers should add up to 50%.

(b) How many possible outcomes are there for rolling two dice?

(c) Complete the table for rolling two dice:

| sum | 2 | 3 | 4 | 5 | 6 | 7 | 8 | 9 | 10 | 11 | 12 |
|---|---|---|---|---|---|---|---|---|---|---|---|
| prob | $\frac{1}{36}$ | | | | | | | | | | |

(d) If you choose 5 cards at random from a deck of cards, without replacement, what is the probability that all five cards will be hearts? ...will be from the same suit?

(e) Repeat the previous problem, but with replacing each card after it is drawn.

(f) Draw four cards at random, without replacement. What is the probability that all four cards are from different suits?

5. Answers to Sample Problems

(a) Suppose you flip a penny, a quarter, and a nickel. What is the probability that all three come up heads? ...that two come up heads? Explain (in terms of the symmetry of heads and tails) why your two answers should add up to 50%.

Since the three coin flips are independent events, the probability of getting three heads is $(\frac{1}{2})(\frac{1}{2})(\frac{1}{2}) = \frac{1}{8}$. Another way to see this is that of the eight possible outcomes, only $HHH$ has all three coins coming up heads.

There are three ways for two coins to come up heads: $HHT, HTH, THH$. So the probability of this event is $\frac{3}{8}$.

The other two possible numbers of heads are zero and one. But obtaining one head is the same event as obtaining two tails. So, by symmetry, the probability of getting one head is the same as the probability of getting two heads. Similarly, the probability of getting no heads (and three tails) is the same as the probability of getting three heads. Since the total probability has to be 1, the sum of our two answers has to be 50% or $\frac{1}{2}$.

(b) How many possible outcomes are there for rolling two dice? There are 36 different outcomes, which are equally likely. If you are measuring the sum of the two dice, then there are eleven different sums, but they are not equally likely.

(c) Complete the table for rolling two dice:

| sum | 2 | 3 | 4 | 5 | 6 | 7 | 8 | 9 | 10 | 11 | 12 |
|---|---|---|---|---|---|---|---|---|---|---|---|
| prob | $\frac{1}{36}$ | $\frac{2}{36}$ | $\frac{3}{36}$ | $\frac{4}{36}$ | $\frac{5}{36}$ | $\frac{6}{36}$ | $\frac{5}{36}$ | $\frac{4}{36}$ | $\frac{3}{36}$ | $\frac{2}{36}$ | $\frac{1}{36}$ |

(d) If you choose 5 cards at random from a deck of cards, without replacement, what is the probability that all five cards will be hearts? ...will be from the same suit?

The probability that the first card is a heart is $\frac{13}{52}$. Assuming that the first card was a heart, there are now only 12 hearts left in the deck of 51 cards. So, the probability that the second card is a heart is $\frac{12}{51}$. Continuing in this way,

$$\left(\frac{13}{52}\right)\left(\frac{12}{51}\right)\left(\frac{11}{50}\right)\left(\frac{10}{49}\right)\left(\frac{9}{48}\right) = \frac{33}{66,640} \approx 0.000495$$

is the probability that all five cards will be hearts.

The probability that all five cards will be from the same suit is four times this quantity, because there are four suits, or $\frac{33}{16,660} \approx 0.00198$.

(e) Repeat the previous problem, but with replacing each card after it is drawn.

This means that for each card, the probability of drawing a heart is $\frac{1}{4}$. So, the probability that all five cards will be hearts is $(\frac{1}{4})^5 = \frac{1}{1024} \approx 0.000977$. The probability that all five cards will be from the same suit is thus $\frac{4}{1024} = \frac{1}{256} \approx 0.0039$.

(f) Draw four cards at random, without replacement. What is the probability that all four cards are from different suits?

The first card could be anything. So the probability of selecting an OK card is 1. However, once the first card is drawn, you can no longer draw a card from that suit. So there are 39 "good" cards left out of the 51 remaining cards. The probability that the second card is OK is thus $\frac{39}{51} = \frac{13}{17}$. The probability that the third card is OK is thus $\frac{26}{50} = \frac{13}{25}$. And finally, the probability that the fourth card is OK is $\frac{13}{49}$. Hence, the probability that all four cards are from different suits is

$$\left(\frac{13}{17}\right)\left(\frac{13}{25}\right)\left(\frac{13}{49}\right) = \frac{2197}{20,825} \approx 0.1055,$$

or almost 11%.

## c. Use and explain the concept of conditional probability

1. What is conditional probability?

Conditional probability deals with probabilities of events happening under certain conditions, i.e., when certain information is known. The notation $P(A|B)$ means the probability of event $A$ happening when event $B$ has already happened. The basic formula is:

$$P(A|B) = \frac{P(A \cap B)}{P(B)}.$$

Notice that if $A$ and $B$ are independent events, then $P(A|B) = P(A)$, which makes sense.

2. How is conditional probability used?

One common example where conditional probability is important lies in medical testing. For instance, suppose that there is an HIV test that is 95% accurate, meaning that in 95% of tests, the test results match the actual HIV status of the subject. Now suppose that you take an HIV test and the result comes back positive. What is the likelihood that you have HIV?

It might surprise you to know that the answer is less than 95%, and that in fact, the answer depends on the actual percentage of the population that has HIV. In order to make the numbers easier, let's assume that the probability that a randomly chosen individual in the population has HIV is 1%. We will now calculate the probability of a false positive test result. Let's assume that 1 million people take the HIV test.

(a) How many of those people actually have HIV? How many people do not have HIV?

ANS: Since we are assuming that 1% of the population has HIV, 10,000 have HIV, which means that 990,000 do not have HIV.

(b) Of those that have HIV, how many tested positive? (That is, how many true positives were there?)

ANS: Of those that have HIV, 95% of them got a test score which matched their status. So, there were 9,500 true positive test results.

(c) Of those that do not have HIV, how many tested positive? (That is, how many false positives were there?)

ANS: Again, 95% obtained a test result that matched their status. So, 5% got a false reading, for a total of $(0.05)(990,000) = 49,500$ false positive test results.

(d) Looking at the previous two answers, how many total positive test results were there?
ANS: There were $9,500 + 49,500 = 59,000$ total positive test results.

(e) What is the probability that a given positive test result is false?
ANS: The probability that a given positive test result is false is therefore $\frac{49,500}{59,000} \approx 0.839$, or almost 84%.

In the language of conditional probability, we would say that the probability that a person is HIV negative, given a positive test result, is 0.839 or 83.9% . This may seem counterintuitive, but there are far more false positive test results in this artificial example than there are true positive test results.

3. Sample Problems

(a) In the previous example, we said that the HIV test was 95% accurate. State what this means in terms of conditional probability.

(b) In the HIV example, find $P(T+)$, the probability of a positive test result.

(c) If two dice are rolled, find the probability that their sum is 8, given that each die has an even number showing.

(d) Flip two coins. What is the probability that both are heads, given that at least one of them is heads?

4. Answers to Sample Problems

(a) In the previous example, we said that the HIV test was 95% accurate. State what this means in terms of conditional probability.

This means that the probability of getting a positive test result, given that the person is HIV+, is 95%. It also means that the probability of getting a negative test result, given that the person is HIV-, is 95%.

(b) In the HIV example, find $P(T+)$, the probability of a positive test result.

**Method #1:** There were a total of 59,000 positive test results out of 1,000,000 tests. So, the probability of getting a positive test result is 0.059. This means that 5.9% of the people taking the test got a positive test result.

**Method #2:** We will use the basic formula twice. Notice that

$$P(T+\,|+) = \frac{P(T+\,\cap+)}{P(+)}, \text{ and } P(+|T+) = \frac{P(+\cap T+)}{P(T+)}.$$

From these two equations, it follows that $P(T+\,|+)P(+) = P(+|T+)P(T+)$, because both sides are equal to $P(T+\cap+)$. We know that $P(T+\,|+) = 0.95$ and $P(+) = 0.01$, and we found in the example above that $P(+|T+)$, the probability of being HIV+ given a positive test result, is $\frac{9{,}500}{59{,}000} \approx 0.161$. Putting all this together, we get

$$P(T+) = \frac{P(T+\,|+)P(+)}{P(+|T+)} = \frac{(0.95)(0.01)}{0.161} = 0.059.$$

(c) If two dice are rolled, find the probability that their sum is 8, given that each die has an even number showing.

**Method #1:** If we know that there are two even numbers showing, then the only possible sums are 4, 6, 8, 10, and 12. Their probabilities can be calculated directly.

| sum | 4 | 6 | 8 | 10 | 12 |
|------|---------------|---------------|---------------|---------------|---------------|
| prob | $\frac{1}{9}$ | $\frac{2}{9}$ | $\frac{3}{9}$ | $\frac{2}{9}$ | $\frac{1}{9}$ |

So, the probability of getting an 8, given that there are two even numbers showing, is $\frac{1}{3}$.

**Method #2:** Let $A$ be the event that the dice add up to 8. Let $B$ be the event that each die has an even number showing. Then $P(A \cap B) = \frac{3}{36} = \frac{1}{12}$ and $P(B) = \frac{1}{4}$. Therefore,

$$P(A|B) = \frac{1/12}{1/4} = \frac{1}{3}.$$

(d) Flip two coins. What is the probability that both are heads, given that at least one of them is heads?

**Method #1:** Since we know that at least one of the two coins was heads, the only possibilities are: $HH$, $HT$, and $TH$, each of which is equally likely. So, the probability that both are heads is $\frac{1}{3}$.

**Method #2:** Let $A$ be the event of getting two heads and let $B$ be the event of getting at least one head. Then $P(A \cap B) = \frac{1}{4}$ and $P(B) = \frac{3}{4}$. Therefore,

$$P(A|B) = \frac{1/4}{3/4} = \frac{1}{3}.$$

**d. Interpret the probability of an outcome**
**e. Use normal, binomial, and exponential distributions to solve and interpret probability problems**

1. What are some ways to interpret the probability of an outcome?

   As we have seen already, probabilities can be interpreted as a ratio. The first part of the ratio is the number of events in which a desired outcome occurs, while the second part of the ratio is the total number of events. For example, the probability of rolling a 7 on two dice is $\frac{1}{6}$ because, in six of the 36 possible rolls, the two dice add up to 7.

Probability can also be interpreted as the likelihood of a given event occurring on a given trial. For example, if you toss a coin, you would expect a heads in about half of all trials.

2. What is the normal distribution? When and how is it used?

The normal distribution (or bell curve) is very important in statistics, as we will see later. For the purposes of probability, the normal curve is centered at the mean value of your variable and the standard deviation is the horizontal distance from the center to the steepest point on the curve (inflection point).

Probabilities are equal to areas under the bell curve and are interpreted using the 68-95-99.7 rule: approximately 68% of the area under the curve lies within one standard deviation of the mean, 95% within two standard deviations, and 99.7% within three standard deviations. For an example, suppose that heights of adults in the US are distributed normally with mean 178cm and standard deviation 7cm. This means that about 68% of adults in the US have heights between 171cm and 185cm (178±7), 95% are between 164cm and 192cm tall (178±14) and only 0.3% are shorter than 157cm or taller than 199cm (178 ± 21).

3. What is the binomial distribution? When and how is it used?

The binomial distribution is used when you have several independent trials, each with the same probability of "success," such as flipping a coin several times, or rolling a die several times. Here, we use the binomial distribution to count $B(n, k, p)$, the probability of having $k$ successes in $n$ trials, if each trial's probability of success is $p$. The formula is:

$$B(n, k, p) = {}_nC_k \, p^k (1 - p)^{n-k}.$$

As an example, the probability of getting three heads when you flip a coin ten times is $B(10, 3, 0.5) = {}_{10}C_3 (0.5)^3 (0.5)^7 = \frac{120}{1024} \approx 0.117$, or almost 12%. The probability of getting 6 heads when you flip a coin 20 times is $B(20, 6, 0.5) \approx 0.037$, which is less than 4%.

4. What is the exponential distribution? When and how is it used?

Suppose there is an event that happens randomly but at a constant average rate. Then the time between events is a random variable that is exponentially distributed. For example, if you are studying a radioactive element, and you are measuring the time between two decay events, you would find that the time between events follows the exponential distribution. The time you have to wait until your next phone call might also be exponentially distributed (assuming that phone calls occur at a constant average rate).

5. Sample Problems

   (a) When the weather report says a 20% chance of rain tomorrow, what does that mean?

   (b) What does it mean to say that the probability of a positive test result, given that the subject has HIV, is 95%?

   (c) Find the probability of getting less than two heads on six coin tosses.

(d) We saw earlier that the probability of getting three heads on ten coin tosses was almost 12%, while the probability of getting six heads on twenty coin tosses was less than 4%. Why aren't these two binomial probabilities equal? After all, both represent a 30% heads rate on the coin.

(e) Find the probability of getting exactly 30 heads on 100 coin tosses.

(f) Scores on a common IQ test are normally distributed with mean 100 and about 68% of people scoring between 85 and 115. What is the standard deviation of the scores on this test?  *15*

(g) Suppose that the heights of US women (age 18-24) are distributed normally with mean 65.5in and standard deviation 2.5in. Find the percentage of US women (age 18-24) who are between 65.5in and 70.5in.

6. Answers to Sample Problems

(a) When the weather report says a 20% chance of rain tomorrow, what does that mean?

This means that historically, similar climate conditions have led to rainfall in about 20% of previous cases.

(b) What does it mean to say that the probability of a positive test result, given that the subject has HIV, is 95%?

This means that if a person has HIV and takes this test repeatedly, they will receive a positive test result in about 95% of trials. It also means that if 100 people had HIV and they each took this HIV test, the expected number of positive test results would be 95.

(c) Find the probability of getting less than two heads on six coin tosses.

We can find this probability by adding the probability of getting zero heads to the probability of getting one head.

$$B(6,0,0.5) + B(6,1,0.5) = (0.5)^6 + 6(0.5)^6 = 0.109375,$$

or about 11%.

(d) We saw earlier that the probability of getting three heads on ten coin tosses was almost 12%, while the probability of getting six heads on twenty coin tosses was less than 4%. Why aren't these two binomial probabilities equal? After all, both represent a 30% heads rate on the coin.

These two numbers are not equal because of the way probability works in a large number of trials. In only ten trials, getting three heads is not too unlikely. If only two more coin tosses had gone the other way, then you would have had exactly 50% heads. But with twenty coin tosses, getting six heads means that you are four coin tosses away from 50%, which is less likely to happen. Notice in the next question how small the probability is of getting 30 heads out of 100 coin tosses. As the number of trials increases, we expect the number of heads to get closer and closer to 50%.

(e) Find the probability of getting exactly 30 heads on 100 coin tosses.

$$B(100,30,0.5) = {}_{100}C_{30}(0.5)^{100} = 0.00002317.$$

(f) Scores on a common IQ test are normally distributed with mean 100 and about 68% of people scoring between 85 and 115. What is the standard deviation of the scores on this test? 15

(g) Suppose that the heights of US women (age 18-24) are distributed normally with mean 65.5in and standard deviation 2.5in. Find the percentage of US women (age 18-24) who are between 65.5in and 70.5in.

Since the standard deviation is 2.5in, about 95% of women are between 60.5in and 70.5in tall. Assuming from the symmetry of the normal distribution that half of these are above the mean and half are below, 47.5% of women are between 65.5in and 70.5in tall.

# 4.2 Statistics

## a. Compute and interpret the mean, median, and mode of both discrete and continuous distributions

1. What is a discrete distribution? What is a continuous distribution?

   A discrete distribution describes a variable that can only take on discrete values, that is, values which are separated by some finite distance. In a continuous distribution, the variable can take on any real number value over some interval.

2. What notation will we be using?

   In the following discrete distributions, we will assume that our data set is finite: $\{x_1, x_2, \ldots, x_n\}$. In the continuous distributions, we will assume that our data set is infinite: $x$ is a real number. In each case, we will assume that our random variable $x$ has a probability density function given by $p(x)$.

   For $p(x)$ to be a discrete probability density function, we must have $p(x_i) \geq 0$ (meaning the probability of the variable taking the value $x_i$ is non-negative) and $\sum_{i=1}^{n} p(x_i) = 1$ (meaning the probability that the variable takes a value in the set $\{x_1, x_2, \ldots, x_n\}$ is 100%).

   For $p(x)$ to be a continuous probability density function, we must have $p(x) \geq 0$ for all values of $x$ (meaning that probability of the variable taking the value $x$ is non-negative) and $\int_{-\infty}^{\infty} p(x)\, dx = 1$ (meaning that the probability that the variable takes a value between negative and positive infinity is 100%).

3. What is the mean of a discrete distribution? What is the mean of a continuous distribution?

   The mean of the discrete data is $\dfrac{1}{n} \sum_{i=1}^{n} x_i = \dfrac{x_1 + x_2 + \ldots + x_n}{n}$.

   The mean of a continuous distribution is the "center of mass" or "balancing point" of the distribution. In calculus, the mean is $\int_{-\infty}^{\infty} xp(x)\, dx$. Another name for the mean is the "average" or "expected" value.

4. What is the median of a discrete distribution? What is the median of a continuous distribution?

   The median of a discrete distribution is the middle value, when all the values are listed in order, except that the median is not counted in either half of the data. So, half (or almost half) of the data points lie below the median and half above. For example, in $\{1, 2, 4, 7, 9\}$, the median is 4. In $\{1, 2, 4, 7, 9, 11\}$, the median is 5.5, the average of 4 and 7.

   In a continuous distribution, the median is the $x$-value which separates the area under the distribution in half. In calculus terms, $M$ is the median if and only if $\int_{-\infty}^{M} p(x)\, dx = \dfrac{1}{2}$.

5. What is the mode of a discrete distribution? What is the mode of a continuous distribution?

   The mode is the value of your data that is most likely to be sampled. The mode of a discrete distribution is the most common number in the list. If there is more than one such number, then there is more than one mode.

   The mode of a continuous distribution is the value of $x$ for which $p(x)$ is maximal. Again, there may be more than one mode.

6. Sample Problems

   (a) Suppose that your driver's license number is 5686788. Find the mean, median, and mode of the digits in your driver's license.

   (b) Assume that you have five data points: 1, 4, 5, 7, and $x$, where we do not know $x$, but we do know that $3 \le x \le 13$.

      i. What are the possible values of the mean of this data?
      ii. What are the possible values of the median of this data?
      iii. What are the possible values of the mode of this data?

   (c) List data in which the mean is equal to the median.

   (d) List data in which the mean is greater than the median.

   (e) List data in which mode > median > mean.

   (f) In real estate, why are median home prices listed, rather than mean home prices?

7. Answers to Sample Problems

   (a) Suppose that your driver's license number is 5686788. Find the mean, median, and mode of the digits in your driver's license.

      The mean is $\frac{1}{7}(5+6+8+6+7+8+8) = \frac{48}{7} \approx 6.86$. The median is 7. The mode is 8.

   (b) Assume that you have five data points: 1, 4, 5, 7, and $x$, where we do not know $x$, but we do know that $3 \le x \le 13$.

      i. What are the possible values of the mean of this data? The mean is $\frac{17+x}{5}$, which will lie between 4 and 6.
      ii. What are the possible values of the median of this data? The median is either 4 (if $x \le 4$), 5 if ($x \ge 5$), or $x$ (if $4 < x < 5$).
      iii. What are the possible values of the mode of this data? The mode could be 4, 5, or 7, if $x$ is equal to any of those numbers. Otherwise, each of the five numbers is equally likely.

   (c) List data in which the mean is equal to the median. Answers may vary. The data set $\{1, 2, 3\}$ has mean 2 and median 2.

   (d) List data in which the mean is greater than the median. Answers may vary. The data set $\{1, 2, 6\}$ has mean 3 and median 2.

   (e) List data in which mode > median > mean. Answers may vary. The data set $\{1, 9, 10, 10\}$ has mode 10, median 9.5, and mean 7.5.

(f) In real estate, why are median home prices listed, rather than mean home prices? The reason that median home prices are listed is that the median is a better measure of the typical home price in this case. Home prices are rarely normally distributed. Instead, there are often several homes near the lower end of the market, and a few very expensive homes (ranches, farms, large estates, etc.). These few expensive homes could noticeably raise the mean home price, but they would have little effect on the median home price.

## b. Compute and interpret quartiles, range, variance, and standard deviation of both discrete and continuous distributions

1. What are the quartiles of a discrete distribution? ... of a continuous distribution?

   In both discrete and continuous distributions, the first quartile is the median of the set of data points that are less than the original median. The third quartile is the median of the set of data points that are bigger than the original median. [The original median is also called the second quartile.] This means that one-fourth of the data lies below the first quartile, one-fourth between the first quartile and the original median, one-fourth between the original median and the third quartile, and one-fourth above the third quartile.

2. What is the range of a discrete distribution? ... of a continuous distribution?

   The range of a discrete distribution is the maximum value of the data minus the minimum value. In a continuous distribution, the range is the difference between the maximum and minimum $x$-values for which $p(x) > 0$. The range of a continuous distribution could be infinite.

3. What is the variance of a discrete distribution? ... of a continuous distribution?

   The variance is a measure of how spread out your data are. The variance of a set of discrete data with mean $\mu$ is $\dfrac{1}{n}\sum_{i=1}^{n}(x_i - \mu)^2$.

   The variance of a continuous variable with mean $\mu$ is $\displaystyle\int_{-\infty}^{\infty}(x - \mu)^2 p(x)\,dx$.

4. What is the standard deviation of a discrete distribution? ... of a continuous distribution?

   The standard deviation is the square root of the variance. It is a commonly used measure for the spread of your data. Recall from the previous section on Probability that if data is normally distributed, then about 68% of the population lies within one standard deviation from the mean, 95% within two standard deviations, and 99.7% within three standard deviations.

5. Sample Problems

   (a) Consider the data sets $\{1, 2, 3, 4, 3, 2, 1\}$ and $\{10, 20, 30, 40, 30, 20, 10\}$. Which data set has a larger standard deviation? Why?

   (b) If your data is $\{1, 3, 4, 4, 6, 9, 12, 13, 13, 14, 15, 15\}$, then list the mean, median, mode, quartiles, and range.

   (c) If you add 100 to each element in the set above, then find the new mean, median, mode, quartiles, and range. Would the variance or standard deviation of your new set be different from their values for the old set? Why or why not?

(d) Calculate the mean and variance of the probability distribution of a six-sided die.

6. Answers to Sample Problems

(a) Consider the data sets $\{1, 2, 3, 4, 3, 2, 1\}$ and $\{10, 20, 30, 40, 30, 20, 10\}$. Which data set has a larger standard deviation? Why?

From the formula for variance, it follows that the variance of the second set is 100 times larger than the variance of the first set because the data points are ten times larger. So, the standard deviation of the second set will be ten times larger than the standard deviation of the first set.

(b) If your data is $\{1, 3, 4, 4, 6, 9, 12, 13, 13, 14, 15, 15\}$, then list the mean, median, mode, quartiles, and range.

The mean is $\frac{109}{12} \approx 9.08$. The median is 10.5. There are three modes: 4, 13, and 15. The first quartile is 4 and the third quartile is 13.5. The range is $15 - 1 = 14$.

(c) If you add 100 to each element in the set above, then find the new mean, median, mode, quartiles, and range. Would the variance or standard deviation of your new set be different from their values for the old set? Why or why not?

The new mean, median, mode, and quartiles would be increased by 100. The new range would be the same as the old range. The variance and standard deviation would not be changed, since they measure how spread out the data are. Adding 100 to each data point does not spread them out at all. Looking at the formula for variance, you can see that if you add 100 to each $x_i$ and to $\mu$, then each difference $(x_i - \mu)$ is unchanged.

(d) Calculate the mean and variance of the probability distribution of a six-sided die.

The mean is $\frac{1}{6}(1) + \frac{1}{6}(2) + \ldots + \frac{1}{6}(6) = \frac{21}{6} = 3.5$. The variance is thus

$$\frac{1}{6}\sum_{i=1}^{6}(i - 3.5)^2 = \frac{17.5}{6} \approx 2.92.$$

## c. Select and evaluate sampling methods appropriate to a task (e.g., random, systematic, cluster, convenience sampling) and display the results

1. What is a sample?

A sample is a subset of the population. Often you want to examine a sample because it is simpler than taking a census, which involves examining the entire population.

2. What are some different sampling methods?

One familiar method is the Voluntary Response Sample, in which individuals are asked to respond if they wish. This is a form of convenience sampling, in which the people conducting the survey are surveying those individuals for whom it is convenient to do so. Such a sampling method is almost guaranteed to be biased.

A Simple Random Sample (SRS) of $n$ individuals from a population is defined to be a sample chosen in such a way that every subset of $n$ individuals is equally likely to be chosen as the sample.

A Stratified Random Sample is one in which the population is broken into groups (or strata), and then an SRS is chosen from each stratum and combined into the overall sample.

An example of systematic sampling is perhaps to select every 25th item on a list and then put those items into your sample. That is, you are taking a systematic (not entirely random) approach to constructing the sample.

Cluster sampling occurs when individuals are divided into clusters (often geographically), and then certain clusters are chosen at random to belong to the sample, (or individuals are chosen at random from the randomly-chosen clusters).

3. Which methods are appropriate for which situations?

A lot of statistical sampling is driven by cost or time constraints. With sufficient resources, we would just survey the entire population for data. A stratified random sample or a cluster sample might be more appropriate than a simple random sample if you would like your sample to contain members of different groups. The stratification takes advantage of the assumption that individuals within a group are similar to each other, thereby eliminating the need to have a large sample from within each group.

Convenience sampling is certainly convenient, but it rarely gives usable conclusions. Worse still is to ask people to participate in a certain survey, because it almost guarantees that the only responses to your survey will be from individuals with strong opinions.

4. How are data displayed?

To display one-variable quantitative data, we use histograms, stem and leaf plots, and box plots. To display one-variable categorical data, we use percentage counts, bar graphs, and pie charts. To display two-variable data, we often plot points on coordinate axes. The independent variable (if there is one) goes on the $x$-axis.

5. Sample Problems

   (a) Suppose that Congress decided to change the law about the Census taken every 10 years. Of the following, which sampling method is best?

      i. They should systematically contact every 500th Social Security Number holder and ask that person survey questions.

      ii. They should set up a phone line and a website for people to enter their census data because it will be most convenient.

      iii. They should combine some stratification with cluster sampling to try to obtain individuals from all sorts of different living situations.

      iv. They should take a simple random sample of the entire US population in order to be completely random.

   (b) Suppose that Johnny wants to determine which battery lasts longer: Battery A or Battery B. So Johnny goes down to the store and buys one package of Battery A and one of Battery B.

      i. What sampling method did Johnny use?

ii. How could Johnny improve the validity of his results? (What would be a better way to sample?)

(c) Big Giant News Corporation conducts an online poll after a recent political debate. They find that 65% favored candidate $P$, while 33% favored candidate $Q$, and 2% were undecided. Are these results reliable? Why or why not?

(d) Suppose that, of 100 randomly selected workplace accidents, 21 occurred on a Monday, 16 on a Tuesday, 13 on a Wednesday, 17 on a Thursday, and 33 on a Friday. How would you display these results visually?

6. Answers to Sample Problems

(a) Suppose that Congress decided to change the law about the Census taken every 10 years. Of the following, which sampling method is best?

i. They should systematically contact every 500th Social Security Number holder and ask that person survey questions.

ii. They should set up a phone line and a website for people to enter their census data because it will be most convenient.

iii. They should combine some stratification with cluster sampling to try to obtain individuals from all sorts of different living situations.

iv. They should take a simple random sample of the entire US population in order to be completely random.

ANS: iii. It is important to have data about people from all different walks of life in order to build a reliable data set. The systematic approach relies too heavily on Social Security Number, which may not be randomly assigned. Also, not everyone has a Social Security Number. Phone lines and web surveys are bad because not all people have a phone line or access to the web, and even those with access may not respond. An SRS might underrepresent certain groups, sort of like the way in which choosing a random sample of congress members might leave out the smaller states entirely.

(b) Suppose that Johnny wants to determine which battery lasts longer: Battery A or Battery B. So Johnny goes down to the store and buys one package of Battery A and one of Battery B.

i. What sampling method did Johnny use? Johnny used a form of convenience sampling. He purchased batteries from a single nearby store.

ii. How could Johnny improve the validity of his results? (What would be a better way to sample?) Johnny could at least sample different packages of batteries from different stores. Ideally, he could pick up a random selection of batteries from the factory. But he shouldn't tell them when he's coming. A dishonest battery manufacturer might give Johnny only their best batteries to be tested.

(c) Big Giant News Corporation conducts an online poll after a recent political debate. They find that 65% favored candidate $P$, while 33% favored candidate $Q$, and 2% were undecided. Are these results reliable? Why or why not?

Online polls (voluntary sampling polls) are rarely, if ever, reliable. People are far more likely to respond if they have a strong opinion on the subject and a strong desire to make their opinion known. A more random sampling method would be better.

(d) Suppose that, of 100 randomly selected workplace accidents, 21 occurred on a Monday, 16 on a Tuesday, 13 on a Wednesday, 17 on a Thursday, and 33 on a Friday. How would you display these results visually?

These data may appear quantitative, but they are really categorical. One could use a bar graph or a pie chart to show the data. The pie chart makes it easy to see that more than 50% of workplace accidents happened on a Monday or a Friday.

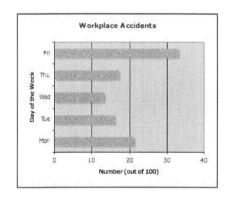
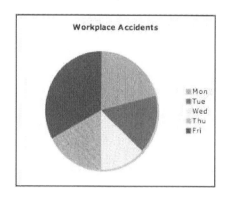

## d. Know the method of least squares and apply it to linear regression and correlation

1. What is correlation?

The correlation of two variables is a number that measures the direction and strength of the linear relationship between them. If there are $n$ data points: $(x_1, y_1), (x_2, y_2), \ldots, (x_n, y_n)$, then the formula for the correlation $r$ is

$$r = \frac{1}{n-1} \sum_{i=1}^{n} \left( \frac{x_i - \overline{x}}{s_x} \right) \left( \frac{y_i - \overline{y}}{s_y} \right),$$

where $\overline{x}$ [respectively, $\overline{y}$] is the mean of the $x$ [resp., $y$] data, and $s_x$ [resp., $s_y$] is the standard deviation of the $x$ [resp., $y$] data.

One result of this formula is that $-1 \le r \le 1$. The sign of $r$ is determined by the slope of the linear relationship. The closer $r$ is to zero, the less correlated the data are. Thus, a scatterplot that lacks a linear relationship has a correlation close to zero, whereas a scatterplot that looks close to a downward-sloping line has a correlation close to $-1$.

2. What is linear regression?

Regression is done on scatterplots when you have an independent (explanatory) variable and a dependent (response) variable. Then you can find the equation of the regression line (or line of best fit) and use it to make predictions.

3. What is the method of least squares? How do you apply least squares to regression?

To find the line of best fit, we use the method of least squares, which minimizes the sum of the squares of the vertical distances of the data points to the line. For a discrete data set,

$\{(x_1, y_1), (x_2, y_2), \ldots, (x_n, y_n)\}$, suppose the line of best fit is $y = mx + b$. Then the values of $m$ and $b$ are chosen to minimize

$$\sum_{i=1}^{n} (y_i - (mx_i + b))^2 .$$

After some calculus, it follows that

$$m = \frac{\sum_{i=1}^{n}(x_i - \overline{x})(y_i - \overline{y})}{\sum_{i=1}^{n}(x_i - \overline{x})^2} \quad \text{and} \quad b = \overline{y} - m\overline{x}.$$

One consequence of these formulas is that the point $(\overline{x}, \overline{y})$ always lies on the regression line.

4. How are correlation and regression related?

Recall that the correlation coefficient $r$ is between $-1$ and $1$. So, $0 \le r^2 \le 1$. In terms of regression, $r^2$ measures the fraction of the variation in the $y$-values that is explained by the least-squares regression line. For instance, if there is a perfect linear fit, then $r^2 = 1$, and so 100% of the variation in $y$-values is explained by this linear relationship. On the other extreme, if $r^2$ is very close to zero, then there is almost no discernible linear relationship between the two variables. So, the regression line would explain very little of the variation in $y$-values.

5. Sample Problems

(a) Suppose that the following data sets have correlations of $-0.8, -0.1, 0.3,$ and $0.9$. Match each picture with its corresponding correlation coefficient.

(b) Find the formula for the regression line through the following data:
$\{(1, 1), (2, 2), (3, 4), (4, 5), (5, 8)\}$.

(c) Suppose that a class measured each student's armspan and height. Then they calculated the following least-squares regression line predicting armspan ($y$, in cm), given an individual's height ($x$, also in cm): $y = -42.7 + 1.3x$.

   i. Johnny is 180cm tall. What would you predict his armspan to be? 191.3

   ii. Suppose that the mean armspan of students in the class was 170.3cm. What, if anything, can be said about the mean height of students in the class?

163

(d) Janey found that for a certain regression line, $r = -0.9$. She concluded that her regression line explained 90% of the variation in her data. Calculate $r^2$. Then interpret $r$ and $r^2$ for Janey. $r^2 = .81 \Rightarrow \text{the}$

6. Answers to Sample Problems

(a) Suppose that the following data sets have correlations of $-0.8$, $-0.1$, $0.3$, and $0.9$. Match each picture with its corresponding correlation coefficient.

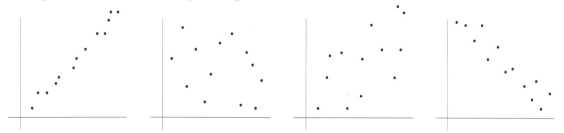

The correlation coefficients are, respectively, $0.9$, $-0.1$, $0.3$, and $-0.8$.

(b) Find the formula for the regression line through the following data:
$\{(1,1),(2,2),(3,4),(4,5),(5,8)\}$.
First, we calculate $\overline{x} = 3$ and $\overline{y} = 4$. So, $(3,4)$ is on the regression line. Next, we have

$$m = \frac{\displaystyle\sum_{i=1}^{5}(x_i - 3)(y_i - 4)}{\displaystyle\sum_{i=1}^{5}(x_i - 3)^2} = \frac{6 + 2 + 0 + 1 + 8}{4 + 1 + 0 + 1 + 4} = \frac{17}{10} = 1.7.$$

Thus the $y$-intercept is $\overline{y} - m\overline{x} = 4 - (1.7)(3) = -1.1$. So the regression line is $y = 1.7x - 1.1$.

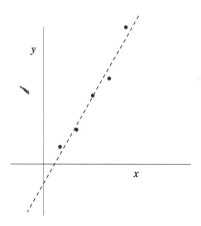

(c) Suppose that a class measured each student's armspan and height. Then they calculated the following least-squares regression line predicting armspan ($y$, in cm), given an individual's height ($x$, also in cm): $y = -42.7 + 1.3x$.

    i. Johnny is 180cm tall. What would you predict his armspan to be? Using the formula, his armspan is predicted to be $-42.7 + 1.3(180) = 191.3$cm.

ii. Suppose that the mean armspan of students in the class was 170.3cm. What, if anything, can be said about the mean height of students in the class? We know that $(\overline{x}, \overline{y})$ is always on the regression line. So, if $\overline{y} = 170.3$, then

$$170.3 = -42.7 + 1.3\overline{x} \Rightarrow \overline{x} = \frac{170.3 + 42.7}{1.3} \approx 163.8\text{cm}.$$

So the average height of students in the class was 163.8cm.

(d) Janey found that for a certain regression line, $r = -0.9$. She concluded that her regression line explained 90% of the variation in her data. Calculate $r^2$. Then interpret $r$ and $r^2$ for Janey.

Janey confused $r$ and $r^2$. In her case, $r^2 = 0.81$, which means that 81% of the variation in the data is explained by the linear relationship between her variables. Her value of $r$ describes the direction of the relationship, which in this case would be a negative correlation (sloping downward). As the explanatory variable gets bigger, the response variable gets smaller.

## e. Know and apply the chi-square test

1. What is the chi-square test?

The chi-square ($\chi^2$ or $X^2$) test is a test of statistical inference, which means that you are evaluating how likely a certain data set would be under certain assumptions. The chi-square test applies to two-way tables in which two categorical variables are being compared. The null hypothesis is that the two variables are not related. In that case, you would expect your population to be distributed a certain way throughout the table. The chi-square test statistic tells you the probability of encountering your data set given that this null hypothesis is true.

2. How do you apply the chi-square test?

To calculate $X^2$, you need to calculate the expected count within each cell of the table. Then, summing over all the cells in the table, you calculate:

$$X^2 = \sum_{\text{all cells}} \frac{(\text{observed count} - \text{expected count})^2}{\text{expected count}}.$$

You also need to find the number of degrees of freedom,

$$df = (\#\text{ rows} - 1)(\#\text{ columns} - 1).$$

3. How do you interpret the chi-square test?

Once you have your test statistic, $X^2$ and your degrees of freedom, $df$, you can look up your $p$-value in a table (or on your calculator). This $p$-value is the probability of getting your data if the null hypothesis is true, that is, if there is no relationship between the two variables. So, a high $p$-value means that your data is very likely under this assumption, and therefore the assumption might well be valid. A low $p$-value means that your data would be very rare under this assumption, and so the assumption might be invalid. A low $p$-value would lead you to suspect that the two variables are, in fact, related.

4. What is an example of the chi-square test?

   The following table represents the grades received by 50 students in a calculus course. Is there good evidence for a relationship between the sex of the student and the grade she or he received in the course?

   | Observed Counts | A | B | C | D | F | Total |
   |---|---|---|---|---|---|---|
   | Female | 9 | 9 | 4 | 0 | 0 | 22 |
   | Male | 2 | 11 | 10 | 4 | 1 | 28 |
   | Total | 11 | 20 | 14 | 4 | 1 | 50 |

   We begin by filling in the expected count for each cell, based on the null hypothesis that there is no relationship between the sex of the student and the grade she or he received in the course. In each case, we use the formula:

   $$\text{expected count} = \frac{(\text{row total})(\text{column total})}{(\text{table total})}.$$

   For instance, the expected number of female students getting an A would be $\frac{(22)(11)}{(50)} = 4.84$.

   | Expected Counts | A | B | C | D | F | Total |
   |---|---|---|---|---|---|---|
   | Female | 4.84 | 8.8 | 6.16 | 1.76 | 0.44 | 22 |
   | Male | 6.16 | 11.2 | 7.84 | 2.24 | 0.56 | 28 |
   | Total | 11 | 20 | 14 | 4 | 1 | 50 |

   Notice that $df = (5-1)(2-1) = 4$. Using a calculator to find $X^2$, we get $X^2 = 11.674$, with $p = 0.020$. This means that if there were no relationship between the sex of the student and the grade she or he received, then the likelihood of this data is about 2%, which is not very likely. Therefore, we have good evidence that there really is some relationship between the sex of the student and the grade she or he received in the calculus course.

   It is important to note that statistically, we have only shown that there is probably a relationship. We have not shown that the relationship is one of *causation*. Thus, one should NOT conclude from this data that women are better at calculus than men. Perhaps the female students worked harder and completed more of the homework, or perhaps the instructor graded the men more harshly. In any case, there is good evidence for a relationship, but much more research is needed to determine what that relationship may entail.

5. What is another example of the chi-square test?

   [This example comes from a standard textbook, Moore and McCabe[2], (p. 644).] Suppose that a company had a large work force and unfortunately had to fire some employees. Someone suspects that the company was more likely to fire older employees rather than younger ones. Are their suspicions valid? The following table has the data separated by age group and termination status.

---

[2]Moore and McCabe, *Introduction to the Practice of Statistics*. Fourth ed. W.H. Freeman and Company: New York, 2003.

| Observed Counts | Under 40 | Over 40 | Total |
|---|---|---|---|
| Fired | 16 | 78 | 94 |
| Not Fired | 585 | 765 | 1350 |
| Total | 601 | 843 | 1444 |

The first thing we need to do is calculate the expected counts in each cell. As before, this is done by looking at the totals in each row and column and figuring out how the numbers would be evenly distributed, given these totals. So, in the first cell (upper left), we would expect $(94)(601)/(1444)$ or 39.12. Continuing in this way, we obtain:

| Expected Counts | Under 40 | Over 40 | Total |
|---|---|---|---|
| Fired | 39.12 | 54.88 | 94 |
| Not Fired | 561.88 | 788.12 | 1350 |
| Total | 601 | 843 | 1444 |

Now we calculate $X^2$, the chi-square test statistic, and the degrees of freedom, $df = (2-1)(2-1) = 1$. You should get $X^2 = 25.04$. Then you go to the table (or use your calculator) to find that $p$ is VERY small ($p < 0.0005$). So, if there were no relationship between the age of the employee and their termination status, then data like ours would happen with a likelihood of less than 0.05%. This is excellent evidence that in fact, the age of the employee *is* related to their termination status.

6. Sample Problems

   (a) In the calculus class data given above, suppose that students need a C or better to take the next class. Then we could make the following table.

   | Observed Counts | Passing | Not Passing | Total |
   |---|---|---|---|
   | Female | 22 | 0 | 22 |
   | Male | 23 | 5 | 28 |
   | Total | 45 | 5 | 50 |

   Does this table present good evidence that there is a relationship between the sex of the student and whether or not the student passed the course? Calculate the chi-square test statistic and corresponding $p$-value to support your answer.

   (b) Suppose that someone comes to you and claims that their teacher is not grading the male students fairly. They ran a chi-square test on the relevant data and came up with $X^2 = 1.31$, with $p = 0.8597$. Do you believe their claim? Why or why not? Interpret their $p$-value.

   (c) (from Moore & McCabe, *ibid.*, p. 647) A survey was sent to three groups: those who received a preliminary letter about the survey, those who received a preliminary phone call about the survey, and those who received no contact prior to the survey. The numbers in the table refer to how many people returned the survey within two weeks.

| Observed Counts | Letter | Phone | None | Total |
|---|---|---|---|---|
| Within 2 weeks | 171 | 146 | 118 | 435 |
| Not within 2 weeks | 220 | 68 | 455 | 743 |
| Total | 391 | 214 | 573 | 1178 |

Fill in the Expected Counts table below. Then calculate the chi-square test statistic and its corresponding *p*-value. Interpret your results.

| Expected Counts | Letter | Phone | None | Total |
|---|---|---|---|---|
| Within 2 weeks | | | | 435 |
| Not within 2 weeks | | | | 743 |
| Total | 391 | 214 | 573 | 1178 |

7. Answers to Sample Problems

   (a) In the calculus class data given above, suppose that students need a C or better to take the next class. Then we could make the following table.

| Observed Counts | Passing | Not Passing | Total |
|---|---|---|---|
| Female | 22 | 0 | 22 |
| Male | 23 | 5 | 28 |
| Total | 45 | 5 | 50 |

   Does this table present good evidence that there is a relationship between the sex of the student and whether or not the student passed the course? Calculate the chi-square test statistic and corresponding *p*-value to support your answer.

   First, we will find the expected counts in each cell.

| Expected Counts | Passing | Not Passing | Total |
|---|---|---|---|
| Female | 19.8 | 2.2 | 22 |
| Male | 25.2 | 2.8 | 28 |
| Total | 45 | 5 | 50 |

   So, the chi-square test statistic is

$$\frac{(22 - 19.8)^2}{19.8} + \frac{(0 - 2.2)^2}{2.2} + \frac{(23 - 25.2)^2}{25.2} + \frac{(5 - 2.8)^2}{2.8} = 4.365.$$

   We also have $df = 1$. Thus, the *p*-value, according to the calculator, is 0.0367. This means that if there were no relationship between the sex of the student and whether or not they passed the class, then our data would happen with a likelihood of about 3.7%, which is not very likely. So there is good evidence of a relationship between the sex of the student and whether or not they passed the class.

   (b) Suppose that someone comes to you and claims that their teacher is not grading the male students fairly. They ran a chi-square test on the relevant data and came up with $X^2 = 1.31$, with $p = 0.8597$. Do you believe their claim? Why or why not? Interpret their *p*-value.

They have not presented good evidence to support their claim. Their $p$-value means that if there were no relationship between the sex of the student and their grade, then the likelihood of obtaining their data is about 86%, which is highly likely. This data does NOT support the claim of unfair treatment.

(c) A survey was sent to three groups: those who received a preliminary letter about the survey, those who received a preliminary phone call about the survey, and those who received no contact prior to the survey. The numbers in the table refer to how many people returned the survey within two weeks.

| Observed Counts | Letter | Phone | None | Total |
|---|---|---|---|---|
| **Within 2 weeks** | 171 | 146 | 118 | 435 |
| **Not within 2 weeks** | 220 | 68 | 455 | 743 |
| **Total** | 391 | 214 | 573 | 1178 |

Fill in the Expected Counts table below. Then calculate the chi-square test statistic and its corresponding $p$-value. Interpret your results.

| Expected Counts | Letter | Phone | None | Total |
|---|---|---|---|---|
| **Within 2 weeks** | 144.38 | 79.02 | 211.59 | 435 |
| **Not within 2 weeks** | 246.62 | 134.98 | 361.41 | 743 |
| **Total** | 391 | 214 | 573 | 1178 |

Running the chi-square test on the calculator (with $df = 2$) gives: $X^2 = 163.412$ and $p = 3.28 \times 10^{-36}$, which is quite small. Therefore, we do have good evidence of a relationship between how the person was contacted beforehand and whether or not the survey was returned within two weeks.

# Subtest III:
# Calculus
# History of Mathematics

# 5.1 Trigonometry

**a. Prove that the Pythagorean Theorem is equivalent to the trigonometric identity $\sin^2 x + \cos^2 x = 1$ and that this identity leads to $1 + \tan^2 x = \sec^2 x$ and $1 + \cot^2 x = \csc^2 x$**

1. What are the six basic trigonometric ratios?

   The six basic trigonometric ratios are sine, cosine, tangent, cotangent, secant, and cosecant. Actually, the "co-" prefix is an abbreviation of "complement's." So, "cosine" means the "complement's sine," that is, the sine of the complementary angle. Use this to complete the following figure.

   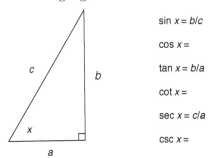

   $\sin x = b/c$

   $\cos x =$

   $\tan x = b/a$

   $\cot x =$

   $\sec x = c/a$

   $\csc x =$

   ANS: $\cos x = \frac{a}{c}$, $\cot x = \frac{a}{b}$, $\csc x = \frac{c}{b}$. From these ratios, it follows that

   $$\tan x = \frac{\sin x}{\cos x}, \quad \cot x = \frac{\cos x}{\sin x}, \quad \sec x = \frac{1}{\cos x}, \quad \text{and} \quad \csc x = \frac{1}{\sin x}.$$

2. Sample Problems

   (a) Draw and label a right triangle with an acute angle $x$. Write down the Pythagorean Theorem. Divide both sides of the equation by $c^2$, where $c$ is the hypotenuse length. What do you obtain, in terms of trigonometric functions of $x$?

   (b) Now divide both sides of the Pythagorean Theorem by $a^2$, where $a$ is one of the legs. What do you obtain, in terms of trigonometric functions of $x$?

   (c) Deduce the third Pythagorean Identity. How did you do it?

   (d) One consequence of this standard is that any of these three trigonometric equations is equivalent to any other one. How can you transform $1 + \tan^2 x = \sec^2 x$ into $\sin^2 x + \cos^2 x = 1$ in one step?

3. Answers to Sample Problems

   (a) Draw and label a right triangle with an acute angle $x$. Write down the Pythagorean Theorem. Divide both sides of the equation by $c^2$, where $c$ is the hypotenuse length. What do you obtain, in terms of trigonometric functions of $x$?

See the picture above.

$$\frac{a^2 + b^2}{c^2} = \frac{c^2}{c^2}$$

$$\frac{a^2}{c^2} + \frac{b^2}{c^2} = 1$$

$$\left(\frac{a}{c}\right)^2 + \left(\frac{b}{c}\right)^2 = 1$$

$$\cos^2 x + \sin^2 x = 1$$

(b) Now divide both sides of the Pythagorean Theorem by $a^2$, where $a$ is one of the legs. What do you obtain, in terms of trigonometric functions of $x$?

$$\frac{a^2 + b^2}{a^2} = \frac{c^2}{a^2} \Rightarrow 1 + \left(\frac{b}{a}\right)^2 = \left(\frac{c}{a}\right)^2 \Rightarrow 1 + \tan^2 x = \sec^2 x.$$

(c) Deduce the third Pythagorean Identity. How did you do it?

By dividing both sides of the Pythagorean Theorem by $b^2$, we obtain $\cot^2 x + 1 = \csc^2 x$.

(d) One consequence of this standard is that any of these three trigonometric equations is equivalent to any other one. How can you transform $1 + \tan^2 x = \sec^2 x$ into $\sin^2 x + \cos^2 x = 1$ in one step? We can multiply both sides by $\cos^2 x$.

$$\cos^2 x (1 + \tan^2 x) = (\sec^2 x) \cos^2 x$$

$$\cos^2 x + \cos^2 x \left(\frac{\sin^2 x}{\cos^2 x}\right) = \frac{\cos^2 x}{\cos^2 x}$$

$$\cos^2 x + \sin^2 x = 1.$$

**b. Prove the sine, cosine, and tangent sum formulas for all real values, and derive special applications of the sum formulas (e.g., double angle, half angle)**

1. What are the sine, cosine, and tangent sum formulas?

$$\sin(x + y) = \sin x \cos y + \cos x \sin y$$

$$\cos(x + y) = \cos x \cos y - \sin x \sin y$$

$$\tan(x + y) = \frac{\tan x + \tan y}{1 - \tan x \tan y}$$

2. How are the sine, cosine, and tangent sum formulas derived?

Usually, one of the formulas is derived and then the others follow as a consequence. We will outline a proof of the formula for $\cos(A - B)$ and then use it to derive the others. (Later, we'll see how to derive these formulas from DeMoivre's Theorem.)

Suppose angle $A$ is bigger than angle $B$ and consider the following points on the unit circle: $(\cos A, \sin A)$, $(\cos B, \sin B)$, $(\cos(A - B), \sin(A - B))$, and $(1, 0)$.

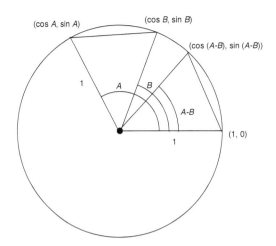

Since both chords have central angle $A - B$, the distance from $(\cos A, \sin A)$ to $(\cos B, \sin B)$ is equal to the distance from $(1,0)$ to $(\cos(A - B), \sin(A - B))$. Setting these two distances equal (then squaring both sides) gives:

$$(\cos A - \cos B)^2 + (\sin A - \sin B)^2 = (\cos(A - B) - 1)^2 + \sin^2(A - B)$$
$$\cos^2 A - 2\cos A \cos B + \cos^2 B + \sin^2 A - 2 \sin A \sin B + \sin^2 B =$$
$$= \cos^2(A - B) - 2\cos(A - B) + 1 + \sin^2(A - B)$$
$$2 - 2\cos A \cos B - 2\sin A \sin B = 2 - 2\cos(A - B),$$

where we have repeatedly used the Pythagorean identity $\cos^2 x + \sin^2 x = 1$. It follows that

$$\cos(A - B) = \cos A \cos B + \sin A \sin B.$$

Now, to find $\cos(x + y)$, use the formula with $A = x$ and $B = -y$.

See the Sample Problems for how to use these cosine formulas to derive the others.

3. How are the double angle formulas deduced?

   Each of the double angle formulas is deduced by calculating $\sin(x + x)$, $\cos(x + x)$, and $\tan(x + x)$ using the sum formulas above.

   - $\sin 2x = \sin(x + x) = \sin x \cos x + \cos x \sin x = 2 \sin x \cos x$
   - $\cos 2x = \cos x \cos x - \sin x \sin x = \cos^2 x - \sin^2 x = 2\cos^2 x - 1 = 1 - 2\sin^2 x$
   - $\tan 2x = \frac{\sin(2x)}{\cos(2x)} = \frac{2 \sin x \cos x}{\cos^2 x - \sin^2 x} \left[ \frac{\sec^2 x}{\sec^2 x} \right] = \frac{2 \tan x}{1 - \tan^2 x}$, where the answer is in terms of $\tan x$

4. How are the half angle formulas deduced?

   The half angle formulas stem from the three forms of the $\cos(2x)$ identity. For example, to obtain the formula for $\sin(x/2)$, we start with $\cos(2\theta) = 1 - 2\sin^2 \theta$ and then we solve the equation for $\sin \theta$.

$$\cos(2\theta) = 1 - 2\sin^2 \theta \Rightarrow 2\sin^2 \theta = 1 - \cos(2\theta) \Rightarrow \sin^2 \theta = \frac{1 - \cos(2\theta)}{2}$$

$$\sin\theta = \sqrt{\frac{1-\cos(2\theta)}{2}}$$

Now, if we let $\theta = \frac{x}{2}$, then we obtain $\sin(x/2) = \sqrt{\frac{1-\cos x}{2}}$. We might need the negative square root, depending on the quadrant in which $\frac{x}{2}$ lies.

The $\cos(x/2)$ formula is derived similarly.

$$\cos(2\theta) = 2\cos^2\theta - 1 \Rightarrow \ldots$$

$$\cos(x/2) =$$

ANS: $\cos(x/2) = \sqrt{\frac{1+\cos x}{2}}$. Again, we might need the negative square root, depending on the quadrant in which $\frac{x}{2}$ lies.

Dividing these two leads to a half-angle formula for tangent.

$$\tan(x/2) =$$

ANS: $\tan(x/2) = \sqrt{\frac{1-\cos x}{1+\cos x}}$. Again, we might need the negative square root, depending on the quadrant in which $\frac{x}{2}$ lies.

5. Sample Problems

   (a) Using the identity $\sin x = \cos(\frac{\pi}{2}-x)$ and the formula for the cosine of a sum or difference, derive the formula for $\sin(x+y)$.

   (b) Derive formulas for $\sin(x-y)$, $\cos(x-y)$, and $\tan(x-y)$ from the sum formulas.

   (c) Show that $\cos(0) = 1$ and that $\sin(0) = \tan(0) = 0$. [Hint: find $\cos(x-x)$.]

   (d) Write down several different expressions, each of which is equal to $\cos(4x)$.

   (e) Write down three different expressions, each of which is equal to $\sin^2(2x)$.

   (f) We know that in general, $\sin(x+y) \neq \sin x + \sin y$. But can you find specific values of $x$ and $y$ that would make the equation true?

   (g) We know that in general, $\cos(x+y) \neq \cos x + \cos y$. But can you find specific values of $x$ and $y$ that would make the equation true?

   (h) Derive formulas for $\cot(x+y)$ and $\csc(2x)$.

6. Answers to Sample Problems

   (a) Using the identity $\sin x = \cos(\frac{\pi}{2}-x)$ and the formula for the cosine of a sum or difference, derive the formula for $\sin(x+y)$.

$$
\begin{aligned}
\sin(x+y) &= \cos\left(\frac{\pi}{2}-(x+y)\right) = \cos\left(\left(\frac{\pi}{2}-x\right)-y\right) \\
&= \cos\left(\frac{\pi}{2}-x\right)\cos y + \sin\left(\frac{\pi}{2}-x\right)\sin y \\
&= \sin x \cos y + \cos x \sin y
\end{aligned}
$$

(b) Derive formulas for $\sin(x-y)$, $\cos(x-y)$, and $\tan(x-y)$ from the sum formulas.

$$\sin(x-y) = \sin(x+(-y)) = \sin x \cos(-y) + \cos x \sin(-y) = \sin x \cos y - \cos x \sin y.$$

$$\cos(x-y) = \cos x \cos(-y) - \sin x \sin(-y) = \cos x \cos y + \sin x \sin y.$$

$$\tan(x-y) = \frac{\tan x + \tan(-y)}{1 - \tan x \tan(-y)} = \frac{\tan x - \tan y}{1 + \tan x \tan y}.$$

(c) Show that $\cos(0) = 1$ and that $\sin(0) = \tan(0) = 0$. [Hint: find $\cos(x-x)$.]

$$\cos(0) = \cos(x-x) = \cos^2 x + \sin^2 x = 1.$$

$$\sin(0) = \sin(x-x) = \sin x \cos x - \cos x \sin x = 0.$$

$$\tan(0) = \tan(x-x) = \frac{\tan x - \tan x}{1 + \tan^2 x} = \frac{0}{\sec^2 x} = 0.$$

(d) Write down several different expressions, each of which is equal to $\cos(4x)$. Answers include: $\cos^2(2x) - \sin^2(2x)$, $2\cos^2(2x) - 1$, $1 - 2\sin^2(2x)$, $2(2\cos^2 x - 1)^2 - 1 = 8\cos^4 x - 8\cos^2 x + 1$. There are more.

(e) Write down three different expressions, each of which is equal to $\sin^2(2x)$. Answers include: $4\sin^2 x \cos^2 x$, $1 - \cos^2(2x)$, $4(1 - \cos^2 x)\cos^2 x = 4\cos^2 x - 4\cos^4 x$, $4\sin^2 x - 4\sin^4 x$, etc.

(f) We know that in general, $\sin(x+y) \neq \sin x + \sin y$. But can you find specific values of $x$ and $y$ that would make the equation true? Yes, if $x$ (or $y$) is equal to any multiple of $2\pi$, then the equation is true.

(g) We know that in general, $\cos(x+y) \neq \cos x + \cos y$. But can you find specific values of $x$ and $y$ that would make the equation true? Yes, if $x = \frac{\pi}{3}$ and $y = -\frac{\pi}{3}$, then $x + y = 0$. So, $\cos(x+y) = 1$ and $\cos(\frac{\pi}{3}) + \cos(-\frac{\pi}{3}) = \frac{1}{2} + \frac{1}{2} = 1$. There are others.

(h) Derive formulas for $\cot(x+y)$ and $\csc(2x)$. Answers may vary.

$$\cot(x+y) = \frac{\cos(x+y)}{\sin(x+y)} = \frac{\cos x \cos y - \sin x \sin y}{\sin x \cos y + \cos x \sin y} = \frac{\cot x \cot y - 1}{\cot x + \cot y}.$$

$$\csc 2x = \frac{1}{\sin 2x} = \frac{1}{2\sin x \cos x} = \frac{1}{2}\csc x \sec x.$$

## c. Analyze properties of trigonometric functions in a variety of ways (e.g., graphing and solving problems)

1. What are some properties of the sine and cosine functions? How do these properties show up on a graph?

   Sine and cosine functions are periodic with fundamental period $2\pi$. That means that, for any value of $x$, $f(x+2\pi) = f(x)$ whenever $f$ is a basic sine or cosine function. These functions are also bounded between $-1$ and $1$, which means that for any value of $x$, $-1 \leq f(x) \leq 1$. Also, sine and cosine are defined for all real values of $x$; that is, each one has a domain consisting of all real numbers. Sine is odd, and $\sin(0) = 0$, whereas cosine is even and $\cos(0) = 1$.

On a graph, $y = \sin x$ and $y = \cos x$ are typical "wave" functions. They oscillate regularly between the horizontal lines $y = 1$ and $y = -1$ and extend infinitely in both the positive and negative $x$-directions. The graph of $y = \sin x$ is shown below.

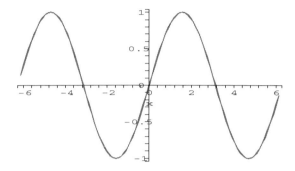

2. What are some properties of the tangent and cotangent functions? How do these properties show up on a graph?

Tangent and cotangent functions are periodic with fundamental period $\pi$. These functions are unbounded. In fact, each function has a range consisting of all real numbers. Tangent is not defined whenever cosine is zero (i.e., at $\frac{\pi}{2} + k\pi$), while cotangent is not defined whenever sine is zero (i.e., at $k\pi$), where $k$ is any integer.

On a graph, these functions consist of several branches, each of which is a copy of the fundamental branch (between $-\frac{\pi}{2}$ and $\frac{\pi}{2}$ for tangent, between $0$ and $\pi$ for cotangent) that has been translated by an integer multiple of $\pi$. The branches have vertical asymptotes at the values for which they are undefined. The graph of $y = \tan x$ is shown below.

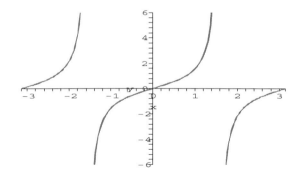

3. What are some properties of the secant and cosecant functions? How do these properties show up on a graph?

Secant and cosecant functions are periodic with fundamental period $2\pi$. Secant (like tangent) is not defined when cosine is zero (odd multiples of $\frac{\pi}{2}$), whereas cosecant (like cotangent) is not defined when sine is zero (multiples of $\pi$). Each of the basic functions has a range of $(-\infty, -1] \cup [1, \infty)$.

On a graph, secant and cosecant have vertical asymptotes where they are not defined. They consist of disjoint U-shaped pieces, either positive and opening upward or negative and opening downward. The graph of $y = \sec x$ is shown below.

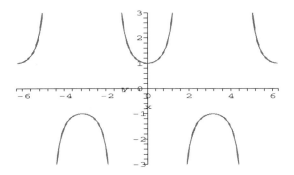

4. What are some problems that can be solved using these properties?

   - $\sin x = 0$ ($x = k\pi$, where $k$ is any integer)
   - $\sin(2x) = 1$ ($2x = \dfrac{\pi}{2} + 2k\pi \Rightarrow x = \dfrac{\pi}{4} + k\pi$, where $k$ is any integer)
   - $\tan x = \sqrt{3}$ ($x = \dfrac{\pi}{3} + k\pi$, where $k$ is any integer)
   - $\sec^2 x = 2$ ($x = \dfrac{\pi}{4} + \dfrac{k\pi}{2}$, where $k$ is any integer)

   For more examples of solving trigonometry problems, see the next subsection on inverse trigonometric functions.

5. What are some problems that can be shown to be unsolvable using these properties?

   - $\sin 2x = 2$ is unsolvable because the range of sine is $[-1, 1]$.
   - $\cot \pi = x$ is unsolvable because cot is not defined at $\pi$ ($\sin \pi = 0$)
   - $\csc x = 0$ is unsolvable because $|\csc x| \geq 1$.

6. What is the formula for a typical sinusoidal function?

   One form of the typical sinusoidal function is

   $$f(x) = A\cos(B(x - C)) + D,$$

   where $A$ is the amplitude, $D$ is the midline (or average value), $C$ is the horizontal shift, and the period is $\frac{2\pi}{B}$. The maximum value of $f$ is _____ and the minimum value of $f$ is _____.

   ANS: maximum value is $D + A$, minimum value is $D - A$

7. Sample Problems

(a) Which of the six basic trigonometric functions are even (meaning $f(-x) = f(x)$)? Which are odd (meaning $f(-x) = -f(x)$)? Which are neither? [Hint: write them in terms of sine and cosine.]

(b) Solve the following equations for $x$. List all solutions on $[0, 2\pi]$.

    i. $\cos x = \dfrac{\sqrt{2}}{2}$

    ii. $\cos 3x = \dfrac{\sqrt{3}}{2}$

    iii. $\tan^4 x - 4\tan^2 x + 3 = 0$

    iv. $\sec x = \dfrac{1}{2}$

    v. $(\sin 2x)(\cos 2x) = \dfrac{1}{4}$

(c) List three different trig functions that have period $\pi$.

(d) List two different trig functions that have period 1 and have asymptotes at $x = n$ for any integer $n$.

(e) Sketch the graph of $y = -B\sin(\pi x) + B$. Label one maximum point on the graph, one minimum, and all intercepts.

(f) Johnny observed a population of rabbits for one year. He counted a minimum of 1500 rabbits at the beginning of February and a maximum of 2700 rabbits at the beginning of August. Since he was looking for a population model, he decided on

$$P(t) = 2700\cos\left(\frac{t-2}{12}\right) + 1500,$$

where $t$ is in months and $t = 0$ corresponds to January. Correct all of Johnny's mistakes. Identify each mistake by name and provide the correct value in each instance.

8. Answers to Sample Problems

(a) Which of the six basic trigonometric functions are even (meaning $f(-x) = f(x)$)? Which are odd (meaning $f(-x) = -f(x)$)? Which are neither? [Hint: write them in terms of sine and cosine.] The functions $\sin x$, $\tan x$, $\cot x$ and $\csc x$ are ODD, while $\cos x$ and $\sec x$ are EVEN.

(b) Solve the following equations for $x$. List all solutions on $[0, 2\pi]$.

    i. $\cos x = \dfrac{\sqrt{2}}{2}$; $x = \dfrac{\pi}{4}, \dfrac{7\pi}{4}$

    ii. $\cos 3x = \dfrac{\sqrt{3}}{2}$; $3x = \dfrac{\pi}{6} + 2k\pi$ or $\dfrac{11\pi}{6} + 2k\pi$; $x = \dfrac{\pi}{18}, \dfrac{11\pi}{18}, \dfrac{13\pi}{18}, \dfrac{23\pi}{18}, \dfrac{25\pi}{18}, \dfrac{35\pi}{18}$

    iii. $\tan^4 x - 4\tan^2 x + 3 = 0$; $(\tan^2 x - 1)(\tan^2 x - 3) = 0$; $\tan x = \pm 1, \pm\sqrt{3}$; $x = \dfrac{\pi}{4}, \dfrac{\pi}{3}, \dfrac{2\pi}{3}, \dfrac{3\pi}{4}, \dfrac{5\pi}{4}, \dfrac{4\pi}{3}, \dfrac{5\pi}{3}, \dfrac{7\pi}{4}$

    iv. $\sec x = \dfrac{1}{2}$; No solutions. ($|\sec x| \geq 1$)

v. $(\sin 2x)(\cos 2x) = \dfrac{1}{4}$; $\sin 4x = \dfrac{1}{2}$; $x = \dfrac{\pi}{24}, \dfrac{5\pi}{24}, \dfrac{13\pi}{24}, \dfrac{17\pi}{24}, \dfrac{25\pi}{24}, \dfrac{29\pi}{24}, \dfrac{37\pi}{24}, \dfrac{41\pi}{24}$

(c) List three different trig functions that have period $\pi$. Answers include $\tan x$, $\cot x$, $\sin 2x$, $\cos 2x$, etc.

(d) List two different trig functions that have period 1 and have asymptotes at $x = n$ for any integer $n$. Answers include $\cot(\pi x)$, $\tan(\pi x - \frac{\pi}{2})$, $\csc(2\pi x)$, etc.

(e) Sketch the graph of $y = -B\sin(\pi x) + B$. Label one maximum point on the graph, one minimum, and all intercepts.

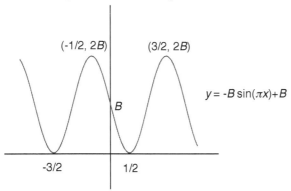

(f) Johnny observed a population of rabbits for one year. He counted a minimum of 1500 rabbits at the beginning of February and a maximum of 2700 rabbits at the beginning of August. Since he was looking for a population model, he decided on

$$P(t) = 2700\cos\left(\dfrac{t-2}{12}\right) + 1500,$$

where $t$ is in months and $t = 0$ corresponds to January. Correct all of Johnny's mistakes. Identify each mistake by name and provide the correct value in each instance.

i. Johnny has an incorrect amplitude of 2700. It should be 600.

ii. Johnny has an incorrect midline of 1500. It should be 2100.

iii. Johnny has an incorrect period of $24\pi$. It should be 12.

iv. Johnny has an incorrect horizontal shift. It should be 1.

v. Johnny should be using a negative cosine graph with a horizontal shift of 1, so that he is starting at a population minimum.

vi. The correct formula should be $P(t) = -600\cos(\frac{2\pi}{12}(t-1)) + 2100$.

## d. Know and apply the definitions and properties of inverse trigonometric functions (i.e., arcsin, arccos, and arctan)

1. What is the definition of an inverse trigonometric function? What are some properties of inverse trigonometric functions?

Inverse trigonometric functions are just inverse functions of trigonometric functions. For example, $\sin(\pi/4) = \sqrt{2}/2$. Therefore, $\arcsin(\sqrt{2}/2) = \pi/4$. The inverse sine (or arcsine) of $x$

is the angle measure (usually in radians) whose sine is equal to $x$. Other inverse trigonometric functions are similarly defined.

$$y = \arccos x \Leftrightarrow x = \cos y, \quad y = \arctan x \Leftrightarrow x = \tan y, \ etc.$$

The general inverse trigonometric functions are technically not functions at all because they are multi-valued. For example, $\arcsin(0)$ could be $0$, $\pi$, $-\pi$, $2\pi$, $5\pi$, etc. So, in order to guarantee that the inverse trigonometric functions are honest-to-goodness functions, we agree on one of the many correct values for the function and we call it the "principal" value (denoted as Arcsin, for instance). $\text{Arcsin}\left(-\dfrac{\sqrt{3}}{2}\right) = -\dfrac{\pi}{3}$ instead of $\dfrac{4\pi}{3}$ or $\dfrac{5\pi}{3}$, even though these satisfy $\sin\theta = -\dfrac{\sqrt{3}}{2}$.

WARNING! There are four different notations for each inverse trigonometric function. The first two are identical: $\arcsin x = \sin^{-1} x$; each one means an angle whose sine is equal to $x$. The principal arcsine, $\text{Arcsin}\, x = \text{Sin}^{-1} x$ is the angle between $-\dfrac{\pi}{2}$ and $\dfrac{\pi}{2}$ whose sine is $x$. Notice that the $\text{Arcsin}\, x$ has only one answer.

WARNING! $\sin^{-1} x \neq \dfrac{1}{\sin x}$. To say $\dfrac{1}{\sin x}$, one would write $\csc x$ or $(\sin x)^{-1}$.

The following table lists domains and ranges of the principal inverse trigonometric functions.

| Function | Domain | Range |
|---|---|---|
| Arcsin $x$ | $[-1, 1]$ | $\left[-\dfrac{\pi}{2}, \dfrac{\pi}{2}\right]$ |
| Arccos $x$ | $[-1, 1]$ | $[0, \pi]$ |
| Arctan $x$ | all reals | $\left(-\dfrac{\pi}{2}, \dfrac{\pi}{2}\right)$ |
| Arccot $x$ | all reals | $(0, \pi)$ |
| Arcsec $x$ | $(-\infty, -1] \cup [1, \infty)$ | $\left[0, \dfrac{\pi}{2}\right) \cup \left(\dfrac{\pi}{2}, \pi\right]$ |
| Arccsc $x$ | $(-\infty, -1] \cup [1, \infty)$ | $\left[-\dfrac{\pi}{2}, 0\right) \cup \left(0, \dfrac{\pi}{2}\right]$ |

2. How can you apply the definitions and properties to solve problems?

As an example, we'll find all the solutions to $\sin(5x) = 0.5$ with $0 \le x \le 2\pi$. First, we have $5x = \text{Arcsin}(0.5) + 2k\pi = \dfrac{\pi}{6} + 2k\pi$. Solving for $x$ gives $x = \dfrac{\pi}{30} + \dfrac{2k\pi}{5}$. Notice that if $k = 0, 1, 2, 3, 4$, then the value of $x$ still lies between $0$ and $2\pi$. So we get five answers, one for each value of $x$. Namely, $x$ is in the set $\left\{\dfrac{\pi}{30}, \dfrac{13\pi}{30}, \dfrac{5\pi}{6}, \dfrac{37\pi}{30}, \dfrac{49\pi}{30}\right\}$.

But is that all the answers possible? Actually, if we look at the sine graph, there are TWO possible values for $\arcsin(0.5)$, $\dfrac{\pi}{6}$ and $\dfrac{5\pi}{6}$. So we could get $5x = \dfrac{5\pi}{6} + 2k\pi$. Again, notice that we get five values for $x$, corresponding to $k = 0, 1, 2, 3, 4$. This gives us five more solutions: $\dfrac{\pi}{6}, \dfrac{17\pi}{30}, \dfrac{29\pi}{30}, \dfrac{41\pi}{30}, \dfrac{53\pi}{30}$.

So, there are ten solutions to $\sin(5x) = 0.5$ between 0 and $2\pi$. The solution set is

$$\left\{ \frac{\pi}{30}, \frac{\pi}{6}, \frac{13\pi}{30}, \frac{17\pi}{30}, \frac{5\pi}{6}, \frac{29\pi}{30}, \frac{37\pi}{30}, \frac{41\pi}{30}, \frac{49\pi}{30}, \frac{53\pi}{30} \right\}.$$

3. Sample Problems

 (a) Sketch graphs of $y = \arcsin x$, $y = \arccos x$, and $y = \arctan x$.

 (b) Sketch graphs of $y = \operatorname{Arcsin} x$, $y = \operatorname{Arccos} x$, and $y = \operatorname{Arctan} x$, and compare to the previous graphs.

 (c) Simplify, if possible.

   i. $\operatorname{Arcsin}(-\frac{1}{2})$

   ii. $\operatorname{Arctan}(1)$

   iii. $\operatorname{Arctan}(\sqrt{3}) + \operatorname{Arccos}(-1)$

   iv. $\operatorname{Arcsin}(2)$

   v. $\cos(\pi - \operatorname{Arccos}(-\frac{\sqrt{3}}{2}))$

   vi. $\operatorname{Arcsin}(\cos(\frac{5\pi}{6}))$

   vii. $\operatorname{Arcsec}(-1) - \operatorname{Arctan}(\tan(\pi))$

 (d) True or False? If true, explain why. If false, give a counterexample. Remember, in math, "true" means "always true."

   i. $\sin(\operatorname{Arcsin} x) = x$.

   ii. $\operatorname{Arctan}(\tan x) = x$.

   iii. $\operatorname{Arctan}(\frac{\pi}{2})$ is undefined.

   iv. $\arctan x = 1$ has two solutions between 0 and $2\pi$.

   v. $\operatorname{Arctan} x = -3$ has two solutions between 0 and $2\pi$.

   vi. $\tan(\operatorname{Arccos} x) = \dfrac{\sqrt{1 - x^2}}{x}$.

   vii. The value of $\sin x$ is never negative on the range of $\operatorname{Arccos} x$.

4. Answers to Sample Problems

 (a) Sketch graphs of $y = \arcsin x$, $y = \arccos x$, and $y = \arctan x$.

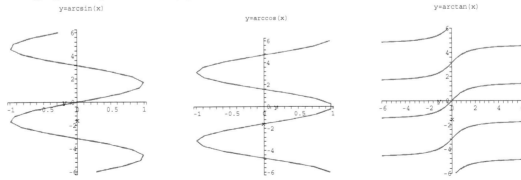

(b) Sketch graphs of $y = \text{Arcsin}\, x$, $y = \text{Arccos}\, x$, and $y = \text{Arctan}\, x$, and compare to the previous graphs.

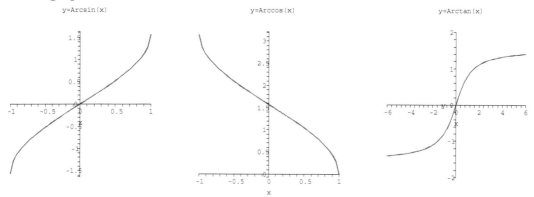

The difference is that the principal arc-graphs are single-valued. For every value of $x$, there is only one value of $y$. This makes the principal inverse trigonometric functions into actual functions. The other graphs are merely relations.

(c) Simplify, if possible.

i. $\text{Arcsin}(-\frac{1}{2}) = -\frac{\pi}{6}$

ii. $\text{Arctan}(1) = \frac{\pi}{4}$

iii. $\text{Arctan}(\sqrt{3}) + \text{Arccos}(-1) = \frac{\pi}{3} + \pi = \frac{4\pi}{3}$

iv. $\text{Arcsin}(2)$ is not defined because $\sin x$ cannot equal 2.

v. $\cos(\pi - \text{Arccos}(-\frac{\sqrt{3}}{2})) = \cos(\pi - \frac{5\pi}{6}) = \frac{\sqrt{3}}{2}$

vi. $\text{Arcsin}(\cos(\frac{5\pi}{6})) = -\frac{\pi}{3}$

vii. $\text{Arcsec}(-1) - \text{Arctan}(\tan(\pi)) = \pi - 0 = \pi$

(d) True or False? If true, explain why. If false, give a counterexample. Remember, in math, "true" means "always true."

i. $\sin(\text{Arcsin}\, x) = x$. TRUE. $\text{Arcsin}\, x$ is an angle whose sine is $x$.

ii. $\text{Arctan}(\tan x) = x$. FALSE. $\text{Arctan}(\tan \pi) = \text{Arctan}(0) = 0 \neq \pi$.

iii. $\text{Arctan}(\frac{\pi}{2})$ is undefined. FALSE. The tangent of $\frac{\pi}{2}$ is undefined. $\text{Arctan}(\frac{\pi}{2})$ is close to 1 because $\tan(1) \approx \frac{\pi}{2}$.

iv. $\arctan x = 1$ has two solutions between 0 and $2\pi$. TRUE. $x = \frac{\pi}{4}, \frac{5\pi}{4}$.

v. $\text{Arctan}\, x = -3$ has two solutions between 0 and $2\pi$. FALSE. $\text{Arctan}\, x = -3$ has only one solution, due to the definition of the principal arctangent function.

vi. $\tan(\text{Arccos}\, x) = \dfrac{\sqrt{1-x^2}}{x}$. TRUE. If $y = \text{Arccos}\, x$, then $\cos y = x$ and $0 \leq y \leq \pi$. So, $\sin y = \sqrt{1 - \cos^2 y} = \sqrt{1 - x^2}$. Hence $\tan y = \frac{\sqrt{1-x^2}}{x}$.

vii. The value of $\sin x$ is never negative on the range of $\text{Arccos}\, x$. TRUE. The range of $\text{Arccos}\, x$ is $[0, \pi]$, on which sine is positive. Similarly, cosine is never negative on the range of $\text{Arcsin}\, x$.

### e. Understand and apply polar representations of complex numbers (e.g., DeMoivre's Theorem)

1. What are polar coordinates?

   Polar coordinates are another way to describe points on the plane (rather than using Cartesian $(x, y)$ coordinates). A point is described by the ordered pair $(r, \theta)$, where $r$ describes how far the point is from the origin, and $\theta$ describes the angle formed by the ray leading from the origin to the point and the ray of the positive $x$-axis (measured counter-clockwise). As examples, the Cartesian point $(0, -2)$ corresponds to the polar point $(2, \frac{3\pi}{2})$ (or possibly $(2, -\frac{\pi}{2})$), and the Cartesian point $(3, 3)$ corresponds to the polar point $(3\sqrt{2}, \frac{\pi}{4})$.

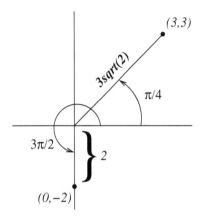

   The formulas for writing $x$ and $y$ as functions of $r$ and $\theta$ are therefore...

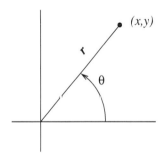

   - $x =$

   - $y =$

   ANS: $x = r \cos \theta$, $y = r \sin \theta$.

2. How do you connect trigonometry to complex numbers?

   Often, complex numbers (e.g., $2 - 3i$) can be graphed as points on a Cartesian plane (e.g., $(2, -3)$). The $a + bi$ notation is helpful when adding or subtracting complex numbers. But the polar coordinates are often more helpful when multiplying, dividing, or finding roots of complex numbers. Using the two examples listed in the previous section on polar coordinates, we can write complex numbers in terms of $r$ and $\theta$. First we factor out $r = \sqrt{a^2 + b^2}$ and then we write the other factor in terms of trigonometric functions of $\theta$.

- $(0, -2) \to -2i = 2(0 + i(-1)) = 2(\cos(\frac{3\pi}{2}) + i\sin(\frac{3\pi}{2}))$
- $(3, 3) \to 3 + 3i = 3\sqrt{2}(\frac{\sqrt{2}}{2} + i\frac{\sqrt{2}}{2}) = 3\sqrt{2}(\cos(\frac{\pi}{4}) + i\sin(\frac{\pi}{4}))$

3. What is DeMoivre's Theorem? How can we use it?

   **DeMoivre's Theorem:** If $x$ is a real number, and if $n$ is an integer, then

   $$(\cos x + i\sin x)^n = \cos(nx) + i\sin(nx),$$

   where $i^2 = -1$. If $(\cos x + i\sin x)$ is abbreviated cis $x$, then the theorem says $(\text{cis } x)^n = \text{cis}(nx)$.

   One way to use this theorem is to derive the multiple angle formulas using complex multiplication. (See Sample Problems, below.) Another way to use the theorem is to find roots of complex numbers. For example, to find the three solutions to the equation $z^3 = 8$, we first think of $z$ as a complex number. Then, using polar coordinates, we can write $z = r\cos\theta + ir\sin\theta = r\,\text{cis}(\theta)$ Then

   $$8 = z^3 = r^3(\text{cis }\theta)^3 = r^3\,\text{cis}(3\theta).$$

   By comparing real and imaginary parts, we see that $r$ must be a real cube root of 8, i.e. $r = 2$, and $\cos(3\theta) = 1$. [We also need $\sin(3\theta) = 0$, but this is redundant if $\cos(3\theta) = 1$.] So, $3\theta = 0, 2\pi, 4\pi$, which means $\theta = 0, \frac{2\pi}{3}, \frac{4\pi}{3}$. Therefore, the three cube roots of 8 are:

   - $2\,\text{cis}(0) = 2(1 + 0i) = 2$
   - $2\,\text{cis}\left(\frac{2\pi}{3}\right) = 2\left(-\frac{1}{2} + i\frac{\sqrt{3}}{2}\right) = -1 + i\sqrt{3}$
   - $2\,\text{cis}\left(\frac{4\pi}{3}\right) = 2\left(-\frac{1}{2} - i\frac{\sqrt{3}}{2}\right) = -1 - i\sqrt{3}$

4. Sample Problems

   (a) Multiply $-2i$ and $3 + 3i$ using polar coordinates. Use the fact that $\text{cis }x\,\text{cis }y = \text{cis}(x + y)$.

   (b) Find formulas for the polar coordinates $r$ and $\theta$ in terms of $x$ and $y$.

   (c) Explain why the expression $\cos\theta + i\sin\theta$ comes up when converting from Cartesian to polar representations of complex numbers.

   (d) Derive formulas for $\cos(2x)$ and $\sin(2x)$ using DeMoivre's Theorem. That is, we know $\text{cis}(2x) = (\text{cis }x)^2 = (\cos x + i\sin x)^2 = \dots$. Multiply out and simplify. Then equate the real parts and the imaginary parts of your answer with the real parts and imaginary parts of $\text{cis}(2x)$.

   (e) Find all the fourth roots of $-1$.

   (f) Find all the sixth roots of 64.

   (g) Find all square roots of i.

   (h) Find all cube roots of i.

(i) Explain how you know that you will be able to explicitly write down all complex $n$-th roots of positive real numbers (i.e., all solutions to $x^n = a > 0$) whenever $n$ is 1, 2, 3, 4, 6, 8, or 12.

(j) Derive formulas for $\cos(3x)$ and $\sin(3x)$ using DeMoivre's Theorem. How far can you go?

(k) A generalization of DeMoivre's Theorem can be found in Euler's Formula: $e^{ix} = \operatorname{cis} x$. Show that $\operatorname{cis} x \operatorname{cis} y = \operatorname{cis}(x + y)$ and then use your answer to verify the formulas for $\cos(x + y)$ and $\sin(x + y)$.

5. Answers to Sample Problems

(a) Multiply $-2i$ and $3 + 3i$ using polar coordinates. Use the fact that $\operatorname{cis} x \operatorname{cis} y = \operatorname{cis}(x+y)$. First, we write the numbers in polar form: $-2i = 2 \operatorname{cis} \frac{3\pi}{2}$ and $3 + 3i = 3\sqrt{2} \operatorname{cis} \frac{\pi}{4}$. Then we multiply magnitudes and add angles, giving:

$$
\begin{aligned}
(-2i)(3 + 3i) &= \left(2 \operatorname{cis} \frac{3\pi}{2}\right)\left(3\sqrt{2} \operatorname{cis} \frac{\pi}{4}\right) = 6\sqrt{2} \operatorname{cis} \frac{7\pi}{4} \\
&= 6\sqrt{2}\left(\frac{\sqrt{2}}{2} - i\frac{\sqrt{2}}{2}\right) = 6 - 6i.
\end{aligned}
$$

(b) Find formulas for the polar coordinates $r$ and $\theta$ in terms of $x$ and $y$.

$$
r = \sqrt{x^2 + y^2}; \quad \theta = \arctan\left(\frac{y}{x}\right)
$$

(c) Explain why the expression $\cos\theta + i\sin\theta$ comes up when converting from Cartesian to polar representations of complex numbers. This expression occurs because complex numbers are graphed on a Cartesian plane in $x + iy$ form, which in polar coordinates becomes $r\cos\theta + ir\sin\theta = r(\cos\theta + i\sin\theta)$.

(d) Derive formulas for $\cos(2x)$ and $\sin(2x)$ using DeMoivre's Theorem. That is, we know $\operatorname{cis}(2x) = (\operatorname{cis} x)^2 = (\cos x + i\sin x)^2 = \ldots$. Multiply out and simplify. Then equate the real parts and the imaginary parts of your answer with the real parts and imaginary parts of $\operatorname{cis}(2x)$.

$$
\begin{aligned}
\operatorname{cis}(2x) &= (\operatorname{cis} x)^2 = (\cos x + i\sin x)^2 \\
&= \cos^2 x + 2i\sin x\cos x + i^2\sin^2 x \\
&= (\cos^2 x - \sin^2 x) + i(2\sin x\cos x), \\
\text{but by definition, } \operatorname{cis}(2x) &= \cos 2x + i\sin 2x,
\end{aligned}
$$

which means that $\cos 2x = \cos^2 x - \sin^2 x$ and $\sin 2x = 2\sin x\cos x$.

(e) Find all the fourth roots of $-1$. We must solve $z^4 = -1$. Note that $-1 = \operatorname{cis}\pi$. Let $z = r \operatorname{cis}\theta$. Then $z^4 = r^4 \operatorname{cis} 4\theta$. Hence $\operatorname{cis}\pi = r^4 \operatorname{cis} 4\theta$, which means $r^4 = 1$ and $4\theta = \pi + 2k\pi$. So, $r = 1$ and $\theta = \frac{\pi}{4}, \frac{3\pi}{4}, \frac{5\pi}{4}, \frac{7\pi}{4}$. Hence $z = \pm\frac{\sqrt{2}}{2} \pm i\frac{\sqrt{2}}{2}$ (where all sign combinations are possible).

(f) Find all the sixth roots of 64. We must solve $z^6 = 64$. Again, note that $64 = 64\operatorname{cis}(0)$. Let $z = r\operatorname{cis}\theta$. Then $z^6 = r^6\operatorname{cis}6\theta$. Hence $64\operatorname{cis}0 = r^6\operatorname{cis}6\theta$. Thus $r^6 = 64$ and $6\theta = 0 + 2k\pi$. So, $r = 2$ and $\theta = 0, \frac{\pi}{3}, \frac{2\pi}{3}, \pi, \frac{4\pi}{3}, \frac{5\pi}{3}$. Therefore, $z = \pm 2$ or $\pm 1 \pm i\sqrt{3}$ (again, with all possible sign combinations).

(g) Find all square roots of i. We must solve $z^2 = i$. Note that $i = \operatorname{cis}(\frac{\pi}{2})$. Following the same method as above, we obtain $r^2 = 1$ and $2\theta = \frac{\pi}{2} + 2k\pi$. So $r = 1$ and $\theta = \frac{\pi}{4}$ or $\frac{5\pi}{4}$, which means that the square roots of i are $\pm(\frac{\sqrt{2}}{2} + i\frac{\sqrt{2}}{2})$.

(h) Find all cube roots of i. We must solve $z^3 = i$. Starting similarly to the previous problem, we find that $r = 1$ and $3\theta = \frac{\pi}{2} + 2k\pi$, which means $\theta = \frac{\pi}{6}, \frac{5\pi}{6}, \frac{3\pi}{2}$. Therefore, the cube roots of i are $\frac{\sqrt{3}}{2} + i(\frac{1}{2})$, $-\frac{\sqrt{3}}{2} + i(\frac{1}{2})$ and $-i$.

(i) Explain how you know that you will be able to explicitly write down all complex $n$-th roots of positive real numbers (i.e., all solutions to $x^n = a > 0$) whenever $n$ is 1, 2, 3, 4, 6, 8, or 12.

We know that we will be able to write down all $n$-th roots of a positive real number whenever $\theta = \frac{2\pi}{n}$ is one of the "nice" angles for which sine and cosine have known values, that is for any multiples of $\frac{\pi}{4}$ or $\frac{\pi}{6}$. This means that $n$ is any factor of 8 or 12.

(j) Derive formulas for $\cos(3x)$ and $\sin(3x)$ using DeMoivre's Theorem. How far can you go? We could go as far as we want, so long as we can multiply out the resulting binomial. For this problem, we want to compare $\operatorname{cis}3x$, that is, $\cos 3x + i\sin 3x$, with the equal expression $(\operatorname{cis}x)^3 = (\cos x + i\sin x)^3$.

$$\begin{aligned}(\cos x + i\sin x)^3 &= \cos^3 x + 3i\cos^2 x\sin x + 3i^2\cos x\sin^2 x + i^3\sin^3 x \\ &= \cos^3 x + 3i\cos^2 x\sin x - 3\cos x\sin^2 x - i\sin^3 x \\ &= \cos^3 x - 3\cos x\sin^2 x + i(3\cos^2 x\sin x - \sin^3 x),\end{aligned}$$

which means $\cos 3x = \cos^3 x - 3\cos x\sin^2 x$ and $\sin 3x = 3\cos^2 x\sin x - \sin^3 x$. There are other forms of these expressions, based on $\sin^2 x + \cos^2 x = 1$.

(k) A generalization of DeMoivre's Theorem can be found in Euler's Formula: $e^{ix} = \operatorname{cis}x$. Show that $\operatorname{cis}x\operatorname{cis}y = \operatorname{cis}(x+y)$ and then use your answer to verify the formulas for $\cos(x+y)$ and $\sin(x+y)$.

$$\cos(x+y) + i\sin(x+y) = \operatorname{cis}(x+y) = e^{i(x+y)} = e^{ix}e^{iy} = \operatorname{cis}x\operatorname{cis}y.$$

Also, we know that

$$\begin{aligned}\operatorname{cis}x\operatorname{cis}y &= (\cos x + i\sin x)(\cos y + i\sin y) \\ &= \cos x\cos y + i\cos x\sin y + i\sin x\cos y + i^2\sin x\sin y \\ &= (\cos x\cos y - \sin x\sin y) + i(\cos x\sin y + \sin x\cos y),\end{aligned}$$

which means that $\cos(x+y)$ must be the real part, which equals $\cos x\cos y - \sin x\sin y$. Similarly, $\sin(x+y)$ must be the imaginary part, which equals $\cos x\sin y + \sin x\cos y$. These are precisely the angle sum formulas for cosine and sine.

# 5.2 Limits and Continuity

### a. Derive basic properties of limits and continuity, including the Sum, Difference, Product, Constant Multiple, and Quotient Rules, using the formal definition of a limit

1. What is the formal definition of a limit?

   The notion of a limit provides one way to describe precisely the behavior of functions near asymptotes or as the variable value increases without bound. It is a way of talking about the infinite without using infinity. We say $\lim_{x \to c} f(x) = L$ if and only if, for any $\epsilon > 0$, there exists a $\delta > 0$ satisfying: if $0 < |x - c| < \delta$ then $|f(x) - L| < \epsilon$. Informally, we write $f(x) \to L$ as $x \to c$.

   This means that no matter how close you want the values of $f(x)$ to get to $L$, you can always find a small enough interval around $x = c$ so that every function value for $x$ in that interval (except maybe at $c$) lies within your desired closeness to $L$.

   An example: $\lim_{x \to 2} 2x = 4$. Here's why. Say you want to find a small interval on the $x$-axis, centered at 2, on which $2x$ is within 0.1 of 4. Can you do it? Yes. You can pick $\delta = 0.05$. Can you always find such an interval, regardless of how accurate your estimate needs to be? (Yes, if you pick $\delta = \frac{\epsilon}{2}$.) So the limit is equal to 4.

2. How are limits related to continuity of functions? How do discontinuities relate to limits?

   While the practical idea of continuity relates to the real world ("You can draw the graph without lifting your pencil."), the mathematical definition of continuity depends on limits. We say that $f(x)$ is continuous at $x = c$ if $\lim_{x \to c} f(x) = f(c)$.

   From the fact that $\lim_{x \to 2} 2x = 4 = 2(2)$, you can determine that $2x$ is continuous at $x = 2$. You can also see that $\frac{1}{x}$ must be discontinuous at $x = 0$, because $f(0) = \frac{1}{0}$ is not defined.

3. What are the basic properties of limits and continuity?

   The basic properties are that, when each individual limit is defined, then you can perform arithmetic on them. Limits can be added, subtracted, multiplied, divided, and raised to powers (provided these operations are defined). Suppose that $\lim_{x \to c} f(x) = F$ and $\lim_{x \to c} g(x) = G$.

$$
\begin{aligned}
\lim_{x \to c}(f(x) + g(x)) &= \lim_{x \to c} f(x) + \lim_{x \to c} g(x) = F + G \\
\lim_{x \to c}(f(x) - g(x)) &= F - G \\
\lim_{x \to c}(f(x)g(x)) &= FG \\
\lim_{x \to c}\frac{f(x)}{g(x)} &= \frac{F}{G}, \quad \text{if } G \neq 0 \\
\lim_{x \to c}(kf(x)) &= kF \\
\lim_{x \to c}(f(x))^m &= F^m, \quad \text{if } F > 0
\end{aligned}
$$

When applied to continuous functions, the properties of limits become properties of continuous functions. Namely: the sum, difference, or product of continuous functions is continuous; the quotient of continuous functions is continuous, except where the denominator is zero; a constant multiple of a continuous function is continuous; and any power or root of a positive continuous function is continuous.

4. How are these properties derived from the definitions?

   We'll look at the first one: $\lim_{x \to c}(f(x) + g(x)) = F + G$. [The others are similar.] Let $\epsilon > 0$. Then $\epsilon/2 > 0$. So, there exists $\delta_f > 0$ such that, if $0 < |x - c| < \delta_f$, then $|f(x) - F| < \epsilon/2$. There also exists $\delta_g > 0$ with similar properties for $g$. Pick $\delta$ to be the smaller of $\delta_f$ and $\delta_g$. Suppose that $0 < |x - c| < \delta$. Then

   $$|(f(x) + g(x)) - (F + G)| = |(f(x) - F) + (g(x) - G)| \leq |f(x) - F| + |g(x) - G| < \frac{\epsilon}{2} + \frac{\epsilon}{2} = \epsilon.$$

   So, $\lim_{x \to c}(f(x) + g(x)) = F + G$. $\square$

   Notice that we used a form of the Triangle Inequality: $|A + B| \leq |A| + |B|$.

5. Sample Problems

   (a) Find the following limits, if they exist.
       i. $\lim_{x \to 3} \sqrt{x^2 + 5x + 1}$
       ii. $\lim_{x \to 1} \cos(\pi x)$
       iii. $\lim_{x \to 2} \dfrac{2x + 4}{3x - 6}$
       iv. $\lim_{x \to \infty} \dfrac{x^2 - 4}{3x^2 + x + 7}$
       v. $\lim_{x \to 7} \dfrac{|x - 7|}{x - 7}$
       vi. $\lim_{x \to -2} \dfrac{x^2 - 4}{x + 2}$

   (b) Explain why $\lim_{x \to 0} \dfrac{|x|}{x}$ does not exist, whereas $\lim_{x \to 0} \dfrac{x}{x}$ does exist.

   (c) Using $\epsilon = 0.1$, find a value of $\delta$ that allows you to justify that $\lim_{x \to 3}(4x + 1) = 13$.

6. Answers to Sample Problems

   (a) Find the following limits, if they exist.
       i. $\lim_{x \to 3} \sqrt{x^2 + 5x + 1} = 5$
       ii. $\lim_{x \to 1} \cos(\pi x) = -1$
       iii. $\lim_{x \to 2} \dfrac{2x + 4}{3x - 6}$ does not exist.
       iv. $\lim_{x \to \infty} \dfrac{x^2 - 4}{3x^2 + x + 7} = \lim_{x \to \infty} \dfrac{x^2 - 4}{3x^2 + x + 7} \left(\dfrac{\frac{1}{x^2}}{\frac{1}{x^2}}\right) = \lim_{x \to \infty} \dfrac{1 - \frac{4}{x^2}}{3 + \frac{1}{x} + \frac{7}{x^2}} = \dfrac{1}{3}.$

v. $\lim\limits_{x \to 7} \dfrac{|x-7|}{x-7}$ does not exist. The fraction takes the value 1 if $x > 7$ and $-1$ if $x < 7$. So the limit does not exist. See (b) below for a similar example.

vi. $\lim\limits_{x \to -2} \dfrac{x^2-4}{x+2} = \lim\limits_{x \to -2} \dfrac{(x+2)(x-2)}{(x+2)} = \lim\limits_{x \to -2}(x-2) = -4.$

(b) Explain why $\lim\limits_{x \to 0} \dfrac{|x|}{x}$ does not exist, whereas $\lim\limits_{x \to 0} \dfrac{x}{x}$ does exist.

Examine what happens for values of $x$ that are close to zero. If we pick a small positive value of $x$, then both expressions are equal to 1. This means that 1 might be the value of each limit. However, if we pick a negative value of $x$ that happens to be close to zero (such as $-0.001$, for instance), then the first expression is equal to $-1$ while the second expression is equal to 1. To summarize, the first expression is equal to 1 for positive $x$-values and $-1$ for negative $x$-values. So $\frac{|x|}{x}$ does not have a limit as $x \to 0$. However, $\frac{x}{x} = 1$ for all positive and negative values of $x$. So it has a limit of 1 as $x \to 0$.

(c) Using $\epsilon = 0.1$, find a value of $\delta$ that allows you to justify that $\lim\limits_{x \to 3}(4x+1) = 13$. Since the slope of this line is 4, we will choose $\delta = \frac{\epsilon}{4} = 0.025$. Thus, if $|x-3| < 0.025$, then

$$
\begin{aligned}
-0.025 <\ & x-3 & < 0.025 \\
2.975 <\ & x & < 3.025 \\
11.9 <\ & 4x & < 12.1 \\
-0.1 <\ & 4x-12 & < 0.1,
\end{aligned}
$$

which means that $|4x+1-13| < 0.1$, which is what we wanted.

## b. Show that a polynomial function is continuous at a point

1. How do you show that polynomials are continuous at EVERY real number?

To show continuity at $x = c$, we need to show that $\lim\limits_{x \to c} f(x) = f(c)$. The following example demonstrates how this can be done for polynomials. We will show that $f(x) = x^2 - 2x + 5$ is continuous at $x = 3$. Provide reasons for each equality.

$$
\begin{aligned}
\lim_{x \to 3} f(x) &= \lim_{x \to 3}(x^2 - 2x + 5) \\
&= \lim_{x \to 3} x^2 - \lim_{x \to 3} 2x + \lim_{x \to 3} 5 \\
&= \left(\lim_{x \to 3} x\right)^2 - 2\left(\lim_{x \to 3} x\right) + \lim_{x \to 3} 5 \\
&= (3)^2 - 2(3) + 5 \\
&= f(3).
\end{aligned}
$$

ANS: The reasons are (in order): definition of $f$, limit of a sum [respectively, difference] is the sum [resp., difference] of limits, limit of a product is the product of limits (and the limit of a constant is equal to that constant), $\lim\limits_{x \to 3} x = 3$, and the definition of $f$.

2. Sample Problems

(a) Find $\lim_{x \to 2}(x^7 - 4x^6 + x^5 + x^4 - 6x^2 - 7x + 12)$.

(b) Explain how you would show that ANY polynomial is continuous at any point.

(c) Is $f(x) = \dfrac{4x^3 - 4x + 1}{x^2 + 3}$ continuous at every point of its domain? Why or why not? [Hint: Can the denominator be zero?]

3. Answers to Sample Problems

(a) Find $\lim_{x \to 2}(x^7 - 4x^6 + x^5 + x^4 - 6x^2 - 7x + 12) = -106$.

(b) Explain how you would show that ANY polynomial is continuous at any point.

The steps in the example can be repeated for a general polynomial, $f(x)$. That is, the limit of the sum of terms is the sum of the limits of the individual terms. Then, the limit of $x^n$ is just the $n$-th power of the limit of $x$. Finally, the limit of $x$ as $x \to c$ is just $c$. So $\lim_{x \to c} f(x) = f(c)$, for any polynomial $f(x)$.

(c) Is $f(x) = \dfrac{4x^3 - 4x + 1}{x^2 + 3}$ continuous at every point of its domain? Why or why not? [Hint: Can the denominator be zero?] Since the denominator is always positive, there are no discontinuities in the domain of this rational function.

## c. Know and apply the Intermediate Value Theorem, using the geometric implications of continuity

1. What does the Intermediate Value Theorem say? How can you use geometry to demonstrate the Intermediate Value Theorem?

The Intermediate Value Theorem says that if $f$ is continuous, then $f(x)$ attains every value in between $f(a)$ and $f(b)$. That is, if $w$ is in the interval $[f(a), f(b)]$, then there exists at least one value $c$ in the interval $[a, b]$ satisfying $f(c) = w$.

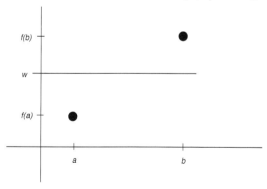

Geometrically speaking: No matter how you continuously connect $(a, f(a))$ to $(b, f(b))$, you must cross the line $y = w$ at least once.

2. What are some geometric implications of continuity?

My personal favorite is that the Intermediate Value Theorem can prove that, at any given time, there are two points on the Equator, directly opposite the earth from each other (antipodal points), that have the same temperature.

To see this, first, let $T(x)$ be the difference in temperature between the point on the equator that is $x$ degrees east of $0°$ and the point $(x+180)$ degrees east of $0°$. [That is $T(x) = \text{temp}(x) - \text{temp}(x+180)$.] Suppose also that $T(0)$ is positive. Then $T(180)$ must be negative. Assuming temperature changes continuously, then there must be some value of $c$ where $T(c) = 0$. See Sample Problems to fill in the missing details of the proof.

3. Sample Problems

   (a) Explain why $2x^4 - x - 21$ has to have a root between 1 and 2.

   (b) Suppose $f$ is a polynomial, with $f(-2) = 6$, $f(0) = -3$, $f(1) = 1$, and $f(4) = 0$. What is the smallest possible degree of $f(x)$?

   (c) Fill in the details of the proof that there are antipodal points at the same temperature. For instance, what happens if $T(0) < 0$? How do you know for sure that $T(0)$ and $T(180)$ have different signs?

   (d) Show that there must be two antipodal points on the Equator which have the same relative humidity.

4. Answers to Sample Problems

   (a) Explain why $2x^4 - x - 21$ has to have a root between 1 and 2.

   $2(1)^4 - 1 - 21 = -6 < 0$, while $2(2)^4 - 2 - 21 = 9 > 0$. Since polynomials are continuous, the Intermediate Value Theorem says that this function must equal zero somewhere between 1 and 2.

   (b) Suppose $f$ is a polynomial, with $f(-2) = 6$, $f(0) = -3$, $f(1) = 1$, and $f(4) = 0$. What is the smallest possible degree of $f(x)$? Three. We can deduce the existence of three zeroes, one between $-2$ and $0$, one between $0$ and $1$, and one at $4$.

   (c) Fill in the details of the proof that there are antipodal points at the same temperature. For instance, what happens if $T(0) < 0$? How do you know for sure that $T(0)$ and $T(180)$ have different signs?

   If $T(0) < 0$, then the argument is similar. In this case, $T(180)$ would be positive. So again, there must be a value of $c$ for which $T(c) = 0$. Since 360 and 0 describe the same point, we have

   $$T(180) = \text{temp}(180) - \text{temp}(360) = \text{temp}(180) - \text{temp}(0) = -T(0).$$

   So the signs of $T(0)$ and $T(180)$ have to be different. By the way, if $T(0)$ happens to equal zero, then $x = 0$ and $x = 180$ are the antipodal points at the same temperature.

   (d) Show that there must be two antipodal points on the Equator which have the same relative humidity.

   The proof is very similar to the proof regarding temperature. Simply replace "temperature" with "relative humidity."

# 5.3 Derivatives and Applications

## a. Derive the rules of differentiation for polynomial, trigonometric, and logarithmic functions using the formal definition of derivative

1. What does the derivative represent?

   The derivative of $f$ at $x = c$ represents the *instantaneous rate of change* of $f$ at $x = c$. Graphically, the derivative represents the slope of the graph of $y = f(x)$ at $x = c$ (or the slope of the tangent line to $y = f(x)$ at $x = c$).

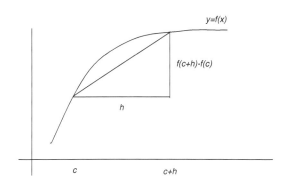 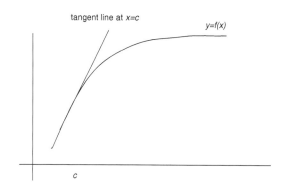

2. What is the formal definition of the derivative at a point?

   Finding the slope usually requires two points. (See left picture.) But to find the slope of a tangent line, you can find the slope between two points and then take the limit as those two points move closer toward each other. (See right picture.) Mathematically, the derivative of $f$ at $c$ is

   $$f'(c) = \lim_{h \to 0} \frac{f(c + h) - f(c)}{h}.$$

   There is an equivalent definition in the Sample Problems. Notice that the numerator and denominator BOTH approach zero, which means that we cannot calculate the limit just by plugging in $h = 0$ immediately. We have to be more thoughtful.

3. What is the formal definition of the derivative function?

   Next we can define a function $f'(x)$ whose value at $x = c$ is the slope of $f(x)$ at $x = c$. That is,

   $$f'(x) = \lim_{h \to 0} \frac{f(x + h) - f(x)}{h}.$$

   The derivative function can also be written as $\dfrac{df}{dx}$.

4. What are some properties of derivatives?

   One can show from the definition that the derivative of $kf(x)$ is $kf'(x)$ if $k$ is a constant. One can also show:

   - the derivative of $f(x) \pm g(x)$ is $f'(x) \pm g'(x)$;

- the derivative of $f(x)g(x)$ is $f'(x)g(x) + f(x)g'(x)$ [Product Rule];
- the derivative of $\dfrac{f(x)}{g(x)}$ is $\dfrac{f'(x)g(x) - f(x)g'(x)}{g(x)^2}$ [Quotient Rule]; and
- the derivative of $f(g(x))$ is $f'(g(x))g'(x)$ [Chain Rule].

5. How do you use the definition to differentiate polynomial and trigonometric functions?

   Probably the most straightforward derivative examples are of the powers of $x$. As an example, let's find the derivative of $f(x) = x^2$ using the definition.

   $$f'(x) = \lim_{h \to 0} \frac{(x+h)^2 - x^2}{h} = \lim_{h \to 0} \frac{x^2 + 2xh + h^2 - x^2}{h} = \lim_{h \to 0} (2x + h) = 2x.$$

   Next we'll consider a trigonometric example. Let's find the derivative of $\sin x$ at $x = 0$.

   $$\lim_{h \to 0} \frac{\sin(0 + h) - \sin 0}{h} = \lim_{h \to 0} \frac{\sin h}{h} = 1.$$

   This means that the slope of the graph $y = \sin x$ is exactly 1 at $x = 0$ (WHEN $x$ IS GIVEN IN RADIANS). [We'll see justification of this fact later, when we talk about L'Hôpital's Rule. You can also find proofs that utilize the "Squeeze Theorem," such as the brilliant online resource http://www.ies.co.jp/math/java/calc/LimSinX/LimSinX.html .]

6. How do you use the definition to differentiate logarithmic functions?

   Here's our plan:

   (a) Look at the derivative of an exponential function.

   (b) Figure out how the derivative of an inverse function relates to the derivative of the original function.

   (c) Find the derivative of a logarithmic function.

   Here we go:

   (a) Let's look at the exponential function $f(x) = e^x$. Its derivative is

   $$f'(x) = \lim_{h \to 0} \frac{e^{x+h} - e^x}{h} = \lim_{h \to 0} \frac{e^x e^h - e^x}{h} = e^x \left( \lim_{h \to 0} \frac{e^h - 1}{h} \right) = e^x.$$

   Yes, as $h \to 0$, the limit of $\frac{e^h - 1}{h}$ is 1. This is related to the fact that $e = \lim_{n \to \infty} \left( 1 + \frac{1}{n} \right)^n$.

   (b) Next, consider $f^{-1}(x)$. Since the graph of $y = f^{-1}(x)$ is the same as the graph of $y = f(x)$ only reflected in the line $y = x$, the slopes at corresponding points are reciprocals of each other (because $\frac{\Delta y}{\Delta x}$ becomes $\frac{\Delta x}{\Delta y}$).

   (c) So, the derivative of $y = \ln x$ at $x = 2$, say, is the reciprocal of the derivative of $y = e^x$ at $y = 2$ (and $x = \ln 2$). Since the derivative of $f(x) = e^x$ is $f'(x) = e^x$, its slope at $\ln 2$ is 2. So the derivative of $\ln x$ at 2 is $\frac{1}{2}$. Similarly, the slope of $y = \ln x$ at $x = c > 0$ is $\frac{1}{c}$. Therefore, the derivative function of $y = \ln x$ is $y' = \frac{1}{x}$.

7. What is implicit differentiation? ... logarithmic differentiation?

Implicit differentiation can be used to find $\dfrac{dy}{dx}$ when $y$ is an implicit function of $x$. The idea is to take the derivative as usual, but remember that $y$ is a function of $x$, and so it requires the Chain Rule to be properly differentiated. For example, to find the slope of the circle $x^2 + y^2 = 5$ at the point $(-1, -2)$, we can use implicit differentiation.

$$x^2 + y^2 = 5 \Rightarrow 2x + 2y\frac{dy}{dx} = 0 \Rightarrow \frac{dy}{dx} = -\frac{x}{y}.$$

So, at $(-1, -2)$, we have $\dfrac{dy}{dx} = -\dfrac{1}{2}$.

Sometimes, one has to take a logarithm of both sides first, which leads some people to use the term "logarithmic differentiation." See Sample Problems for an example.

8. Sample Problems

   (a) Find a formula for the derivative of $y = 3x^2 + x$ using the formal definition.
   (b) Show that the derivative of $x^n$ is $nx^{n-1}$.
   (c) Using the definition of the derivative, find the derivative of $\dfrac{1}{x}$ and of $\dfrac{1}{x^2}$.
   (d) Use the Product Rule to find the derivative of $x^2 = x \cdot x$.
   (e) Use the Quotient Rule to find the derivative of $\tan x = \dfrac{\sin x}{\cos x}$.
   (f) Use the Chain Rule to find the derivative of $\sin(3x^2)$ and $\ln(1 + x^2)$.
   (g) Another way to define the derivative of $f$ at $x = c$ is

   $$f'(c) = \lim_{b \to c} \frac{f(b) - f(c)}{b - c}.$$

   Explain why this definition is equivalent to the one given above. Draw a picture showing your reasoning.
   (h) Using the alternate definition of the derivative, find derivatives of $x^2$ and $\frac{1}{x}$.
   (i) Using the definition of the derivative, find the derivative of $y = \cos x$. You may use the fact that $\lim\limits_{h \to 0} \dfrac{\sin h}{h} = 1$ and $\lim\limits_{h \to 0} \dfrac{\cos h - 1}{h} = 0$.
   (j) Find the derivative of $y = x^x$. [Hint: Use logarithmic differentiation by taking the logarithm of both sides and then implicitly differentiating the resulting equation.]

9. Answers to Sample Problems

   (a) Find a formula for the derivative of $y = 3x^2 + x$ using the formal definition.

   $$\begin{aligned} f'(x) &= \lim_{h \to 0} \frac{3(x+h)^2 + (x+h) - (3x^2 + x)}{h} \\ &= \lim_{h \to 0} \frac{3x^2 + 6xh + 3h^2 + x + h - 3x^2 - x}{h} \\ &= \lim_{h \to 0} \frac{6xh + 3h^2 + h}{h} = \lim_{h \to 0} (6x + 3h + 1) = 6x + 1. \end{aligned}$$

(b) Show that the derivative of $x^n$ is $nx^{n-1}$. Using the formal definition (and the Binomial Theorem), we get:

$$f'(x) = \lim_{h \to 0} \frac{(x+h)^n - x^n}{h}$$

$$= \lim_{h \to 0} \frac{\left[ x^n + \binom{n}{1} x^{n-1}h + \binom{n}{2} x^{n-2}h^2 + \ldots \right] - x^n}{h}$$

$$= \lim_{h \to 0} \frac{nx^{n-1}h + \frac{n(n-1)}{2}x^{n-2}h^2 + \ldots}{h}$$

$$= \lim_{h \to 0} \left[ nx^{n-1} + \frac{n(n-1)}{2}x^{n-2}h + \ldots \right] = nx^{n-1}.$$

Notice that all the unwritten terms have a factor of $h$. So, they go to zero as $h \to 0$.

(c) Using the definition of the derivative, find the derivative of $\frac{1}{x}$ and of $\frac{1}{x^2}$.

$$\lim_{h \to 0} \frac{\frac{1}{x+h} - \frac{1}{x}}{h} = \lim_{h \to 0} \frac{\frac{x-(x+h)}{x(x+h)}}{h} = \lim_{h \to 0} \frac{-h}{hx(x+h)} = \lim_{h \to 0} \frac{-1}{x(x+h)} = -\frac{1}{x^2}, \text{ and}$$

$$\lim_{h \to 0} \frac{\frac{1}{(x+h)^2} - \frac{1}{x^2}}{h} = \lim_{h \to 0} \frac{x^2 - (x+h)^2}{hx^2(x+h)^2} = \lim_{h \to 0} \frac{-2xh - h^2}{hx^2(x+h)^2} = \lim_{h \to 0} \frac{-2x - h}{x^2(x+h)^2} = -\frac{2}{x^3}.$$

(d) Use the Product Rule to find the derivative of $x^2 = x \cdot x$.

Since $f(x) = g(x) = x$, we find that the derivative of $x^2$ is $(1)(x) + (x)(1) = 2x$.

(e) Use the Quotient Rule to find the derivative of $\tan x = \dfrac{\sin x}{\cos x}$.

$$\frac{d}{dx}\left(\frac{\sin x}{\cos x}\right) = \frac{\cos x \cos x - (\sin x)(-\sin x)}{\cos^2 x} = \frac{\cos^2 x + \sin^2 x}{\cos^2 x} = \frac{1}{\cos^2 x} = \sec^2 x$$

(f) Use the Chain Rule to find the derivative of $\sin(3x^2)$ and $\ln(1 + x^2)$.

The derivative of $\sin(3x^2)$ is $(\cos(3x^2))(6x) = 6x \cos(3x^2)$.

The derivative of $\ln(1 + x^2)$ is $\dfrac{1}{1+x^2}(2x) = \dfrac{2x}{1+x^2}$.

(g) Another way to define the derivative of $f$ at $x = c$ is

$$f'(c) = \lim_{b \to c} \frac{f(b) - f(c)}{b - c}.$$

Explain why this definition is equivalent to the one given above. Draw a picture showing your reasoning.

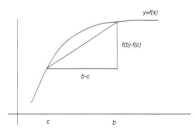

Both definitions lead to the instantaneous rate of change at the point $x = c$. In fact, by letting $b = c + h$, the two definitions are exactly the same.

(h) Using the alternate definition of the derivative, find derivatives of $x^2$ and $\frac{1}{x}$.

$$\lim_{b \to c} \frac{b^2 - c^2}{b - c} = \lim_{b \to c} \frac{(b+c)(b-c)}{b - c} = \lim_{b \to c}(b + c) = 2c, \text{ and}$$

$$\lim_{b \to c} \frac{\frac{1}{b} - \frac{1}{c}}{b - c} = \lim_{b \to c} \frac{\frac{c-b}{bc}}{b - c} = \lim_{b \to c} \frac{-1}{bc} = -\frac{1}{c^2}.$$

(i) Using the definition of the derivative, find the derivative of $y = \cos x$. You may use the fact that $\lim\limits_{h \to 0} \dfrac{\sin h}{h} = 1$ and $\lim\limits_{h \to 0} \dfrac{\cos h - 1}{h} = 0$.

$$\begin{aligned}
\lim_{h \to 0} \frac{\cos(x + h) - \cos x}{h} &= \lim_{h \to 0} \frac{\cos x \cos h - \sin x \sin h - \cos x}{h} \\
&= \lim_{h \to 0} \frac{\cos x(\cos h - 1) - \sin x \sin h}{h} \\
&= \cos x \left( \lim_{h \to 0} \frac{\cos h - 1}{h} \right) - \sin x \left( \lim_{h \to 0} \frac{\sin h}{h} \right) \\
&= (\cos x)(0) - (\sin x)(1) = -\sin x.
\end{aligned}$$

(j) Find the derivative of $y = x^x$. [Hint: Use logarithmic differentiation by taking the logarithm of both sides and then implicitly differentiating the resulting equation.]

$$y = x^x \Rightarrow \ln y = \ln x^x = x \ln x \Rightarrow \frac{1}{y} \frac{dy}{dx} = 1 \ln x + x \left( \frac{1}{x} \right) = \ln x + 1,$$

which means that $\dfrac{dy}{dx} = y(\ln x + 1) = x^x(\ln x + 1)$. Notice that we used a property of logarithms and the Product Rule.

## b. Interpret the concept of derivative geometrically, numerically, and analytically (i.e., slope of the tangent, limit of difference quotients, extrema, Newton's method, and instantaneous rate of change)

1. How is the concept of the derivative related to its definition?

   The derivative represents an instantaneous rate of change of a function $f$. This is reflected in the definition because to find an instantaneous rate of change, you need to compute a rate of change between two points and then examine what happens as the second point approaches the first.

2. What does the derivative mean geometrically? ...numerically? ...analytically?

   Geometrically, the derivative of $f$ at $x = c$ is equal to the slope of the tangent line to $y = f(x)$ at $x = c$. Numerically, this can be approximated by taking the slope between two points that are very close to each other: one at $x = c$ and one very close to $c$ (at $c + h$ for small

$h$). For most functions, the closer the second point is to the first, the better the numerical approximation will be. Analytically, one needs to examine the difference quotient (slope, rate of change) of the function $f$ between the $x$-values of $c$ and $c + h$ and determine the limit of this quotient as $h \to 0$. This is precisely the definition of $f'(c)$.

3. What is Newton's Method? How is it used?

   Newton's Method uses tangent lines to estimate roots of a function. (See picture below.) Suppose you can't solve $f(x) = 0$ exactly. Then you can make a guess: $x_0$. Using this guess, construct the tangent line to $y = f(x)$ at $x_0$. Then determine where this tangent line crosses the $x$-axis, say at $x_1$. (You can always find the $x$-intercept of a non-horizontal line.) Then you can either use $x_1$ as your guess for the solution or you can repeat the process. Construct the tangent line at $x_1$ and then determine where the line meets the $x$-axis, at $x_2$. Continue until you are as close to the solution of $f(x) = 0$ as you wish.

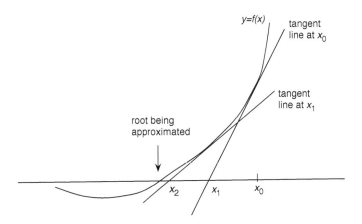

   The formula (which can be deduced from the explanation above – see Sample Problems) for $x_{n+1}$ in terms of $x_n$ is:

   $$x_{n+1} = x_n - \frac{f(x_n)}{f'(x_n)}.$$

4. Sample Problems

   (a) Find the equation of the tangent line to $y = 3x^3$ at the point $x = 2$.

   (b) Find the equation of the tangent line to $y = \frac{6}{x^2}$ at the point $x = 1$.

   (c) Referring to the graphs of $y = \sin x$ and $y = \cos x$, explain why the derivative of $\sin x$ is $\cos x$ and the derivative of $\cos x$ is $-\sin x$.

   (d) Using the data in the table, find a good estimate for $f'(3)$.

   | $x$ | 1 | 2 | 3 | 4 |
   |---|---|---|---|---|
   | $f(x)$ | 5 | 4 | 2 | $-1$ |

   (e) Using Newton's Method, estimate the root of $x^2 - 3$ that lies between 1 and 2. [Review: How do you know there *is* a root between 1 and 2?]

   (f) Deduce the Newton's Method formula. Find the tangent line at $x_0$ and then find $x_1$, its $x$-intercept.

5. Answers to Sample Problems

   (a) Find the equation of the tangent line to $y = 3x^3$ at the point $x = 2$.
   The tangent line is $y = 36x - 48$.

   (b) Find the equation of the tangent line to $y = \frac{6}{x^2}$ at the point $x = 1$.
   The tangent line is $y = -12x + 18$.

   (c) Referring to the graphs of $y = \sin x$ and $y = \cos x$, explain why the derivative of $\sin x$ is $\cos x$ and the derivative of $\cos x$ is $-\sin x$.

   Notice that the slope of $\sin x$ at zero is a positive number. As $x$ increases, the slope of $\sin x$ becomes zero, then negative, then zero again, and then positive again at $2\pi$. If we are in radians, then the maximum slope of $\sin x$ (at $x = 0$) is 1, which is $\cos 0$. So it's not hard to believe that the derivative of $\sin x$ is $\cos x$.

   Similarly, at $x = 0$, the slope of $\cos x$ is zero. As $x$ increases, the slopes become negative, then zero, then positive, then zero again at $2\pi$. This is the opposite behavior of the sine function. So it's not hard to believe that the derivative of $\cos x$ is $-\sin x$.

   (d) Using the data in the table, find a good estimate for $f'(3)$.

   | $x$ | 1 | 2 | 3 | 4 |
   |---|---|---|---|---|
   | $f(x)$ | 5 | 4 | 2 | $-1$ |

   To find the best estimate we can, we will use the smallest interval possible from the given data, which is $\Delta x = 1$. Also, we will average the slopes to the left and to the right of 3. To the left, we get $\frac{f(3)-f(2)}{3-2} = \frac{2-4}{1} = -2$, and to the right, we get $\frac{f(4)-f(3)}{4-3} = -3$. So we will guess $f'(3) = -2.5$. Notice that this is the same result you get when you find the slope between 2 and 4. That is, $\frac{f(4)-f(2)}{4-2} = \frac{-1-4}{2} = -2.5$.

   (e) Using Newton's Method, estimate the root of $x^2 - 3$ that lies between 1 and 2. [Review: How do you know there *is* a root between 1 and 2?] We know there is a root between 1 and 2 because of the Intermediate Value Theorem: $f(1) = -2 < 0$ and $f(2) = 1 > 0$. To find it, we start with a guess. You can use anything between 1 and 2, but I'll start with $x_0 = \frac{3}{2}$. Notice that we need $f(x) = x^2 - 3$ and $f'(x) = 2x$ in the formula. So

   $$x_1 = x_0 - \frac{f(x_0)}{f'(x_0)} = \frac{3}{2} - \frac{\frac{9}{4}-3}{2(\frac{3}{2})} = \frac{3}{2} - \frac{\frac{-3}{4}}{3} = \frac{3}{2} + \frac{1}{4} = \frac{7}{4}; \text{ and}$$

   $$x_2 = \frac{7}{4} - \frac{\frac{49}{16}-3}{2(\frac{7}{4})} = \frac{7}{4} - \frac{\frac{1}{16}}{\frac{7}{2}} = \frac{7}{4} - \frac{1}{56} = \frac{97}{56}$$

   This will be fine, especially since there are no calculators on this part of the CSET! $(\frac{97}{56})^2 = \frac{9409}{3136} = 3 + \frac{1}{3136} \approx 3.00032$, which is pretty close to 3.

   (f) Deduce the Newton's Method formula. Find the tangent line at $x_0$ and then find $x_1$, its $x$-intercept.

   To find the tangent line to $f(x)$ at $x_0$, we need to know the point of tangency: $(x_0, f(x_0))$ and the slope at that point: $f'(x_0)$. Using the point-slope form of the line, we know that the tangent line is $y - f(x_0) = f'(x_0)(x - x_0)$. The $x$-intercept $x_1$ of this line occurs when $y = 0$. So

$$0 - f(x_0) = f'(x_0)(x_1 - x_0) \Rightarrow -\frac{f(x_0)}{f'(x_0)} = x_1 - x_0 \Rightarrow x_1 = x_0 - \frac{f(x_0)}{f'(x_0)}.$$

This procedure works at each and every step, which means $x_{n+1} = x_n - \frac{f(x_n)}{f'(x_n)}$.

## c. Interpret both continuous and differentiable functions geometrically and analytically and apply Rolle's Theorem, the Mean Value Theorem, and L'Hôpital's rule

1. What's the difference between "continuous" and "differentiable" functions?

   A function is called "differentiable" at a point if its derivative is continuous at that point. It can be shown that ALL FUNCTIONS THAT ARE DIFFERENTIABLE EVERYWHERE ARE CONTINUOUS EVERYWHERE. However, not all continuous functions are differentiable. Functions with cusps, corners, and vertical tangents are not differentiable at those points.

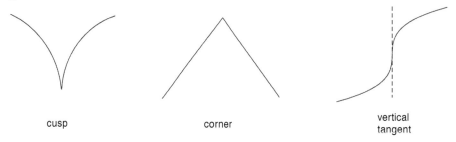

cusp                    corner                    vertical tangent

   Analytically, this means that the limit given in the definition of the derivative does not exist at the point in question. There are two main reasons why the derivative would not exist. Either there is no unique tangent line at the point in question, or the slope of the tangent line is undefined.

2. What does Rolle's Theorem say? How do you interpret it geometrically and analytically?

   Rolle's Theorem: If $f$ is continuous on $[a, b]$ and differentiable on $(a, b)$, and if $f(a) = f(b)$, then there is some number $c$ between $a$ and $b$ satisfying $f'(c) = 0$.

   Geometrically, this means that if you start and end a continuous and differentiable function at the same $y$-value, then you must have turned around (switched from increasing to decreasing or vice versa) at some point. Analytically, Rolle's Theorem means that because there must be a local maximum or local minimum value of the function $f$ on the interval $(a, b)$, then $f'(x)$ must equal zero somewhere on the interval $(a, b)$. In the picture below, there are three possible choices for $c$.

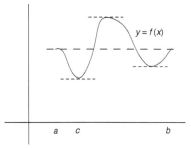

$y = f(x)$

$a \quad c \qquad\qquad b$

3. What does the Mean Value Theorem say? How do you interpret it geometrically and analytically?

   Mean Value Theorem: If $f$ is continuous on $[a, b]$ and differentiable on $(a, b)$, then there is some number $c$ between $a$ and $b$ satisfying

   $$f'(c) = \frac{f(b) - f(a)}{b - a}.$$

   Geometrically, this means that there is some point where the slope of the tangent line of $f$ is equal to the slope between the starting and ending points of $f$.

   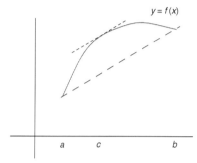

   To prove the Mean Value Theorem analytically, we can subtract the line through $(a, f(a))$ and $(b, f(b))$ from the function $f(x)$ to get a function $g(x)$ which satisfies all the conditions of Rolle's Theorem. Then the value of $c$ making $g'(c) = 0$ is the same value of $c$ making $f'(c) = \frac{f(b)-f(a)}{b-a}$. See Sample Problems.

4. What does L'Hôpital's Rule say? How do you interpret it geometrically and analytically?

   L'Hôpital's Rule is used to evaluate certain limits which cannot be determined at first glance. If you are evaluating a limit of a quotient, and the quotient is "indeterminate," meaning that it is approaching $\frac{\infty}{\infty}$ or $\frac{0}{0}$, then more information is needed. In these cases (and only in these cases)

   $$\lim_{x \to c} \frac{f(x)}{g(x)} = \lim_{x \to c} \frac{f'(x)}{g'(x)}.$$

   For example, $\lim_{x \to 1} \dfrac{x-1}{\ln x} \to \dfrac{0}{0}$, and thus

   $$\lim_{x \to 1} \frac{x-1}{\ln x} = \lim_{x \to 1} \frac{1}{1/x} = 1.$$

5. Sample Problems

   (a) L'Hôpital's Rule works for limits as $x \to \infty$ as well. Write down L'Hôpital's Rule in this case.

   (b) Evaluate these limits. If they do not exist, write "DNE."

   i. $\lim\limits_{x \to \infty} \dfrac{x}{e^x}$

ii. $\displaystyle\lim_{x\to 0}\frac{\cos x - 1}{x^2}$

(c) Verify that $\displaystyle\lim_{x\to 0}\frac{\sin x}{x} = 1$.

(d) How do you know that the *derivative* of $\cos 2x$ has a root between 0 and $\pi$?

(e) Explain how Rolle's Theorem is a special case of the Mean Value Theorem.

(f) Apply the Mean Value Theorem to the function $x^2$ between 0 and 1 to complete the sentence: There must be a point $c$ between 0 and 1 satisfying $f'(c) = \dots.$ Find the point.

(g) Fill in details of the Mean Value Theorem proof.

6. Answers to Sample Problems

(a) L'Hôpital's Rule works for limits as $x \to \infty$ as well. Write down L'Hôpital's Rule in this case.

If $\displaystyle\lim_{x\to\infty}\frac{f(x)}{g(x)} \to \frac{0}{0}$ or $\pm\frac{\infty}{\infty}$, then $\displaystyle\lim_{x\to\infty}\frac{f(x)}{g(x)} = \lim_{x\to\infty}\frac{f'(x)}{g'(x)}$.

(b) Evaluate these limits. If they do not exist, write "DNE."

  i. $\displaystyle\lim_{x\to\infty}\frac{x}{e^x}\left(\to\frac{0}{0}\right) = \lim_{x\to\infty}\frac{1}{e^x} = 0$

  ii. $\displaystyle\lim_{x\to 0}\frac{\cos x - 1}{x^2}\left(\to\frac{0}{0}\right) = \lim_{x\to 0}\frac{-\sin x}{2x}\left(\to\frac{0}{0}\right) = \lim_{x\to 0}\frac{-\cos x}{2} = -\frac{1}{2}$

(c) Verify that $\displaystyle\lim_{x\to 0}\frac{\sin x}{x} = 1$. Using L'Hôpital's Rule, we get

$$\lim_{x\to 0}\frac{\sin x}{x} = \lim_{x\to 0}\frac{\cos x}{1} = 1.$$

(d) How do you know that the *derivative* of $\cos 2x$ has a root between 0 and $\pi$?

Since $\cos(2(0)) = \cos(2\pi) = 1$, Rolle's Theorem says that the derivative of $\cos 2x$ must be zero at some point between 0 and $\pi$.

(e) Explain how Rolle's Theorem is a special case of the Mean Value Theorem.

If we apply the Mean Value Theorem in the special case where $f(a) = f(b)$, then the Mean Value Theorem says that there is a point $c$ between $a$ and $b$ satisfying $f'(c) = \frac{f(b)-f(a)}{b-a} = 0$. This is precisely Rolle's Theorem.

(f) Apply the Mean Value Theorem to the function $x^2$ between 0 and 1 to complete the sentence: There must be a point $c$ between 0 and 1 satisfying $f'(c) = \dots.$ Find the point.

There must be a point $c$ between 0 and 1 satisfying $f'(c) = \frac{1^2-0^2}{1-0} = 1$. Since $f'(x) = 2x$, we can deduce that $c = \frac{1}{2}$.

(g) Fill in details of the Mean Value Theorem proof.

The explanation given above says to subtract the line through $(a, f(a))$ and $(b, f(b))$ from $f(x)$. Explicitly, this line is $y - f(a) = m(x - a)$, where $m = \frac{f(b)-f(a)}{b-a}$. (There are other valid formulas.) So,

$$g(x) = f(x) - [f(a) + m(x - a)] = f(x) - f(a) - \frac{f(b) - f(a)}{b - a}(x - a).$$

Notice that $g(a) = f(a) - f(a) - 0 = 0$ and that $g(b) = f(b) - f(a) - (f(b) - f(a)) = 0$. So, applying Rolle's Theorem to $g(x)$, we know that there must be a value $c$ between $a$ and $b$ satisfying $g'(c) = 0$. But $g'(x) = f'(x) - \frac{f(b)-f(a)}{b-a}$. So, if $g'(c) = 0$, then $f'(c) = \frac{f(b)-f(a)}{b-a}$, which is what we wanted to show.  □

## d. Use the derivative to solve rectilinear motion, related rate, and optimization problems

1. What is rectilinear motion? How can you use the derivative to solve problems?

   Rectilinear motion will mean motion along a straight line. The derivative can be used to describe velocity (and the second derivative, acceleration) of a particle if you know the particle's position as a function of time. For instance, if a particle's $x$-coordinate at time $t$ (in seconds) is $16t^2$ feet, then its velocity is $32t$ feet per second and its acceleration is 32 feet per second per second.

2. What is meant by "related rates?" How can you use the derivative to solve problems?

   If two quantities are related by an equation, then their rates of change (derivatives) are also related. Let's look at a sample question: Suppose you are 6 feet tall and you are walking toward a 15 foot tall streetlight at a constant rate of 2 feet per second. How fast is the length of your shadow changing when you are 10 feet from the base of the streetlight? To solve this, we need to relate the length of the shadow to the distance from you to the lamppost. Then we take derivatives to determine the relationship between the given rates of change. So, let $x$ represent your distance to the lamppost and let $s$ be the length of your shadow.

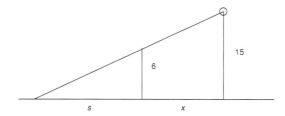

   Using similar triangles (or trigonometry), we get $\frac{s}{6} = \frac{x+s}{15}$ or $15s = 6x + 6s$, which means that $s = \frac{2}{3}x$. So, by taking derivatives, we must have $\frac{ds}{dt} = \frac{2}{3}\frac{dx}{dt} = \frac{2}{3}(2) = \frac{4}{3}$ feet per second. So, when you are 10 feet from the lamppost, or at any point, the length of your shadow is changing at a rate of about 1.333 feet per second.

3. How do you use the derivative to optimize a function?

   If you are trying to optimize a function, then you need to check the places where the derivative is zero or undefined (such as at endpoints of your allowed region). For example, suppose we want to maximize the revenue function $R(x) = 24x - x^2$, where $0 \leq x \leq 24$. We first find the derivative $R'(x) = 24 - 2x$ and set it equal to zero, obtaining $x = 12$. So our critical points (see the next section on maxima and minima) are $x = 0$, 12, and 24. Checking these gives $R(0) = R(24) = 0$, whereas $R(12) = 144$. So the revenue function is optimized when $x = 12$.

4. Sample Problems

   (a) A particle moves up and down on the surface of the water so that its height as a function of time is $\sin t$. Find its velocity.

   (b) The standard formula for the height of a projectile on Earth is $h(t) = h_0 + v_0 t - 16t^2$, where $t$ is in seconds, $h_0$ is the initial height in feet, and $v_0$ is the initial upward velocity in feet per second.

       i. Show that $h(0) = h_0$ by plugging in $t = 0$.

       ii. Show that $v(0) = v_0$ by taking the derivative of $h(t)$ to find $v(t)$.

       iii. Show that the acceleration due to gravity is constant (by taking the derivative of $v(t)$). What is the value of the acceleration due to gravity on Earth? Give units.

   (c) In the related rates example, how fast is the tip of your shadow moving toward the lamppost? [Hint: find out how fast $x + s$ is changing.]

   (d) Sand falls at a constant rate of 20mm³ per second through an hourglass, forming a cone-shaped pile that has a slant angle of $\pi/4$. How fast is the height of the pile changing when the height of the pile is 10mm?

   (e) Find the maximum height reached by an object fired upward from the ground with a velocity of 96 feet per second. [Use the formula above.]

   (f) Repeat the previous problem, but use an initial velocity of $v_0$.

5. Answers to Sample Problems

   (a) A particle moves up and down on the surface of the water so that its height as a function of time is $\sin t$. Find its velocity. $\cos t$

   (b) The standard formula for the height of a projectile on Earth is $h(t) = h_0 + v_0 t - 16t^2$, where $t$ is in seconds, $h_0$ is the initial height in feet, and $v_0$ is the initial upward velocity in feet per second.

       i. Show that $h(0) = h_0$ by plugging in $t = 0$. $h(0) = h_0 + 0 - 0 = h_0$

       ii. Show that $v(0) = v_0$ by taking the derivative of $h(t)$ to find $v(t)$. $v(t) = h'(t) = v_0 - 32t$. So $v(0) = v_0 - 0 = v_0$.

       iii. Show that the acceleration due to gravity is constant (by taking the derivative of $v(t)$). What is the value of the acceleration due to gravity on Earth? Give units. $a(t) = v'(t) = -32$. The acceleration due to gravity of Earth is approximately 32 feet per second per second downward.

(c) In the related rates example, how fast is the tip of your shadow moving toward the lamppost? [Hint: find out how fast $x + s$ is changing.]

$$\frac{d(x+s)}{dt} = \frac{dx}{dt} + \frac{ds}{dt} = 2 + \frac{4}{3} = \frac{10}{3}.$$

So the tip of your shadow is moving toward the lamppost at a rate of $\frac{10}{3}$ feet per second.

(d) Sand falls at a constant rate of 20mm$^3$ per second through an hourglass, forming a cone-shaped pile that has a slant angle of $\pi/4$. How fast is the height of the pile changing when the height of the pile is 10mm?

This is a classic related rates problem. The slant angle of $\pi/4$ means that the cone's height is equal to its radius. Since the volume of a cone in general is $\frac{1}{3}\pi r^2 h$, then the volume of our cone is $V = \frac{1}{3}\pi h^3$. We are told that $\frac{dV}{dt} = 20$. So, taking the derivative with respect to $t$, we get

$$\frac{dV}{dt} = \pi h^2 \frac{dh}{dt} \Rightarrow 20 = \pi(10)^2 \frac{dh}{dt} \Rightarrow \frac{dh}{dt} = \frac{1}{5\pi}.$$

Thus, when the height of the pile is 10mm, the height of the pile is increasing at a rate of $\frac{1}{5\pi}$ mm per second.

(e) Find the maximum height reached by an object fired upward from the ground with a velocity of 96 feet per second. [Use the formula above.] The height is given by $h(t) = 0 + 96t - 16t^2$. So, to maximize the height, we find when $h'(t) = 0$ (i.e., zero velocity). $h'(t) = 96 - 32t = 0$ implies $t = 3$ seconds. The maximum height is thus $h(3) = 96(3) - 16(3)^2 = 288 - 144 = 144$ feet.

(f) Repeat the previous problem, but use an initial velocity of $v_0$.

$$h'(t) = v_0 - 32t = 0 \Rightarrow t = \frac{v_0}{32}$$

So, the maximum height is thus $h(\frac{v_0}{32}) = v_0(\frac{v_0}{32}) - 16(\frac{v_0}{32})^2 = \frac{v_0^2}{64}$ feet.

**e. Use the derivative to analyze functions and planar curves (e.g., maxima, minima, inflection points, concavity)**

1. What are maxima and minima? How do you find them?

An $x$-value $p$ is called a *local maximum* of $f$ if $f(x) \le f(p)$ for all values of $x$ near $p$. The definition of a local minimum is similar. (See Sample Problems.) Local maxima and minima must occur at critical points of $f$; that is, points $c$ where $f'(c)$ is either zero or undefined (such as at endpoints of the domain).

2. What is concavity?

Concavity describes the direction of curvature of the graph of $f$. We say $f$ is concave up if it is shaped like a bowl (or like $y = x^2$, opening upward), and concave down if the graph of $f$ is shaped like a dome (or like $y = -x^2$, opening downward). Straight lines have no concavity.

3. What are inflection points? How do you find them?

   An inflection point is a point where the graph of the function $f$ changes its concavity - which means that $f''(x)$ changes sign at these points. This occurs at critical points of $f'$; that is, points where $f''(x)$ is either zero or undefined.

4. How do you graph a function if you know maxima, minima, inflection points, and concavity?

   These help you find important points on the function, and can tell you important features of the graph. Let's do an example: $y = x^3 - 3x$.

   First, we take derivatives. If $f(x) = x^3 - 3x$, then $f'(x) = 3x^2 - 3$ and $f''(x) = 6x$. To find critical points, we set $f'(x) = 0$. Then $3x^2 - 3 = 0$, which means that there are two critical points, $x = \pm 1$. [Using $f'(-2) = f'(2) = 9$ and $f'(0) = -3$, we see that slopes of $f$ are positive for $x < -1$, then negative from $x = -1$ to $x = 1$, then positive again for $x > 1$.] So, $-1$ is a local maximum and $1$ is a local minimum. Let's plot $(1, f(1))$ and $(-1, f(-1))$ on the graph of $f$. Setting $f''(x) = 0$, we find that $x = 0$ is a possible inflection point. Checking that indeed, $f''(x)$ changes from negative to positive at $x = 0$, then $0$ is an inflection point. In fact $f(x)$ changes from concave down to concave up at that point. Plot $(0, f(0))$ on the graph as well. Now, we can also find zeroes of this function: $0 = x(x^2 - 3)$, which means $x = 0, \pm\sqrt{3}$ are zeroes of $f(x)$. Plotting all these important points, combined with our knowledge of end behavior as $x \to \pm\infty$, we get a graph of $y = f(x)$.

   y=x^3-3x

   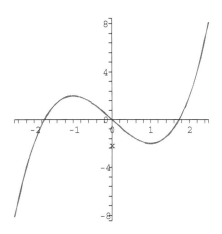

5. Sample Problems

   (a) Find local maxima and minima and inflection points of the following functions.

      i. $x^4 - 2x^2$

      ii. $x^3 - 3x^2 + 2x$

      iii. $e^x$

      iv. $\sin x$ on $[0, 2\pi]$

   (b) Sketch a graph of $y = x^4 - 2x^2$, labeling important points.

   (c) TRUE or FALSE. Explain.

    i. If $f$ is increasing, then $f'$ is positive.

    ii. If $f'$ is concave up, then $f$ is increasing.

    iii. If $f$ is concave up, then $f''$ is increasing.

    iv. If $f'' > 0$, then $f'$ is increasing and $f$ is concave up.

    v. If $f' > 0$, then $f > 0$.

(d) Define what it means for $p$ to be a *local minimum* of $f$.

6. Answers to Sample Problems

(a) Find local maxima and minima and inflection points of the following functions.

    i. $x^4 - 2x^2$ maximum: 0, minima: $-1$ and 1, inflection: $\pm\frac{1}{\sqrt{3}}$

    ii. $x^3 - 3x^2 + 2x$ maximum: $1 - \frac{\sqrt{3}}{3}$, minimum: $1 + \frac{\sqrt{3}}{3}$, inflection: 1

    iii. $e^x$ no maxima, no minima, and no inflection points

    iv. $\sin x$ on $[0, 2\pi]$ maximum: $\frac{\pi}{2}$, minimum: $\frac{3\pi}{2}$, inflection: 0, $\pi$, and $2\pi$.

(b) Sketch a graph of $y = x^4 - 2x^2$, labeling important points.

Maxima, minima, and inflection points were found above. There are also zeroes at 0, $-\sqrt{2}$, and $\sqrt{2}$.

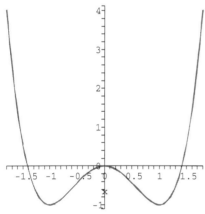

(c) TRUE or FALSE. Explain.

    i. If $f$ is increasing, then $f'$ is positive. TRUE. An increasing function has a positive slope.

    ii. If $f'$ is concave up, then $f$ is increasing. FALSE. $f'$ could be concave up and negative, which would mean that $f$ would be decreasing. The concavity of $f'$ does not relate to whether or not $f$ is increasing.

    iii. If $f$ is concave up, then $f''$ is increasing. FALSE. If $f$ is concave up, then we know $f''$ is positive, but it might not be increasing.

    iv. If $f'' > 0$, then $f'$ is increasing and $f$ is concave up. TRUE. $f'$ increases precisely when $f''$ is positive, and when $f$ is concave up.

v. If $f' > 0$, then $f > 0$. FALSE. If $f' > 0$, then $f$ is increasing. But that does not mean that $f$ has to take positive values.

(d) Define what it means for $p$ to be a *local minimum* of $f$.

An $x$-value $p$ is called a *local minimum* of $f$ if $f(x) \geq f(p)$ for all values of $x$ near $p$.

## f. Solve separable first-order differential equations and apply them to growth and decay problems

1. What is a differential equation?

   A differential equation is one which involves functions and their derivatives. To solve a differential equation means to find the function whose derivatives satisfy the given equation. For example, $y = e^x$ is a solution to the differential equation $\frac{dy}{dx} = y$ because $\frac{dy}{dx} = e^x = y$.

2. What is a separable, first-order differential equation? How do you solve them?

   A separable, first-order differential equation is one which can be solved by (artificially) separating the $dy$ and $dx$ of the derivative so that all the $x$ terms wind up on one side (with $dx$) and all the $y$ terms wind up on the other side (with $dy$). "First-order" means that only the first derivative of $y$ is involved. You can solve a first-order separable equation by separating the variables and integrating each side. This might be a topic for the next section (Integrals), but occasionally you can guess the answer and check it, using only your knowledge of derivatives.

3. How do growth and decay problems relate to separable first-order differential equations? How do you solve growth and decay problems?

   Exponential growth and decay arises mathematically from differential equations. For instance, let's suppose that a population $P$ grows at a rate that is proportional to the population. (This makes sense because maybe a certain percentage of the population is reproducing at any time.) Then $\frac{dP}{dt} = kP$, where $k$ is a constant. The solution to this equation is $P(t) = P_0 e^{kt}$, where $P_0$ represents the initial population, $P(0)$. So, whenever the growth rate is proportional to the population, one has exponential growth. Similarly, if the decay rate is proportional to the amount remaining, then one obtains exponential decay.

4. Sample Problems

   (a) Show that $y = 5e^{-2t}$ is a solution to $\frac{dy}{dt} = -2y$.

   (b) Show that $y = Ae^{-kt}$ is a solution to $\frac{dy}{dt} = -ky$.

   (c) Show that $y = 3x^2$ is a solution to $\frac{dy}{dx} = \frac{2y}{x}$.

   (d) Show that $y = Ax^3$ is a solution to $\frac{dy}{dx} = \frac{3y}{x}$.

   (e) Solve $\frac{dy}{dx} = \cos x$.

(f) Suppose that a population of bacteria grows at a rate proportional to its population, and assume that the constant of proportionality is 0.5hr$^{-1}$. Write down a differential equation stating this assumption. Solve it, assuming that the initial population is 4000 bacteria. Find the doubling time for this population.

(g) The quantity $Q(t)$ of Strontium 90 (Sr-90) remaining at time $t$ (in years) satisfies the differential equation $\frac{dQ}{dt} = -0.0231Q$. Solve to find $Q(t)$ if the initial amount of Sr-90 is 100mg. Find the half-life of Sr-90.

5. Answers to Sample Problems

(a) Show that $y = 5e^{-2t}$ is a solution to $\frac{dy}{dt} = -2y$.

$$\frac{dy}{dt} = 5(-2)e^{-2t} = -2y.$$

(b) Show that $y = Ae^{-kt}$ is a solution to $\frac{dy}{dt} = -ky$.

$$\frac{dy}{dt} = A(-k)e^{-kt} = -ky.$$

(c) Show that $y = 3x^2$ is a solution to $\frac{dy}{dx} = \frac{2y}{x}$.

$$\frac{dy}{dx} = 6x = \frac{6x^2}{x} = \frac{2y}{x}.$$

(d) Show that $y = Ax^3$ is a solution to $\frac{dy}{dx} = \frac{3y}{x}$.

$$\frac{dy}{dx} = 3Ax^2 = \frac{3Ax^3}{x} = \frac{3y}{x}.$$

(e) Solve $\frac{dy}{dx} = \cos x$. $y = \sin x + C$, where $C$ can be any constant.

(f) Suppose that a population of bacteria grows at a rate proportional to its population, and assume that the constant of proportionality is 0.5hr$^{-1}$. Write down a differential equation stating this assumption. Solve it, assuming that the initial population is 4000 bacteria. Find the doubling time for this population.

The differential equation is $\frac{dP}{dt} = \frac{1}{2}P$. The solution is $P = 4000e^{t/2}$. To find the doubling time, we need to find the time when the population is 8000.

$$8000 = 4000e^{t/2} \Rightarrow 2 = e^{t/2} \Rightarrow \ln 2 = \frac{t}{2},$$

which means that the doubling time is $2 \ln 2 \approx 1.4$ hours.

(g) The quantity $Q(t)$ of Strontium 90 (Sr-90) remaining at time $t$ (in years) satisfies the differential equation $\dfrac{dQ}{dt} = -0.0231Q$. Solve to find $Q(t)$ if the initial amount of Sr-90 is 100mg. Find the half-life of Sr-90.

Solving the differential equation, we get $Q(t) = 100e^{-0.0231t}$. The half-life will be the time when there are 50mg remaining.

$$50 = 100e^{-0.0231t} \Rightarrow \frac{1}{2} = e^{-0.0231t} \Rightarrow \ln\frac{1}{2} = -0.0231t,$$

which means that the half-life of Sr-90 is $\frac{\ln 0.5}{-0.0231}$ years. Notice that this quantity is positive because $\ln 0.5$ is a negative number. In fact, using a calculator, we obtain a half life of 30 years.

## 5.4 Integrals and Applications

### a. Derive definite integrals of standard algebraic functions using the formal definition of integral

1. What is the definition of the definite integral?

   The mathematical definition is below. We will see how to use it here, and then investigate what it means in later sections. The definite integral of $f$ from $x = a$ to $x = b$ is:

   $$\int_a^b f(x) \, dx = \lim_{n \to \infty} \left[ \sum_{i=0}^{n-1} f(a + i\Delta x)\Delta x \right] \quad \text{OR} \quad \lim_{n \to \infty} \left[ \sum_{i=1}^{n} f(a + i\Delta x)\Delta x \right],$$

   where $\Delta x = \dfrac{b - a}{n}$. The first comes from the "left-hand sums," while the second comes from the "right-hand sums."

2. How can you evaluate a definite integral using the definition?

   We will integrate $f(x) = x$ from $x = 2$ to $x = 5$ using this definition. First we write down $\Delta x = \dfrac{5 - 2}{n} = \dfrac{3}{n}$. Then we apply the formula:

   $$
   \begin{aligned}
   \int_2^5 x \, dx &= \lim_{n \to \infty} \left[ \sum_{i=1}^{n} f(2 + i\Delta x)\Delta x \right] = \lim_{n \to \infty} \left[ \sum_{i=1}^{n} \left( 2 + \frac{3i}{n} \right) \frac{3}{n} \right] = \\
   &= \lim_{n \to \infty} \left[ \sum_{i=1}^{n} \left( \frac{6}{n} + \frac{9i}{n^2} \right) \right] = \lim_{n \to \infty} \left[ \sum_{i=1}^{n} \frac{6}{n} + \sum_{i=1}^{n} \frac{9i}{n^2} \right] = \\
   &= \lim_{n \to \infty} \left[ \frac{6}{n} \sum_{i=1}^{n} 1 + \frac{9}{n^2} \sum_{i=1}^{n} i \right] = \lim_{n \to \infty} \left[ \frac{6}{n}(n) + \frac{9}{n^2} \left( \frac{n(n+1)}{2} \right) \right] = \\
   &= \lim_{n \to \infty} \left[ 6 + \frac{9}{2} + \frac{9}{2n} \right] = \frac{21}{2} = 10.5.
   \end{aligned}
   $$

3. What other information do we need to know in order to use the definition of the integral?

   As you could tell from the example, we had to know the "closed form" of certain summations. Some helpful ones are listed below:

   $$\sum_{i=1}^{n} 1 = n; \quad \sum_{i=1}^{n} i = \frac{n(n+1)}{2}; \quad \sum_{i=1}^{n} i^2 = \frac{n(n+1)(2n+1)}{6}.$$

   We also had to recall how the distributive property relates to summations: if $k$ doesn't depend on $i$, then $\sum_{i=1}^{n} ka_i = k \sum_{i=1}^{n} a_i$.

4. Sample Problems

(a) Calculate $\int_2^7 (x - 4)\,dx$ using the definition of the definite integral.

(b) Calculate $\int_0^3 x^2\,dx$ using the definition of the definite integral.

5. Answers to Sample Problems

(a) Calculate $\int_2^7 (x - 4)\,dx$ using the definition of the definite integral.

$$
\begin{aligned}
\int_2^7 (x - 4)\,dx &= \lim_{n\to\infty}\left[\sum_{i=1}^n (2 + i\Delta x - 4)\Delta x\right] = \lim_{n\to\infty}\left[\sum_{i=1}^n \left(-2 + \frac{5i}{n}\right)\frac{5}{n}\right] \\
&= \lim_{n\to\infty}\left[\sum_{i=1}^n \left(\frac{-10}{n} + \frac{25i}{n^2}\right)\right] = \lim_{n\to\infty}\left[\sum_{i=1}^n \frac{-10}{n} + \sum_{i=1}^n \frac{25i}{n^2}\right] \\
&= \lim_{n\to\infty}\left[\frac{-10}{n}(n) + \frac{25}{n^2}\sum_{i=1}^n i\right] = \lim_{n\to\infty}\left[-10 + \frac{25}{n^2}\frac{n(n+1)}{2}\right] \\
&= \lim_{n\to\infty}\left[-10 + \frac{25}{2}\frac{n(n+1)}{n^2}\right] = -10 + \frac{25}{2} = \frac{5}{2}.
\end{aligned}
$$

(b) Calculate $\int_0^3 x^2\,dx$ using the definition of the definite integral.

$$
\begin{aligned}
\int_0^3 x^2\,dx &= \lim_{n\to\infty}\left[\sum_{i=1}^n (0 + i\Delta x)^2 \Delta x\right] = \lim_{n\to\infty}\left[\sum_{i=1}^n \left(\frac{3i}{n}\right)^2 \frac{3}{n}\right] \\
&= \lim_{n\to\infty}\frac{27}{n^3}\sum_{i=1}^n i^2 = \lim_{n\to\infty}\frac{27}{n^3}\left(\frac{n(n+1)(2n+1)}{6}\right) \\
&= \frac{27}{6}\lim_{n\to\infty}\left(\frac{n(n+1)(2n+1)}{n^3}\right) = \frac{27}{6}(2) = 9.
\end{aligned}
$$

## b. Interpret the concept of a definite integral geometrically, numerically, and analytically (e.g., limit of Riemann sums)

1. How is the concept of the definite integral related to the definition?

   The integral is most commonly thought of as "area under the curve." There are several ways to approximate the area between a graph of $y = f(x)$ and the $x$-axis, but the two easiest ones to use are the left-hand sums and right-hand sums. In each method, rectangles are used to estimate the area between $y = f(x)$ and the $x$-axis (top and bottom boundaries), and between $x = a$ and $x = b$ (left and right boundaries). Both methods begin by dividing the interval $[a, b]$ into $n$ equal subdivisions, each of width $\Delta x$, which is why $\Delta x = \dfrac{b - a}{n}$.

   The left-hand sums (LHS) form rectangles on each subinterval, with the height of the rectangle being determined by the value of $f$ at the LEFT endpoint of the subinterval. (So, the first rectangle has height $f(a)$, the second $f(a + \Delta x)$, the third $f(a + 2\Delta x)$, etc.)

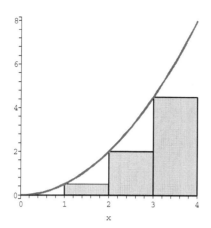 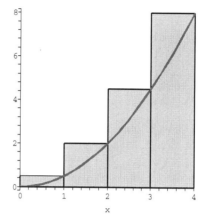

**Example: LHS and RHS approximations to** $\displaystyle\int_0^4 \frac{x^2}{2}\,dx$ **with** $n = 4$

The right-hand sums (RHS) use rectangles whose heights are determined by the value of the function at the RIGHT endpoint of each subinterval. (So, the first rectangle has height $f(a + \Delta x)$, the second $f(a + 2\Delta x)$, the third $f(a + 3\Delta x)$, etc.) Thus, the area obtained by each method is slightly different:

$$\text{LHS} \quad = \quad f(a)\Delta x + f(a + \Delta x)\Delta x + \ldots + f(a + (n-1)\Delta x)\Delta x = \sum_{i=0}^{n-1} f(a + i\Delta x)\Delta x$$

$$\text{RHS} \quad = \quad f(a + \Delta x)\Delta x + f(a + 2\Delta x)\Delta x + \ldots + f(a + n\Delta x)\Delta x = \sum_{i=1}^{n} f(a + i\Delta x)\Delta x$$

However, for suitably "nice" (*integrable*) functions, these two approximations for area approach the same value in the limit as $n$, the number of subdivisions, increases to infinity. Therefore, the definite integral is defined as the limit of these summations as $n$ approaches infinity.

2. What does the definite integral mean geometrically? ... numerically? ... analytically?

   Geometrically, the definite integral refers to the area under the curve. Numerically speaking, one can approximate this area in a variety of ways, usually by using LHS or RHS with a small number of subdivisions. This method works even if you only have a table of function values. (See Sample Problems.) Analytically, one can use the Fundamental Theorem of Calculus to evaluate definite integrals. (See next section.)

3. What are some properties of integrals?

   Let $a$, $b$, and $k$ be constants.

   - $\displaystyle\int_a^b k f(x)\,dx = k \int_a^b f(x)\,dx$

   - $\displaystyle\int_a^b f(x)\,dx = -\int_b^a f(x)\,dx$

- $$\int_a^b f(x)\ dx = \int_a^c f(x)\ dx + \int_c^b f(x)\ dx$$

All of these properties follow from the definition, and can be interpreted in terms of area under the curve.

4. What is a Riemann sum? (pronounced: REE-mahn, not RYE-mahn)

Bernhard Riemann (1826-1866) contributed to the subject of Analysis (the branch of mathematics which includes calculus) when he defined the definite integral as a limit of summations. Today, a sum which approximates the area under a curve is called a Riemann sum. Thus, both the summations given in the above definition of the definite integral are Riemann sums. Riemann was actually more general in his definition, allowing for subintervals which were not necessarily of the same length, and using any point in the subinterval to determine the rectangle height. This gives a more complicated formula, but one which still converges to the same value.

The Riemann integral is thus

$$\int_a^b f(x)\ dx = \lim_{n\to\infty}\sum_{i=1}^n f(c_i)(x_i - x_{i-1}),$$

where $a = x_0 < x_1 < \ldots < x_{n-1} < x_n = b$ and $x_{i-1} \le c_i \le x_i$.

5. Sample Problems

(a) Evaluate $\int_2^5 x\ dx$ using area under the curve.

(b) Evaluate $\int_0^3 \sqrt{9 - x^2}\ dx$ exactly.

(c) Using the following table, estimate $\int_0^{20} f(x)\ dx$ using left-hand sums, and right-hand sums, and then averaging the two estimates.

| $x$ | 0 | 5 | 10 | 15 | 20 |
|---|---|---|---|---|---|
| $f(x)$ | 1 | 3 | 4 | 6 | 11 |

(d) If $\int_2^5 f(x)\ dx = 7$ and $\int_2^9 f(x)\ dx = 5$, then find $\int_5^9 f(x)\ dx$.

(e) Explain how $\int_a^b f\ dx = -\int_b^a f\ dx$ follows from the definition of the definite integral.

6. Answers to Sample Problems

(a) Evaluate $\int_2^5 x\ dx$ using area under the curve. The trapezoid has area $\frac{(2+5)(3)}{2} = \frac{21}{2}$.

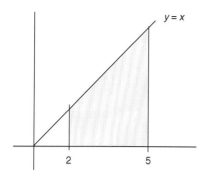

(b) Evaluate $\int_0^3 \sqrt{9 - x^2} \, dx$ exactly. Notice that if $y = \sqrt{9 - x^2}$, then $y^2 = 9 - x^2$, or $x^2 + y^2 = 9$, which is the graph of a circle of radius 3. The quarter circle described has area $\frac{1}{4}\pi(3)^2 = \frac{9\pi}{4}$.

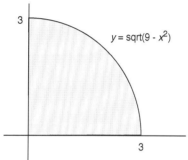

(c) Using the following table, estimate $\int_0^{20} f(x) \, dx$ using left-hand sums, and right-hand sums, and then averaging the two estimates.

| $x$ | 0 | 5 | 10 | 15 | 20 |
|---|---|---|---|---|---|
| $f(x)$ | 1 | 3 | 4 | 6 | 11 |

Using left hand sums, we have four boxes, each of width 5, with heights 1, 3, 4, and 6. So the area is

$$5(1) + 5(3) + 5(4) + 5(6) = 5(1 + 3 + 4 + 6) = 5(14) = 70.$$

Similarly, the right hand sums give an area of $5(3 + 4 + 6 + 11) = 5(24) = 120$. The average of these two estimates is 95.

(d) If $\int_2^5 f(x) \, dx = 7$ and $\int_2^9 f(x) \, dx = 5$, then find $\int_5^9 f(x) \, dx$.
One property of definite integrals implies that

$$\int_2^5 f(x) \, dx + \int_5^9 f(x) \, dx = \int_2^9 f(x) \, dx.$$

So, $7 + \int_5^9 f(x) \, dx = 5$, which means $\int_5^9 f(x) \, dx = -2$.

(e) Explain how $\int_a^b f \, dx = -\int_b^a f \, dx$ follows from the definition of the definite integral.

Recall the definition of the definite integral:

$$\int_a^b f(x)\ dx = \lim_{n \to \infty} \left[ \sum_{i=0}^{n-1} f(a + i\Delta x)\Delta x \right] \quad \text{OR} \quad \lim_{n \to \infty} \left[ \sum_{i=1}^{n} f(a + i\Delta x)\Delta x \right],$$

where $\Delta x = \dfrac{b-a}{n}$. So, if we switch $a$ and $b$, we wind up changing the sign of $\Delta x$. This introduces a negative sign in every term of the sum. (It also means that we sum the boxes from right to left, but that alone would not change the sign of the answer.) Therefore, $\displaystyle\int_a^b f\ dx = -\int_b^a f\ dx$.

## c. Prove the Fundamental Theorem of Calculus, and use it to interpret definite integrals as antiderivatives

1. What does the Fundamental Theorem of Calculus (FTOC) say?

   In the last section, we studied derivatives, and this section, we are studying integrals. These are the two main concepts of Calculus. They arise in different ways (slopes of tangent lines vs. areas under curves), yet they are intimately related through the most important theorem of calculus:

   Part 1: If $f$ is continuous on $[a, b]$ then $F(x) := \displaystyle\int_a^x f(t)\ dt$ is continuous on $[a, b]$, differentiable on $(a, b)$, and $F'(x) = f(x)$.

   Part 2: If $f$ is continuous on $[a, b]$ and if $F$ is any antiderivative of $f$ (that is, $F' = f$), then $\displaystyle\int_a^b f(t)\ dt = F(b) - F(a)$.

2. How do you prove the FTOC?

   We will prove Part 1 by using the definition of the derivative and our ideas about area. The main result of Part 1 is that the derivative of $F$ is $f$. So let's start with the definition of the derivative of $F$ and see where we go.

   $$F'(x) = \lim_{h \to 0} \frac{F(x+h) - F(x)}{h} = \lim_{h \to 0} \frac{\int_a^{x+h} f(t)\ dt - \int_a^x f(t)\ dt}{h}$$

   $$= \lim_{h \to 0} \frac{1}{h} \left( \int_x^{x+h} f(t)\ dt \right)$$

   Let's think about what's happening here. Since $f$ is continuous, we know that as $h \to 0$, $f(x+h) \to f(x)$, which means that this integral can be approximated by a rectangle of height $f(x)$ and width $h$. So,

   $$\lim_{h \to 0} \frac{1}{h} \left( \int_x^{x+h} f(t)\ dt \right) = \lim_{h \to 0} \frac{1}{h}[f(x)h] = f(x).$$

   So, $F'(x) = f(x)$, which is what we set out to prove. [Note: we can be more precise. In fact, because $f$ is continuous, there is some value $c$ between $x$ and $x + h$ that makes

$\int_x^{x+h} f(t) \, dt = f(c)h$. Then as $h \to 0$, $f(c) \to f(x)$. But the hand-wavy argument has the same spirit.] $\square$

We will prove Part 2 using Part 1. Since $f$ is continuous, we know from Part 1 that the function $G(x) = \int_a^x f(t) \, dt$ is an antiderivative of $f$. So, $(F - G)' = F' - G' = f - f = 0$, which means that $F - G$ must be a constant. So, $F(x) = G(x) + C$. Therefore,

$$F(b) - F(a) = [G(b) + C] - [G(a) + C] = G(b) - G(a) =$$
$$= \int_a^b f(t) \, dt - \int_a^a f(t) \, dt = \int_a^b f(t) \, dt,$$

which is what we set out to prove. $\square$

3. How does the FTOC allow you to interpret definite integrals as antiderivatives?

   Part 2 is the way that most definite integrals are evaluated. All you have to do is find any antiderivative of the integrand and then evaluate at $b$ and at $a$ and take the difference. As an example, let us consider the definite integral we did at the beginning: $\int_2^5 x \, dx$. Using FTOC Part 2, we need to find an antiderivative of $x$. It's not too hard to see that $F(x) = \dfrac{x^2}{2}$ works, because $F'(x) = x$. Therefore

   $$\int_2^5 x \, dx = \frac{x^2}{2}\Big|_2^5 = \frac{5^2}{2} - \frac{2^2}{2} = \frac{21}{2} = 10.5.$$

   This method is much faster than using the definition to evaluate definite integrals.

4. Sample Problems

   (a) Calculate the following definite integrals.

      i. $\int_0^4 x^2 \, dx$

      ii. $\int_0^\pi \sin x \, dx$

      iii. $\int_0^\pi \cos x \, dx$ [Why?]

      iv. $\int_0^1 x^n \, dx$

      v. $\int_0^3 e^x \, dx$

      vi. $\int_3^8 \frac{7}{x^2} \, dx$

      vii. $\int_3^5 (3x^2 + 2x - 1) \, dx$

      viii. $\int_{-2}^2 (x^4 - 5x^2 + 4) \, dx$

(b) Differentiate the following functions.

i. $F(x) = \int_2^x (4t^3 - t^2 + t + 1) \, dt$

ii. $F(x) = \int_x^{10} (e^t + 24 \sin t - \ln t) \, dt$

iii. $F(x) = \int_2^4 (t^3 - t) \, dt$

iv. $F(x) = \int_x^{x+5} (e^{3t} + \sqrt{7t - 2}) \, dt$

(c) Calculate the following definite integrals.

i. $\int_0^1 e^{5x} \, dx$

ii. $\int_0^{\pi/3} \sin 3x \, dx$

iii. $\int_2^5 \frac{x}{x^2 + 1} \, dx$

5. Answers to Sample Problems

(a) Calculate the following definite integrals.

i. $\int_0^4 x^2 \, dx = \frac{x^3}{3} \Big|_0^4 = \frac{64}{3}$

ii. $\int_0^\pi \sin x \, dx = (-\cos x)|_0^\pi = 2$

iii. $\int_0^\pi \cos x \, dx = 0$, because if you look at the graph, the area above the $x$-axis is equal to the area below the $x$-axis.

iv. $\int_0^1 x^n \, dx = \frac{x^{n+1}}{n+1} \Big|_0^1 = \frac{1}{n+1}$

v. $\int_0^3 e^x \, dx = e^x|_0^3 = e^3 - 1$

vi. $\int_3^8 \frac{7}{x^2} \, dx = -\frac{7}{x} \Big|_3^8 = -\frac{7}{8} + \frac{7}{3} = \frac{35}{24}$

vii. $\int_3^5 (3x^2 + 2x - 1) \, dx = (x^3 + x^2 - x)\big|_3^5 = 112$

viii. $\int_{-2}^2 (x^4 - 5x^2 + 4) \, dx = \left( \frac{x^5}{5} - \frac{5x^3}{3} + 4x \right) \Big|_{-2}^2 = \frac{32}{15}$

(b) Differentiate the following functions.

i. $F(x) = \int_2^x (4t^3 - t^2 + t + 1) \, dt$; $F'(x) = 4x^3 - x^2 + x + 1$.

ii. $F(x) = \int_x^{10} (e^t + 24\sin t - \ln t)\, dt$; $F'(x) = -e^x - 24\sin x + \ln x$.

iii. $F(x) = \int_2^4 (t^3 - t)\, dt$; $F'(x) = 0$ (because $F(x)$ is a constant).

iv. $F(x) = \int_x^{x+5} (e^{3t} + \sqrt{7t-2})\, dt$

If we separate into two integrals (at $x = 0$, say), we have

$$F(x) = \int_x^0 (e^{3t} + \sqrt{7t-2})\, dt + \int_0^{x+5} (e^{3t} + \sqrt{7t-2})\, dt.$$

Therefore,

$$\begin{aligned}
F'(x) &= -(e^{3x} + \sqrt{7x-2}) + e^{3(x+5)} + \sqrt{7(x+5)-2} \\
&= e^{3x+15} - e^{3x} + \sqrt{7x+33} - \sqrt{7x-2}.
\end{aligned}$$

(c) Calculate the following definite integrals.

i. $\displaystyle\int_0^1 e^{5x}\, dx = \frac{1}{5}e^{5x}\Big|_0^1 = \frac{1}{5}e^5 - \frac{1}{5}$

ii. $\displaystyle\int_0^{\pi/3} \sin 3x\, dx = -\frac{1}{3}\cos 3x\Big|_0^{\pi/3} = \frac{1}{3} + \frac{1}{3} = \frac{2}{3}$

iii. $\displaystyle\int_2^5 \frac{x}{x^2+1}\, dx = \frac{1}{2}\ln(x^2+1)\Big|_2^5 = \frac{1}{2}\ln(26) - \frac{1}{2}\ln(5) = \frac{1}{2}\ln\left(\frac{26}{5}\right)$

If it is difficult to guess the antiderivative in these problems, you can use the method of Substitution. In the third problem, we can let $u = x^2 + 1$. Everything else follows from this choice of $u$. Then $\frac{du}{dx} = 2x$, which means that $x\, dx = \frac{du}{2}$. Next, the limits need to be changed. When $x = 2$, $u = 5$, and when $x = 5$, $u = 26$. Thus,

$$\int_2^5 \frac{x\, dx}{x^2+1} = \int_5^{26} \frac{1}{u}\frac{du}{2} = \frac{1}{2}\int_5^{26} \frac{1}{u}\, du = \frac{1}{2}\ln(u)\Big|_5^{26} = \frac{1}{2}\ln(26) - \frac{1}{2}\ln(5).$$

**d. Apply the concept of integrals to compute the length of curves and the areas and volumes of geometric figures**

1. How is the concept of the integral applied to other problems?

   The main idea of the definite integral is that it is a way to add up a lot of tiny contributions to a quantity, giving the total amount of that quantity, even if the individual contributions are not constant over time or across space. For instance, physicists use integration to calculate work done, distance traveled, etc.

2. How does integration apply to rectilinear motion?

   Since velocity is the derivative of displacement (i.e., position), then one can determine how far an object has traveled if one integrates its velocity function. For example, if a particle has a velocity of $4t$ m/s from $t = 0$ to $t = 3$ seconds, then the object travels

   $$\int_0^3 4t\, dt = 2t^2\Big|_0^3 = 18 \text{ meters}.$$

3. How can you use the definite integral to measure area between two curves?

   By breaking the region into rectangles, one can deduce that the area between the graphs of $f(x)$ and $g(x)$, between $x = a$ and $x = b$ is $\int_a^b [f(x) - g(x)]dx$, assuming $f(x) > g(x)$. For example, the area between $y = \sin x$ and $y = \cos x$ from $x = \pi/4$ to $x = 5\pi/4$ is

   $$\int_{\pi/4}^{5\pi/4} (\sin x - \cos x)dx = [-\cos x - \sin x]\Big|_{\pi/4}^{5\pi/4} = +\frac{\sqrt{2}}{2} + \frac{\sqrt{2}}{2} + \frac{\sqrt{2}}{2} + \frac{\sqrt{2}}{2} = 2\sqrt{2}.$$

4. How can you use the definite integral to measure the length of a function curve (arc length)?

   By breaking a curve into small straight lines, one can deduce that the arc length of $y = f(x)$ above the interval $[a, b]$ is $\int_a^b \sqrt{1 + (f'(x))^2}\, dx$. The problem is that there are very few functions for which the arc length works out nicely. The length of $y = \frac{2}{3}x^{3/2}$ from $x = 0$ to $x = 2$ can be worked out. Note that $f'(x) = x^{1/2}$.

   $$L = \int_0^2 \sqrt{1 + x}\, dx = \int_1^3 u^{1/2}\, du = \frac{2}{3}u^{3/2}\Big|_1^3 = \frac{2}{3}[3^{3/2} - 1] = 2\sqrt{3} - \frac{2}{3},$$

   where we used the substitution method of integration (with $u = 1 + x$) to evaluate the integral.

5. How can you use the definite integral to measure the surface area of a solid of revolution?

   The formula for surface area is similar to that of arc length, only it takes into account the radius of revolution (which is just $y = f(x)$ when the axis of revolution is the $x$-axis). The surface area of the solid formed by rotating $f(x)$ around the $x$-axis is $\int_a^b 2\pi f(x)\sqrt{1 + (f'(x))^2}\, dx$. Like arc length, surface area integrals rarely work out nicely.

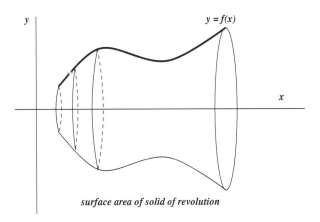

*surface area of solid of revolution*

As an example, we can rotate $y = \frac{1}{3}x^3$ from $x = 1$ to $x = 4$ around the $x$-axis and find the surface area of the solid generated. Notice that $f'(x) = x^2$ here, and again, we need substitution.

$$\begin{aligned}
SA &= \int_1^4 2\pi \left(\frac{x^3}{3}\right)\sqrt{1 + x^4}\, dx = \frac{2\pi}{12}\int_1^4 4x^3\sqrt{1 + x^4}\, dx \\
&= \frac{\pi}{6}\left(\frac{2}{3}(1 + x^4)^{3/2}\right)\Big|_1^4 = \frac{\pi}{9}(257^{3/2} - 2^{3/2}).
\end{aligned}$$

6. How can you use the definite integral to measure the volume of a solid of revolution?

   To measure the volume of a solid of revolution, one can think of the solid as being divided into small slices (usually disks or washers). Then one can find the area of each slice. By integrating the area over all possible slices, one obtains the volume. For example, if $y = f(x) > 0$ is rotated around the $x$-axis, the volume generated between $a$ and $b$ is $\int_a^b \pi(f(x))^2 \, dx$.

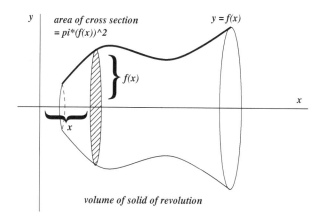

*volume of solid of revolution*

   For example, rotating the curve $y = \sqrt{x}$ around the $x$-axis between $x = 4$ and $x = 9$ gives a volume of:
   $$V = \int_4^9 \pi(\sqrt{x})^2 dx = \int_4^9 \pi x \, dx = \left. \frac{\pi x^2}{2} \right|_4^9 = \frac{65\pi}{2}.$$

7. How can you use the definite integral to measure the volume of a solid that has a consistent cross-sectional shape?

   Suppose that the cross-sections have an area function $A(x)$. Then the volume of the solid (from $x = a$ to $x = b$) is $\int_a^b A(x) \, dx$. For example, if we want to find the volume of a pyramid that is 5 feet tall and has a square base of side length 5 feet, then we can think of the pyramid as being composed of square slices that are parallel to the base. Indeed, the slice that is $x$ feet above the ground has a side length of $5 - x$ feet. So its area is $(5 - x)^2 = 25 - 10x + x^2$. Integrating over all values of $x$, we get the volume:

   $$\begin{aligned} V &= \int_0^5 (25 - 10x + x^2) dx \\ &= \left. \left[ 25x - 5x^2 + \frac{x^3}{3} \right] \right|_0^5 \\ &= 125 - 125 + \frac{125}{3} = \frac{125}{3} \text{ cubic feet.} \end{aligned}$$

8. Sample Problems

   (a) Find the area between $x^2$ and $x^3$, from $x = 0$ to $x = 1$.

(b) Find the arc length of $y = 2x$ from $x = 0$ to $x = 4$ using integration. Then compare your answer to the Pythagorean Theorem.

(c) The following graph represents the velocity of a helicopter. Estimate the distance traveled by the helicopter in the first 20 minutes. ... in the first 60 minutes.

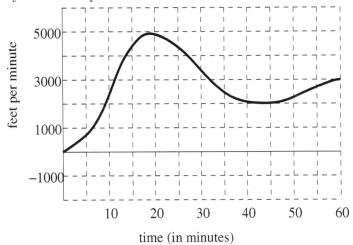

(d) Find the surface area of the solid generated by rotating $y = \frac{1}{3}x$ around the $x$-axis, from $x = 0$ to $x = 7$. What does this solid look like?

(e) Find the volume generated by rotating $y = \sqrt{\sin x}$ from $0$ to $\pi$ around the $x$-axis.

(f) Find the volume generated by rotating $y = 4 - x^2$ from $-2$ to $2$ around the $x$-axis.

(g) Find the volume of the solid whose base is the unit circle, but whose cross-sections perpendicular to the $x$-axis are squares.

(h) Find the area between $x^n$ and $x^m$ ($n > m > 0$), from $x = 0$ to $x = 1$.

(i) Find the surface area of the solid generated by rotating $y = mx$ around the $x$-axis, from $x = 0$ to $x = H$. From this, deduce the formula for the lateral surface area of a cone of height $H$ and radius $R$.

(j) Using the same equations as the previous problem, find the volume of the cone.

9. Answers to Sample Problems

(a) Find the area between $x^2$ and $x^3$, from $x = 0$ to $x = 1$. $\displaystyle\int_0^1 (x^2 - x^3)\, dx = \frac{1}{12}$

(b) Find the arc length of $y = 2x$ from $x = 0$ to $x = 4$ using integration. Then compare your answer to the Pythagorean Theorem. $4\sqrt{5}$

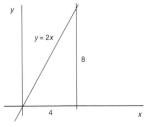

$$\int_0^4 \sqrt{1 + 4}\, dx = 4\sqrt{5} = \sqrt{80} = \sqrt{4^2 + 8^2}$$

(c) The following graph represents the velocity of a helicopter. Estimate the distance traveled by the helicopter in the first 20 minutes. ... in the first 60 minutes.

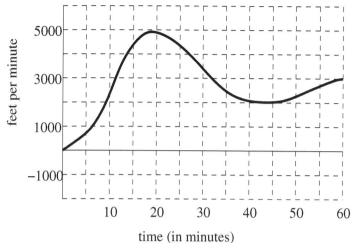

time (in minutes)

Answers may vary. The area between 0 and 20 is about 10 boxes, which means that the helicopter travels approximately $(10)(5)(1000) = 50{,}000$ feet in the first 20 minutes. In the first 60 minutes, the helicopter travels approximately $(23)(5)(1000) = 115{,}000$ feet.

(d) Find the surface area of the solid generated by rotating $y = \frac{1}{3}x$ around the $x$-axis, from $x = 0$ to $x = 7$. What does this solid look like? This solid is a cone. The surface area is

$$\int_0^7 2\pi \left(\frac{x}{3}\right) \sqrt{1 + \left(\frac{1}{3}\right)^2} \; dx = \frac{2\pi\sqrt{10}}{9} \int_0^7 x \; dx = \frac{49\pi\sqrt{10}}{9}.$$

(e) Find the volume generated by rotating $y = \sqrt{\sin x}$ from 0 to $\pi$ around the $x$-axis.

$$\int_0^\pi \pi \sin x \; dx = -\pi \cos x \big|_0^\pi = 2\pi$$

(f) Find the volume generated by rotating $y = 4 - x^2$ from $-2$ to $2$ around the $x$-axis.

$$\int_{-2}^2 \pi (4 - x^2)^2 \; dx = \pi \int_{-2}^2 (16 - 8x^2 + x^4) \; dx = \frac{512\pi}{15}$$

(g) Find the volume of the solid whose base is the unit circle, but whose cross-sections perpendicular to the $x$-axis are squares. A picture of this solid is given below.

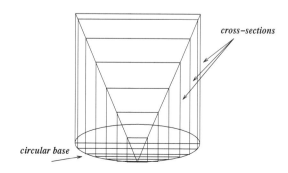

cross–sections

circular base

The circular boundary is $y = \pm\sqrt{1 - x^2}$. So the side length of the square at $x$-coordinate $x$ is $2\sqrt{1 - x^2}$. The volume is thus:

$$\int_{-1}^{1} \left(2\sqrt{1 - x^2}\right)^2 \, dx = \int_{-1}^{1} (4 - 4x^2) \, dx = \left(4x - \frac{4x^3}{3}\right)\Bigg|_{-1}^{1} = \frac{16}{3}$$

(h) Find the area between $x^n$ and $x^m$ $(n > m > 0)$, from $x = 0$ to $x = 1$.

$$\int_0^1 (x^m - x^n) \, dx = \left(\frac{x^{m+1}}{m+1} - \frac{x^{n+1}}{n+1}\right)\Bigg|_0^1 = \frac{1}{m+1} - \frac{1}{n+1} = \frac{n - m}{(m+1)(n+1)}$$

(i) Find the surface area of the solid generated by rotating $y = mx$ around the $x$-axis, from $x = 0$ to $x = H$. From this, deduce the formula for the lateral surface area of a cone of height $H$ and radius $R$.

$$\int_0^H 2\pi mx\sqrt{1 + m^2} \, dx = 2\pi m\sqrt{1 + m^2} \int_0^H x \, dx = \pi m H^2 \sqrt{1 + m^2}$$

Notice that the slope $m$ is equal to $\frac{R}{H}$. So the surface area formula simplifies to

$$\pi m H^2 \sqrt{1 + m^2} = \pi\left(\frac{R}{H}\right) H^2 \sqrt{1 + \left(\frac{R}{H}\right)^2} = \pi R\sqrt{H^2 + R^2} = \pi R\ell,$$

where $\ell$ is the *slant height* of the cone.

(j) Using the same equations as the previous problem, find the volume of the cone.

$$\int_0^H \pi(mx)^2 \, dx = \pi m^2 \left(\frac{x^3}{3}\right)\Bigg|_0^H = \frac{\pi m^2 H^3}{3} = \frac{1}{3}\pi R^2 H,$$

where again we used the fact that $m = \frac{R}{H}$.

## 5.5 Sequences and Series

**a. Derive and apply the formulas for the sums of finite arithmetic series and finite and infinite geometric series (e.g., express repeating decimals as a rational number)**

1. What is the difference between an "arithmetic" sequence and a "geometric" sequence?

   A sequence is "arithmetic" if there is a *common difference* between successive terms. For example, the sequence 1, 4, 7, 10, 13, 16, ... is arithmetic. The formula for the $n$-th term of an arithmetic sequence is linear: $a_n = a_1 + (n-1)d$, where $d$ is the common difference and $a_1$ is the first term.

   A sequence is "geometric" if there is a *common ratio* between successive terms. For example, the sequence $\frac{1}{2}$, 1, 2, 4, 8, ... is geometric. The formula for the $n$-th term of a geometric sequence is exponential: $a_n = a_1 r^{n-1}$, where $r$ is the common ratio and $a_1$ is the first term.

2. How do you derive a formula for the sum of a finite arithmetic sequence?

   Let's do an example first. Suppose we want to find: $1 + 4 + 7 + 10 + 13 + 16$ using a shortcut.

$$
\begin{array}{rrrrrrcl}
1 & +4 & +7 & +10 & +13 & +16 & = & S \\
+16 & +13 & +10 & +7 & +4 & +1 & = & S \\
\hline
17 & +17 & +17 & +17 & +17 & +17 & = & 2S
\end{array}
$$

   And so $S = \dfrac{(17)(6)}{2} = 51$. It's not hard to see that

$$
S_n = a_1 + a_2 + \ldots + a_n = \frac{n}{2}(a_1 + a_n) \quad \text{or} \quad S = \frac{n}{2}(2a_1 + (n-1)d).
$$

3. How do you derive the formula for the sum of a finite geometric sequence?

   Let's do another example first. Suppose we want to add up $\frac{1}{2} + 1 + 2 + 4 + 8$ using a shortcut.

$$
\begin{array}{rrrrrcl}
\frac{1}{2} & +1 & +2 & +4 & +8 & = & S \\
-(1 & +2 & +4 & +8 & +16 & = & 2S) \\
\hline
\frac{1}{2} & +0 & +0 & +0 & -16 & = & -S
\end{array}
$$

   And so $S = \dfrac{\frac{1}{2} - 16}{-1} = \dfrac{31}{2}$. Repeating this in general gives

$$
S_n = a_1 + a_1 r + \ldots + a_1 r^{n-1} = \frac{a_1 - a_1 r^n}{1 - r}.
$$

4. When can you extend the formula for the sum of a finite geometric sequence to an infinite geometric sequence? What do you obtain?

   If $|r| < 1$, then the terms of the geometric series approach 0 as $n \to \infty$. So, if we calculate $S = \lim\limits_{n \to \infty} S_n$, we get $S = \dfrac{a_1}{1 - r}$. If $|r| \geq 1$, then the infinite geometric series does not converge.

CSET Mathematics Study Guide - by Christopher Goff, University of the Pacific                182

5. How can you represent a repeating decimal as a rational number?

   Every repeating decimal is really a geometric series in disguise. For example,

   $$0.\overline{15} = \frac{15}{100} + \frac{15}{10,000} + \frac{15}{1,000,000} + \ldots = \frac{\frac{15}{100}}{1 - \frac{1}{100}} = \frac{15}{99} = \frac{5}{33}.$$

6. Sample Problems

   (a) Find the sum of the first 100 positive integers. [Gauss did this in second grade, according to math legend.]

   (b) Find the sum of the first 100 positive even integers.

   (c) Find the sum of the following series.

      i. $36 + 12 + 4 + \frac{4}{3} + \frac{4}{9} + \frac{4}{27}$

      ii. $36 + 12 + 4 + \frac{4}{3} + \frac{4}{9} + \frac{4}{27} + \ldots$

      iii. $\frac{1}{2} + \frac{1}{4} + \frac{1}{8} + \frac{1}{16} + \ldots$

      iv. $\frac{2}{3} + \frac{4}{9} + \frac{8}{27} + \frac{16}{81} + \ldots$

      v. $1 - 1 + 1 - 1 + \ldots + (-1)^n$

      vi. $1 + 1.1 + 1.21 + 1.331 + 1.4641 + \ldots + (1.1)^{10}$

   (d) Fill in the details to derive the arithmetic sum formula $S_n = \frac{n}{2}(a_1 + a_n)$.

   (e) Fill in the details to derive the geometric sum formula $S_n = \frac{a_1 - a_1 r^n}{1 - r}$.

   (f) Find rational values of the following.

      i. $0.\overline{4}$

      ii. $0.\overline{9}$

      iii. $0.\overline{123}$

      iv. $0.\overline{142857}$

7. Answers to Sample Problems

   (a) Find the sum of the first 100 positive integers. [Gauss did this in second grade, according to math legend.] $\frac{(1+100)(100)}{2} = 5050$.

   (b) Find the sum of the first 100 positive even integers.

      $$2 + 4 + \ldots + 200 = \frac{100}{2}(2 + 200) = 10,100$$

   (c) Find the sum of the following series.

      i. $36 + 12 + 4 + \frac{4}{3} + \frac{4}{9} + \frac{4}{27} = \frac{36 - \frac{4}{81}}{1 - \frac{1}{3}} = \frac{1456}{27}$

ii. $36 + 12 + 4 + \dfrac{4}{3} + \dfrac{4}{9} + \dfrac{4}{27} + \ldots = \dfrac{36}{1 - \frac{1}{3}} = 54$

iii. $\dfrac{1}{2} + \dfrac{1}{4} + \dfrac{1}{8} + \dfrac{1}{16} + \ldots = \dfrac{\frac{1}{2}}{1 - \frac{1}{2}} = 1$

iv. $\dfrac{2}{3} + \dfrac{4}{9} + \dfrac{8}{27} + \dfrac{16}{81} + \ldots = \dfrac{\frac{2}{3}}{1 - \frac{2}{3}} = 2$

v. $1 - 1 + 1 - 1 + \ldots + (-1)^n$. It depends. If $n$ is even, then the sum is 1. If $n$ is odd, then the sum is 0. Notice that this series starts at $n = 0$.

vi. $1 + 1.1 + 1.21 + 1.331 + 1.4641 + \ldots + (1.1)^{10} = \dfrac{1 - (1.1)^{11}}{1 - 1.1} = 10[(1.1)^{11} - 1] \approx 18.53$

(using a calculator)

(d) Fill in the details to derive the arithmetic sum formula $S_n = \dfrac{n}{2}(a_1 + a_n)$. First, notice that $a_1 + a_n = a_2 + a_{n-1}$ because the sequence is arithmetic. In other words:

$$a_2 + a_{n-1} = (a_1 + d) + a_{n-1} = a_1 + (d + a_{n-1}) = a_1 + a_n.$$

It's not hard to see that for all $j$, $a_j + a_{n+1-j} = a_1 + a_n$ for the same reason. So we have

$$
\begin{array}{lllll}
a_1 & +a_2 & +\ldots & +a_n & = & S \\
+a_n & +a_{n-1} & +\ldots & +a_1 & = & S \\
\hline
(a_1 + a_n) & +(a_1 + a_n) & +\ldots & +(a_1 + a_n) & = & 2S
\end{array}
$$

Therefore $S = \dfrac{n}{2}(a_1 + a_n)$.

(e) Fill in the details to derive the geometric sum formula $S_n = \dfrac{a_1 - a_1 r^n}{1 - r}$.

$$
\begin{array}{lllll}
a_1 & +a_1 r & +\ldots & +a_1 r^{n-1} & = & S_n \\
-(a_1 r & +a_1 r^2 & +\ldots & +a_1 r^n & = & r S_n) \\
\hline
a_1 & +0 & +\ldots & -a_1 r^n & = & (1 - r)S_n
\end{array}
$$

Therefore, $S_n = \dfrac{a_1 - a_1 r^n}{1 - r}$.

(f) Find rational values of the following.

i. $0.\overline{4} = \dfrac{4}{9}$

ii. $0.\overline{9} = \dfrac{9}{9} = 1$

iii. $0.\overline{123} = \dfrac{123}{999} = \dfrac{41}{333}$

iv. $0.\overline{142857} = \dfrac{142{,}857}{999{,}999} = \dfrac{1}{7}$

**b. Determine convergence of a given sequence or series using standard techniques (e.g., Ratio, Comparison, Integral Tests)**

1. What does it mean for a sequence to converge?

   The sequence of terms $a_n$ converges if $\lim_{n\to\infty} a_n$ exists. For instance, the sequence $\frac{1}{2}, \frac{2}{3}, \frac{3}{4}, \frac{4}{5}, \ldots$ converges to 1, whereas the sequence $-1, 1, -1, 1, -1, 1, \ldots$ does not converge.

2. What does it mean for a series to converge?

   A series converges if and only if its "sequence of partial sums" converges. That means that the series $\sum_{n=1}^{\infty} a_n$ converges if and only if the sequence

   $$
   \begin{aligned}
   s_1 &= a_1 \\
   s_2 &= a_1 + a_2 \\
   s_3 &= a_1 + a_2 + a_3 \\
   s_4 &= a_1 + a_2 + a_3 + a_4 \\
   s_5 &= a_1 + a_2 + a_3 + a_4 + a_5
   \end{aligned}
   $$
   *etc.*

   converges. We talked about the specific case of an infinite geometric series, which converges if and only if $|r| < 1$. Another type of series which can be summed is called a "telescoping" series, such as $\sum_{n=1}^{\infty}\left(\frac{1}{n} - \frac{1}{n+1}\right)$. This series converges to 1 because its sequence of partial sums is: $\frac{1}{2}, \frac{2}{3}, \frac{3}{4}, \frac{4}{5}, \ldots$, which clearly converges to 1. To see why such a series is called "telescoping," consider the following:

   $$\sum_{n=1}^{\infty}\left(\frac{1}{n} - \frac{1}{n+1}\right) = \left(1 - \frac{1}{2}\right) + \left(\frac{1}{2} - \frac{1}{3}\right) + \left(\frac{1}{3} - \frac{1}{4}\right) + \ldots = 1.$$

   The sum collapses, and all terms cancel except the first.

3. What is the Ratio Test? ... Comparison Test? ... Integral Test?

   All of these tests are used to determine if $\sum_{n=1}^{\infty} a_n$ converges.

   **Ratio Test:** Consider the limit of the absolute value of the ratio of successive terms, that is $\lim_{n\to\infty}\left|\frac{a_{n+1}}{a_n}\right|$. If this limit exists and is less than 1, then the series converges. If this limit exists and is equal to one, then you must use another test because the Ratio Test is inconclusive. In all other cases, the series diverges.

   As an example, let's consider $\sum_{n=1}^{\infty}\frac{2^n}{n!}$. Using the Ratio Test,

   $$\lim_{n\to\infty}\left|\frac{\frac{2^{n+1}}{(n+1)!}}{\frac{2^n}{n!}}\right| = \lim_{n\to\infty}\left|\frac{2^{n+1}}{(n+1)!}\frac{n!}{2^n}\right| = \lim_{n\to\infty}\left|\frac{2}{n+1}\right| = 0 < 1.$$

   Hence this series converges.

**Comparison Test:** If you know that $0 \leq a_n \leq b_n$ for all $n$ and that $\sum_{n=1}^{\infty} b_n$ converges, then you know that $\sum_{n=1}^{\infty} a_n$ also converges (because the $a_n$ sum is smaller than a known convergent series). If on the other hand, you know that $0 \leq b_n \leq a_n$ for all $n$ and that $\sum_{n=1}^{\infty} b_n$ diverges, then you know that $\sum_{n=1}^{\infty} a_n$ also diverges (because the $a_n$ sum is bigger than a known divergent series).

It helps to have a list of known convergent and known divergent series. We know geometric series converge if and only if $|r| < 1$. Also, the series $\sum_{n=1}^{\infty} \frac{1}{n^p}$ converges if and only if $p > 1$ (which can be proved using the Integral Test, below).

As an example of how to use the Comparison Test, let's consider $\sum_{n=1}^{\infty} \frac{2^n}{3^n + n}$. We first notice that $\frac{2^n}{3^n + n} < \frac{2^n}{3^n} = \left(\frac{2}{3}\right)^n$. Therefore, since $\sum_{n=1}^{\infty} \left(\frac{2}{3}\right)^n$ converges (geometric with $|r| < 1$), then the series $\sum_{n=1}^{\infty} \frac{2^n}{3^n + n}$ converges also.

**Integral Test:** Suppose that $f(x) \geq 0$ for all $x \geq 1$. Then the Integral Test says that the series $\sum_{n=1}^{\infty} f(n)$ converges if and only if the improper integral $\int_{1}^{\infty} f(x)\, dx$ converges.

As an example, let's look at the series $\sum_{n=1}^{\infty} \frac{1}{n}$. Does this series converge or diverge? The Integral Test says that we can consider the integral $\int_{1}^{\infty} \frac{1}{x}\, dx$.

$$\int_{1}^{\infty} \frac{1}{x}\, dx = \lim_{B \to \infty} \left[ \int_{1}^{B} \frac{1}{x}\, dx \right] = \lim_{B \to \infty} [\ln x]\big|_{1}^{B} = \lim_{B \to \infty} [\ln B],$$

which does not exist (because it diverges to infinity). Hence the series $\sum_{n=1}^{\infty} \frac{1}{n}$ diverges.

4. Are there any other tests?

There are other tests as well, a few of which are mentioned here.

**Test for Divergence:** If $\lim_{n \to \infty} a_n \neq 0$, then the series $\sum_{n=1}^{\infty} a_n$ diverges.

**Alternating Series Test:** If the series $\displaystyle\sum_{n=1}^{\infty} a_n$ is alternating in sign, then it converges if and only if $\displaystyle\lim_{n\to\infty} a_n = 0$.

**Root Test:** If $\displaystyle\lim_{n\to\infty} \sqrt[n]{|a_n|}$ exists and is less than 1, then the series $\displaystyle\sum_{n=1}^{\infty} a_n$ converges. If the limit is equal to one, then you must use another test because this one is inconclusive. In all other cases, the series diverges.

5. Sample Problems

   (a) Show that the Ratio Test fails for $\displaystyle\sum_{n=1}^{\infty} \frac{1}{n}$.

   (b) Which of the following series converge and which diverge? Which tests did you use?

   i. $\displaystyle\sum_{n=1}^{\infty} \frac{n+1}{n!}$

   ii. $\displaystyle\sum_{n=1}^{\infty} \frac{3^n - 2}{4^n + 2}$

   iii. $\displaystyle\sum_{n=1}^{\infty} \frac{1}{n^2}$

   iv. $\displaystyle\sum_{n=1}^{\infty} \frac{1}{n^2 + n}$

   v. $\displaystyle\sum_{n=1}^{\infty} \frac{1}{\sqrt{n}}$

   vi. $\displaystyle\sum_{n=1}^{\infty} \frac{4n^2}{2^n}$

   vii. $\displaystyle\sum_{n=1}^{\infty} \frac{n}{n+1}$

   viii. $\displaystyle\sum_{n=1}^{\infty} (-1)^n$

   ix. $\displaystyle\sum_{n=1}^{\infty} 5$

   x. $\displaystyle\sum_{n=2}^{\infty} \frac{1}{n^n}$

   (c) If you apply the Ratio Test to a geometric series, what do you obtain? Is this consistent with what we know of geometric series?

6. Answers to Sample Problems

(a) Show that the Ratio Test fails for $\displaystyle\sum_{n=1}^{\infty}\frac{1}{n}$.

$$\lim_{n\to\infty}\left|\frac{\frac{1}{n+1}}{\frac{1}{n}}\right| = \lim_{n\to\infty}\frac{n}{n+1} = 1.$$

Therefore, the Ratio Test is inconclusive.

(b) Which of the following series converge and which diverge? Which tests did you use?

   i. $\displaystyle\sum_{n=1}^{\infty}\frac{n+1}{n!}$ converges. Using the Ratio Test,

$$\lim_{n\to\infty}\left|\frac{(n+2)}{(n+1)!}\frac{n!}{(n+1)}\right| = \lim_{n\to\infty}\frac{n+2}{n^2+2n+1} = 0 < 1.$$

   ii. $\displaystyle\sum_{n=1}^{\infty}\frac{3^n-2}{4^n+2}$ converges. We know that $\frac{3^n-2}{4^n+2} < \frac{3^n}{4^n} = \left(\frac{3}{4}\right)^n$, which is a convergent geometric series. Therefore, the Comparison Test says that $\displaystyle\sum_{n=1}^{\infty}\frac{3^n-2}{4^n+2}$ converges.

   iii. $\displaystyle\sum_{n=1}^{\infty}\frac{1}{n^2}$ converges. Using the Integral Test,

$$\int_1^{\infty}\frac{1}{x^2}\,dx = \lim_{B\to\infty}\int_1^B\frac{1}{x^2}\,dx = \lim_{B\to\infty}\left(-\frac{1}{B}+1\right) = 1.$$

Because the integral converges, the series also converges. [The Integral Test can also show that $\displaystyle\sum_{n=1}^{\infty}\frac{1}{n^p}$ converges for any $p > 1$.]

   iv. $\displaystyle\sum_{n=1}^{\infty}\frac{1}{n^2+n}$ converges by comparison to the previous problem: $\frac{1}{n^2+n} < \frac{1}{n^2}$.

   v. $\displaystyle\sum_{n=1}^{\infty}\frac{1}{\sqrt{n}}$ diverges. Using the Integral Test,

$$\int_1^{\infty}\frac{1}{\sqrt{x}}\,dx = \lim_{B\to\infty}\int_1^B\frac{1}{\sqrt{x}}\,dx = \lim_{B\to\infty}2\sqrt{x}\Big|_1^B = \lim_{B\to\infty}(2\sqrt{B}-2),$$

which diverges. One could also use the fact that $\displaystyle\sum_{n=1}^{\infty}\frac{1}{n^p}$ diverges if $p \leq 1$.

   vi. $\displaystyle\sum_{n=1}^{\infty}\frac{4n^2}{2^n}$ converges. Using the Ratio Test,

$$\lim_{n\to\infty}\left|\frac{4(n+1)^2}{2^{n+1}}\frac{2^n}{4n^2}\right| = \frac{1}{2}\lim_{n\to\infty}\frac{4n^2+8n+4}{4n^2} = \frac{1}{2} < 1.$$

vii. $\sum_{n=1}^{\infty} \dfrac{n}{n+1}$ diverges. Using the Test for Divergence, $\frac{n}{n+1} \to 1$ as $n \to \infty$. Since the size of the terms approaches 1, there is no way for this series to converge.

viii. $\sum_{n=1}^{\infty} (-1)^n$ diverges because the sequence of partial sums: $-1, 0, -1, 0, \ldots$, does not converge.

ix. $\sum_{n=1}^{\infty} 5$ diverges because the sequence of partial sums: $5, 10, 15, \ldots$ does not converge.

x. $\sum_{n=2}^{\infty} \dfrac{1}{n^n}$ converges by comparison to $\frac{1}{n^2}$. Since $n \geq 2$, $\frac{1}{n^n} \leq \frac{1}{n^2}$. Since the series $\sum_{n=2}^{\infty} \dfrac{1}{n^2}$ converges, this series converges. [One could also compare this series to $\frac{1}{2^n}$.]

(c) If you apply the Ratio Test to a geometric series, what do you obtain? Is this consistent with what we know of geometric series?

$$\lim_{n \to \infty} \left| \frac{a_1 r^n}{a_1 r^{n-1}} \right| = \lim_{n \to \infty} |r| = |r|.$$

According to the Ratio Test, this series converges if $|r| < 1$, which is consistent with what we know of geometric series.

## c. Calculate Taylor series and Taylor polynomials of basic functions

1. What is a Taylor polynomial? How is that different from a Taylor series?

A Taylor polynomial is the best polynomial approximation to a given function near a given point. That means that the degree $n$ Taylor polynomial $P_n(x)$ for $f(x)$ at $x = a$ has the same value and the same first $n$ derivatives as the function does at that point. That is, $P_n(a) = f(a)$, $P_n'(a) = f'(a)$, $P_n''(a) = f''(a)$, $\ldots$, $P_n^{(n)}(a) = f^{(n)}(a)$. The general formula for the degree $n$ Taylor polynomial of $f(x)$ near $x = a$ is:

$$f(a) + f'(a)(x-a) + \frac{f''(a)}{2!}(x-a)^2 + \frac{f'''(a)}{3!}(x-a)^3 + \ldots + \frac{f^{(n)}(a)}{n!}(x-a)^n.$$

When $a = 0$, the formula simplifies to:

$$f(0) + f'(0)x + \frac{f''(0)}{2!}x^2 + \frac{f'''(0)}{3!}x^3 + \ldots + \frac{f^{(n)}(0)}{n!}x^n.$$

A Taylor series is an infinite version of a Taylor polynomial. It has *all* the same derivatives at the point as does the original function. The general formula for the Taylor series for $f(x)$ at (or near) $x = a$ is:

$$f(a) + f'(a)(x-a) + \frac{f''(a)}{2!}(x-a)^2 + \frac{f'''(a)}{3!}(x-a)^3 + \ldots + \frac{f^{(n)}(a)}{n!}(x-a)^n + \ldots.$$

When $a = 0$, the formula simplifies to:

$$f(0) + f'(0)x + \frac{f''(0)}{2!}x^2 + \frac{f'''(0)}{3!}x^3 + \ldots + \frac{f^{(n)}(0)}{n!}x^n + \ldots.$$

2. What are the Taylor series of some basic functions?

Here are some commonly used Taylor series at $x = 0$.

$$e^x = 1 + x + \frac{x^2}{2!} + \frac{x^3}{3!} + \dots$$

$$\sin x = x - \frac{x^3}{3!} + \frac{x^5}{5!} - \frac{x^7}{7!} + \dots$$

$$\cos x = 1 - \frac{x^2}{2!} + \frac{x^4}{4!} - \frac{x^6}{6!} + \dots$$

$$\frac{1}{1-x} = 1 + x + x^2 + x^3 + \dots$$

$$\ln(1+x) = x - \frac{x^2}{2} + \frac{x^3}{3} - \frac{x^4}{4} + \dots$$

$$(1+x)^k = 1 + kx + \frac{k(k-1)}{2!}x^2 + \frac{k(k-1)(k-2)}{3!}x^3 + \dots$$

Each of these Taylor series can be manipulated through substitution, multiplication, differentiation and integration. For example, the Taylor series for $e^{-x^2}$ is the same as the Taylor series of $e^x$, but with $-x^2$ substituted in place of $x$:

$$e^{-x^2} = 1 - x^2 + \frac{x^4}{2!} - \frac{x^6}{3!} + \dots.$$

Also

$$\frac{1}{1+x^2} = \frac{1}{1-(-x^2)} = 1 - x^2 + x^4 - x^6 + \dots.$$

These kinds of manipulations work, because $x^2 \to 0$ as $x \to 0$.

3. Sample Problems

   (a) Using Taylor series, show that the derivative of $e^x$ is $e^x$.

   (b) Using Taylor series, show that the derivative of $\sin x$ is $\cos x$ and that the derivative of $\cos x$ is $-\sin x$.

   (c) Using Taylor series, verify that $\lim\limits_{x \to 0} \dfrac{\sin x}{x} = 1$.

   (d) Using Taylor series, find $\lim\limits_{x \to 0} \dfrac{1 - \cos x}{x^2}$.

   (e) Find Taylor series for $\sin 2x$, $\cos 5x$, and $\ln(1-x)$.

   (f) Using the general formula for a Taylor series at $x = 0$, derive the Taylor series for $e^x$.

4. Answers to Sample Problems

   (a) Using Taylor series, show that the derivative of $e^x$ is $e^x$.

$$\begin{aligned}
\frac{d}{dx}e^x &= \frac{d}{dx}\left(1 + x + \frac{x^2}{2!} + \frac{x^3}{3!} + \frac{x^4}{4!} + \dots\right) \\
&= 0 + 1 + \frac{2x}{2!} + \frac{3x^2}{3!} + \frac{4x^3}{4!} + \dots \\
&= 1 + x + \frac{x^2}{2!} + \frac{x^3}{3!} + \dots = e^x
\end{aligned}$$

(b) Using Taylor series, show that the derivative of $\sin x$ is $\cos x$ and that the derivative of $\cos x$ is $-\sin x$.

$$\frac{d}{dx}(\sin x) = \frac{d}{dx}\left(x - \frac{x^3}{3!} + \frac{x^5}{5!} - \frac{x^7}{7!} + \ldots\right) = 1 - \frac{x^2}{2!} + \frac{x^4}{4!} - \frac{x^6}{6!} + \ldots = \cos x$$

$$\frac{d}{dx}(\cos x) = \frac{d}{dx}\left(1 - \frac{x^2}{2!} + \frac{x^4}{4!} - \frac{x^6}{6!} + \ldots\right) = 0 - x + \frac{x^3}{3!} - \frac{x^5}{5!} + \ldots = -\sin x$$

(c) Using Taylor series, verify that $\lim\limits_{x\to 0} \dfrac{\sin x}{x} = 1$.

$$\lim_{x\to 0} \frac{\sin x}{x} = \lim_{x\to 0} \frac{x - \frac{x^3}{3!} + \frac{x^5}{5!} - \frac{x^7}{7!} + \ldots}{x} = \lim_{x\to 0}\left(1 - \frac{x^2}{3!} + \frac{x^4}{5!} - \frac{x^6}{7!} + \ldots\right) = 1$$

(d) Using Taylor series, find $\lim\limits_{x\to 0} \dfrac{1-\cos x}{x^2} \cdot \dfrac{1}{2}$

$$\lim_{x\to 0} \frac{1-\cos x}{x^2} = \lim_{x\to 0} \frac{1 - (1 - \frac{x^2}{2!} + \frac{x^4}{4!} - \frac{x^6}{6!} + \ldots)}{x^2} = \lim_{x\to 0}\left(\frac{1}{2} - \frac{x^2}{4!} + \frac{x^4}{6!} - \ldots\right) = \frac{1}{2}$$

(e) Find Taylor series for $\sin 2x$, $\cos 5x$, and $\ln(1-x)$.

$$\sin 2x = (2x) - \frac{(2x)^3}{3!} + \frac{(2x)^5}{5!} - \frac{(2x)^7}{7!} + \ldots = 2x - \frac{8x^3}{3!} + \frac{32x^5}{5!} - \frac{128x^7}{7!} + \ldots$$

$$\cos 5x = 1 - \frac{25x^2}{2!} + \frac{625x^4}{4!} - \frac{15{,}625x^6}{6!} + \ldots$$

$$\ln(1-x) = \ln(1+(-x)) = -x - \frac{x^2}{2} - \frac{x^3}{3} - \frac{x^4}{4} - \ldots$$

(f) Using the general formula for a Taylor series at $x = 0$, derive the Taylor series for $e^x$. Since every derivative of $e^x$ is equal to $e^x$, $f(0) = f'(0) = \ldots = f^{(n)}(0) = e^0 = 1$. So the Taylor series for $e^x$ is

$$1 + x + \frac{x^2}{2!} + \frac{x^3}{3!} + \ldots + \frac{x^n}{n!} + \ldots$$

# 6.1 Chronological and Topical Development of Mathematics

a. Demonstrate understanding of the development of mathematics, its cultural connections, and its contributions to society

b. Demonstrate understanding of the historical development of mathematics, including the contributions of diverse populations as determined by race, ethnicity, culture, geography, and gender

DISCLAIMER: The field of mathematics history is far richer than can be conveyed in this short space. Thus, I have greatly reduced this vast field of human endeavor to the level of "sound bites." Hopefully, this brief encounter will either jog your memory of some of the stories of mathematics history, or will spur your interest to learn more about this fascinating subject, or ideally, both.

1. What are some key ideas in the development of mathematics?

   - Number Theory: counting numbers and their properties (divisibility, primes, etc.)
   - Geometry: idealized space and the need for "proof"
   - Algebra: symbolic computation and the power of generalization
   - Calculus: both differential and integral – the mathematics of change
   - Probability and Statistics: chance and predictability

2. Who are some of the key people in the development of mathematics?

   - Pythagoras (Geometry and Number Theory)
   - Euclid (Geometry and Number Theory)
   - Archimedes (Geometry and beginnings of Calculus)
   - al-Khwarizmi (Algebra)
   - Descartes (Coordinate Geometry, Algebra, Functions, Philosophy)
   - Pascal (Probability, Pascal's Wager)
   - Newton (Calculus and Physics)
   - Leibniz (Calculus, co-inventor with Newton, Philosophy)
   - Euler (prolific mathematician, blind in later years, $e^{ix} = \cos x + i \sin x$)
   - Gauss (*Wunderkind*, predicted asteroid motion, Gaussian elimination to solve a system of linear equations)
   - Riemann (Calculus, Number Theory)

3. What are some of the historical cultures known for their mathematics?

   - Babylonian - stone tablets, could solve lots of problems, including those involving quadratic and higher powers

- Egyptian - Rhind papyrus, hieroglyphic symbols for powers of ten
- Greek - known for the axiomatic development of mathematical thinking
- Chinese - early version of Pascal's triangle
- Indian - algebra, quadratic formulas and approximations
- Arab - algebra, preservation of much Greek knowledge through the "Dark Ages"
- European - rediscovery of Greek mathematics, cubic and quartic formulas (and impossibility of general quintic formula), non-Euclidean geometries, proliferation of branches of mathematics

4. What are some of mathematics' contributions to society?

Navigation, Architecture, Engineering, Medicine, Science, Social Science, etc.

5. What do race, ethnicity, culture, geography and gender have to do with mathematics?

- issues of access to a good education in mathematics
- stereotypes and their effect on learning
- teacher beliefs/student beliefs about knowledge, ability, and confidence
- Western Aristotelian thought: either $A$ or not $A$, no middle ground
- ethnomathematics: patterns, methods, problem-solving in different cultures

6. Who are some important mathematicians or mathematical ideas who come from different races, ethnicities, cultures, geographical origins, or who are women?

- Banneker, Benjamin (1731-1806) (wrote almanacs, including eclipse information)
- Germain, Sophie (1776-1831) (number theorist, got lecture notes via a male pseudonym)
- Lovelace, Ada (1815-1852) (first computer programmer, for Charles Babbage's Analytical Engine)
- Nightingale, Florence (1820-1910) (early statistician, member of Royal Statistical Society)
- Kovalevsky, Sofia (1850-1891) (Russian, first female full professor in Europe)
- Noether, Emmy (1882-1935) (big name in Abstract Algebra)

7. Sample Problems

   (a) What mathematical word comes from the name "al-Kwarizmi?"
   (b) What is Descartes most known for?
   (c) What is Pascal's Triangle? How and why is it used?
   (d) Who were the two main inventors of Calculus?
   (e) What are Germain primes?

8. Answers to Sample Problems

(a) What mathematical word comes from the name "al-Kwarizmi?" algorithm

(b) What is Descartes most known for?

In mathematics, Descartes is most known for inventing the Cartesian plane. This allowed an entirely different way of looking at functions and other curves. In philosophy, he is most known for the phrase, "I think, therefore I am."

(c) What is Pascal's Triangle? How and why is it used?

Pascal's Triangle contains the binomial coefficients in a nice, recursive format.

$$1$$
$$1 \quad 1$$
$$1 \quad 2 \quad 1$$
$$1 \quad 3 \quad 3 \quad 1$$
$$1 \quad 4 \quad 6 \quad 4 \quad 1$$

In this (slanted) version, each number is the sum of the number above it and the number above and to the left. [E.g., $6 = 3 + 3$.] These numbers show up in many areas of combinatorics (counting) and probability. For instance, when expanding the binomial $(x + y)^4$, we can obtain the coefficients from Pascal's Triangle.

$$(x + y)^4 = x^4 + 4x^3y + 6x^2y^2 + 4xy^3 + y^4$$

(d) Who were the two main inventors of Calculus? Newton and Leibniz. There was a famous priority dispute as to which one was "the" inventor of Calculus.

(e) What are Germain primes? A prime number $p$ is called a "Germain prime" if $2p + 1$ is also prime. So, 3 is a Germain prime because $2(3) + 1 = 7$ is prime. However, 7 is not a Germain prime, because $2(7) + 1 = 15$, which is not prime. Germain primes are mentioned in the play *Proof*, by David Auburn, and the 2005 movie version, starring Gwyneth Paltrow, Anthony Hopkins, Jake Gyllenhaal, and Hope Davis (Dir. John Madden).

Made in the USA
Lexington, KY
16 August 2012